Contents

*Normandy is covered by two Michelin Green Guides:
Normandy Seine Valley and Normandy Cotentin.*

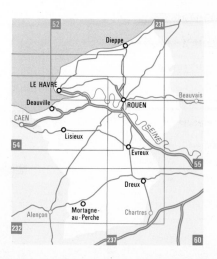

*The Michelin maps
you will need
with this guide
are:*

PRINCIPAL SIGHTS

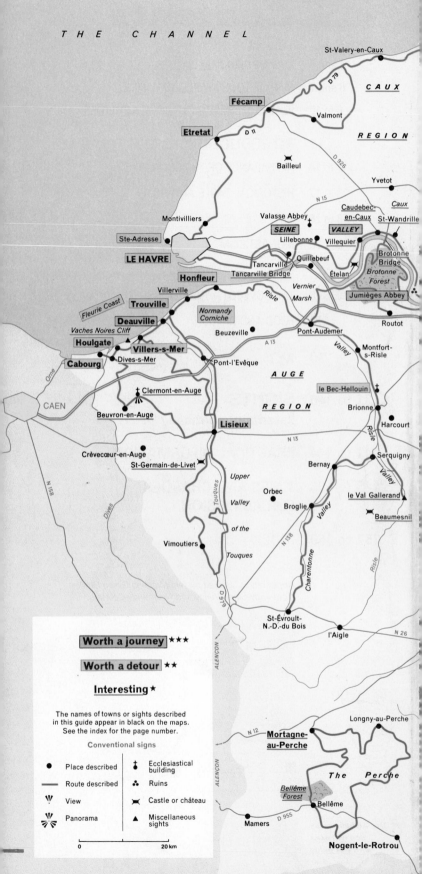

THE CHANNEL

St-Valery-en-Caux

CAUX REGION

Fécamp

Valmont

Etretat

Bailleul

Yvetot

Montivilliers

Caux

Valasse Abbey

Caudebec-en-Caux

St-Wandrille

Ste-Adresse

SEINE **VALLEY**

Lillebonne

Villequier

LE HAVRE

Quilleboeuf

Brotonne Bridge

Tancarville

Tancarville Bridge

Ételan

Brotonne Forest

Honfleur

Villerville

Vernier Marsh

Jumièges Abbey

Routot

Fleurie Coast

Trouville

Risle

Normandy Corniche

Deauville

Vaches Noires Cliff

Beuzeville

Pont-Audemer

Houlgate

A 13

Montfort-s-Risle

Villers-s-Mer

Cabourg

Dives-s-Mer

Pont-l'Evêque

le Bec-Hellouin

Orne

AUGE

Valley

Clermont-en-Auge

Brionne

CAEN

Beuvron-en-Auge

REGION

Harcourt

Lisieux

N 13

Serquigny

Crèvecœur-en-Auge

Risle Valley

St-Germain-de-Livet

Bernay

Dives

Upper

Orbec

le Val Gallerand

N 158

Valley

Broglie

Valley

Beaumesnil

of the

Charentonne

Risle

Touques

Vimoutiers

N 138

Touques

D 916

St-Évroult-N.-D.-du-Bois

l'Aigle

N 26

ALENCON

Longny-au-Perche

N 12

Mortagne-au-Perche

ALENCON

The Perche

Bellême Forest

Bellême

Mamers

D 955

Nogent-le-Rotrou

Worth a journey ★★★

Worth a detour ★★

Interesting ★

The names of towns or sights described in this guide appear in black on the maps. See the index for the page number.

Conventional signs

●	Place described	✝	Ecclesiastical building
—	Route described	♣	Ruins
＼⅂	View	⋈	Castle or château
⅏	Panorama	▲	Miscellaneous sights

0   20 km

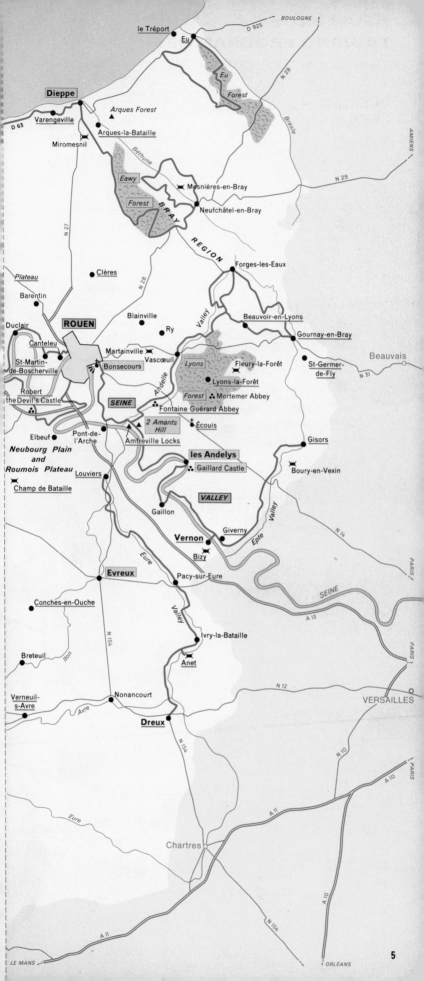

TOURING PROGRAMMES

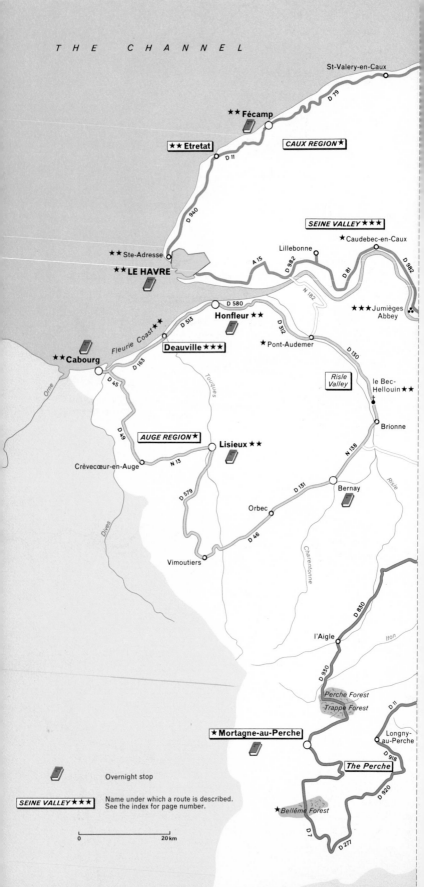

THE CHANNEL

St-Valery-en-Caux

D 79

★★ Fécamp

★★ Etretat

CAUX REGION ★

D 11

SEINE VALLEY ★★★

D 940

Lillebonne

★ Caudebec-en-Caux

★★ Ste-Adresse

A 15

D 982

D 81

D 982

★★ LE HAVRE

N 182

★★★ Jumièges Abbey

D 580

Fleurie Coast ★★★

D 513

Honfleur ★★

D 312

★ Pont-Audemer

D 130

Risle Valley

le Bec-Helluoin ★★

★★ Cabourg

D 163

Deauville ★★★

Orne

D 45

Touques

Brionne

Risle

AUGE REGION ★

Lisieux ★★

N 138

Crèvecœur-en-Auge

N 13

D 579

D 151

Bernay

Dives

Orbec

D 46

Charentonne

Vimoutiers

D 830

Iton

l'Aigle

D 930

Perche Forest
Trappe Forest

D 11

Longny-au-Perche

★ Mortagne-au-Perche

D 918

The Perche

D 920

★ *Bellême Forest*

D 7

D 277

Overnight stop

SEINE VALLEY ★★★ Name under which a route is described.
See the index for page number.

0   20 km

6

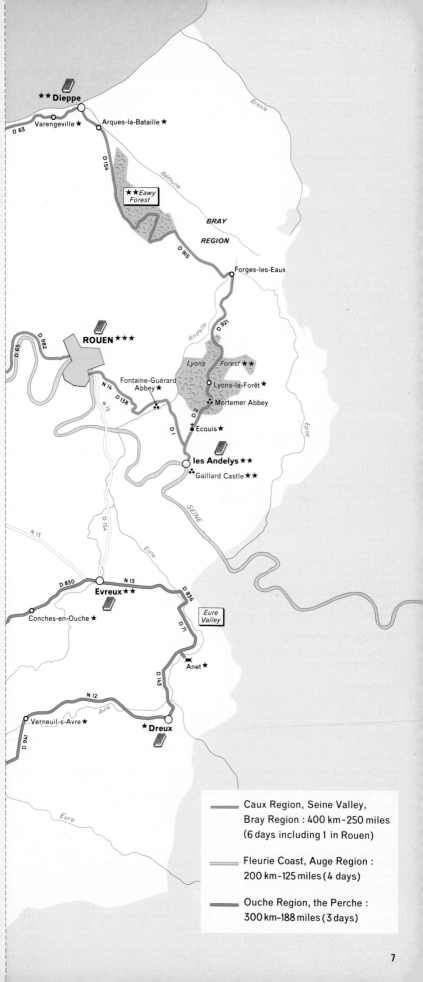

★★ **Dieppe**

Varengeville ★

Arques-la-Bataille ★

D 63

D 154

Bresle

Béthune

★★*Eawy Forest*

BRAY

REGION

D 915

Forges-les-Eaux

D 65

D 982

ROUEN ★★★

Andelle

D 921

Lyons *Forest* ★★

N 14

D 138

Fontaine-Guérard Abbey ★

Lyons-la-Forêt ★

Mortemer Abbey

N 15

D 2

D 1

✝ Ecouis ★

les Andelys ★★

Gaillard Castle ★★

SEINE

Epte

N 13

D 154

Eure

D 830

N 13

Evreux ★★

D 826

Eure Valley

Conches-en-Ouche ★

D 71

Anet ★

D 143

N 12

Avre

Verneuil-s-Avre ★

★ **Dreux**

D 941

Eure

—— Caux Region, Seine Valley, Bray Region : 400 km–250 miles (6 days including 1 in Rouen)

—— Fleurie Coast, Auge Region : 200 km–125 miles (4 days)

—— Ouche Region, the Perche : 300 km–188 miles (3 days)

PLACES TO STAY

The mention Facilities under the individual headings or after place names in the body of the guide refers to the information given on this page.
The map below indicates towns selected for the accommodation and leisure facilities, which they offer to the holidaymaker. To help you plan your route and choose your hotel, restaurant or camping site consult the following Michelin publications.

Accommodation

The **Michelin Red Guide France** of hotels and restaurants and the **Michelin Guide Camping Caravaning France** are annual publications, which present a selection of hotels, restaurants and camping sites. The final choice is based on regular on the spot enquiries and visits.
Both the hotels and camping sites are classified according to the standard of comfort of their amenities. Establishments which are notable for their fortunate setting, their decor, their quiet and secluded location and their warm welcome are distinguished by special symbols. The Michelin Guide France also gives the address and telephone number of local tourist offices and tourist information centres.

Guest-houses

The many farms and manors tucked away in attractive, peaceful settings are one of Normandy's greatest charms. Some of them offer bed, breakfast and evening meal at reasonable prices. Look for the sign *Chambres d'hôte.*

Planning your route, sports and recreation

The **Michelin Maps** at a scale of 1:200 000 cover the whole of France. For those concerning the region see the layout diagram on page 3. In addition to a wealth of road information these maps indicate beaches, bathing spots, swimming pools, golf courses, racecourses, air fields, panoramas and scenic routes.

OUTDOOR ACTIVITIES

For addresses and other details see the chapter Practical Information at the end of the guide.

On the coast

To enjoy their stay to the full visitors should take an interest in the marine life of the region. The first thing to become acquainted with is the rhythm of the tides, a rhythm almost as important as the rising and setting of the sun. The flow or high tide occurs twice every 24 hours. The sea remains at the high water mark for a few hours then subsides with the ebb tide until reaching the low water mark. The cycle then begins over again.
High tide attracts bathers who do not have far to go to reach the water's edge. Beach and water sport enthusiasts display all their energy while others find it is the best time for a drive along the coast or a visit to a port or harbour.
Fishermen and many others wait impatiently for low tide to search for crabs, shrimps, mussels and cockles which lurk among seaweed-covered rocks and in the wet sand.
In stormy weather the attraction of the sea is incomparable. To see and hear the savage sea, its waves thundering against the rocks and sea-walls sending clouds of spray high into the air, is a truly wonderful spectacle. Onlookers approach at their own risk!

Sailing and windsurfing

Sailing clubs abound where lessons are organised at all levels. Yearly regattas take place in the larger resorts.

Landsailing

This sport is performed on a curious three-wheeled cart equipped with sail, a cross between a go-cart and a yacht which can reach speeds of up to 100km - 63 miles per hour. A variant is windskating which is done on skateboards. The lawns of the Boulevard de Verdun in Dieppe attract enthusiasts.

Boating

The Channel coasts are the right places for yachting and outboard motor boat sports. The main pleasure boat harbours are indicated on the map of places to stay *(p 9)*. They have been selected for the large number of places offered and services included: fuelling facilities, drinking water and electricity on the quayside, toilets and showers, crane or elevator handling facilities, repairs and surveillance of craft.

Fishing

From Le Tréport to the mouth of the Orne, the stretches of coastline seem to offer unlimited possibilities for the amateur fisherman whether onshore, offshore or underwater. His line may have one or two hooks, as beyond this limit a declaration must be made with the authorities *(Inscription Maritime)*. Special permission is required for the use of a net.
Angling is possible from rocks or the quayside, using a fishing line and sinker. Shrimping is possible at low tide with a long-handled shrimping net. Armed with spade or rake the holiday-maker can search for clams and cockles hidden in the sand. Mussels, small crabs and winkles are to be found among the rocks.

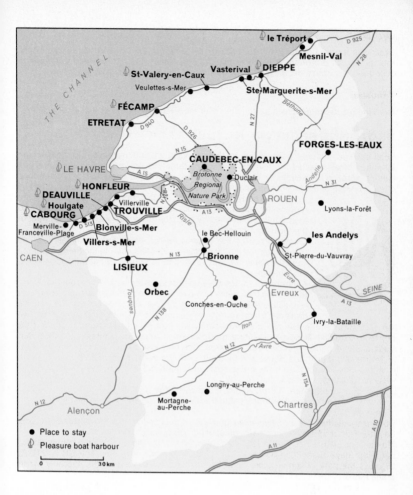

Underwater diving

The coast along the Caux Region provides the right conditions for this sport.

Inland

The Normandy countryside is an ideal place to stay for nature lovers who appreciate the peace and quiet of rural life. Naturalists will find an abundance of flora and fauna, and for the solitary walker there are forests of superb beech trees to be discovered with here and there a country manor house or well-kept farm.

Fresh water fishing

Normandy offers a wealth of rivers, streams, lakes and ponds for anglers in search of trout, pike etc.

Outings on horseback

Horse riding clubs throughout Normandy propose outings in woodland or along the shore. Horse breeding is traditional and contributes to the economic resources of the region.

Rambling

Footpaths clearly marked out with red and white lined posts enable the whole region to be visited.

The main footpaths are:
The **GR 2** Seine Valley.
The **GR 22** Paris-Mont-St-Michel which crosses the region to the southwest as far as Mamers.
The **GR 222** leading through the valleys and forests of the Eure.
The **GR 26** from the Yvelines *département* west of Paris winds through the Eure and Calvados regions before reaching the coast at Deauville.
Footpaths between Rouen and the coast:
The **GR 2** goes alongside the north bank of the Seine and crosses La Londe and Roumare Forests.
The **GR 23** on the south bank crossing Brotonne Forest.
The **GR 21** up the Lézarde Valley reaching the coast at Étretat.
The **GR 211** from the Seine to the coast through Maulévrier Forest.
The **GR 25** around Rouen.
The **GR 225** across the Vexin, Lyons Forest, the Bray Region to the coast near Dieppe.
Ramblers can obtain more details and advice from the topo guides available.

Cycling

Cycling is a very pleasant way to discover the different valleys and woodlands of the region such as Brotonne or Lyons Forest, the Eure Valley, the meanders of the Seine or even the Caux coastline. Bicycles may be hired in many towns and villages.

Canoeing

Even the most energetic will be satisfied with the rivers, lakes and stretches of water.

BROTONNE REGIONAL NATURE PARK

Regional and national parks differ in their conception and purpose. The former are inhabited areas selected for development with a threefold aim; protection of natural and cultural heritage (museums, restoration), economic growth (co-operatives and promotion of local crafts), and education (initiating people to the secrets of nature). They are run by

an official body consisting of local councillors, land-owners and representatives of various local associations. Their projects, but also their limits, are defined by a charter drawn up with the agreement of the local population.

Created in 1974 the **Brotonne Regional Nature Park** stretches over 40 communes and 40 000 hectares – 98 840 acres – in the Seine-Maritime and Eure *départements,* striving to safeguard its natural and architectural wealth.

A number of routes have been signposted so as to enable the visitor to discover the beauty of the region. The thatched cottage route from la Mailleraye-sur-Seine to the Vernier Marsh is worthwhile and the *route des fruits* is particularly enjoyable in spring when the fruits trees

are in bloom. Fruit is sold along the roadside from Jumièges to Duclair. Within the park the **Lower Seine Craft Museum,** in reality a group of small museums, brings back forgotten traditions and trades long since disappeared. One may visit:
– Bourneville (Eure): the House and Museum of Crafts and Trades *(p 130).*
– La Haye-de-Routot (Eure): the bread oven and sabot-maker's workshop *(p 50).*
– Hauville (Eure): the stone mill *(p 130).*
– Ste-Opportune-la-Mare (Eure): Apple House and forge *(p 137).*
– Ételan Château (Seine-Maritime): cultural activities are organised at certain times of the year *(p 128).*
Open-air activities are not neglected and the Jumièges-le-Mesnil Leisure Centre and Country Park proposes tennis, swimming, windsurfing etc.
Mannevilles Nature Reserve *(p 137)* is a privileged spot for flora and fauna conservation. Ramblers have more than 350km - 218 miles of signposted paths. The GR 2, 211 A, 23 cross the park in certain places and horse riding is possible on the specially made bridle paths.

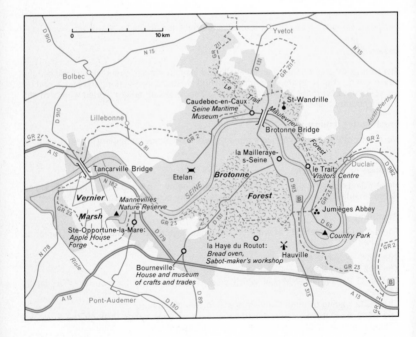

D-Day, the 6 June 1944 a historic date.
Visit the D-Day Beaches
*with the **Michelin Green Guide Normandy Cotentin***
and the Channel Islands.

Introduction
to the tour

Normandy's Seine Valley offers visitors the winding course of the river, the forests of the Eure and Seine-Maritime *départements,* the manors of the Auge Region, the tall cliffs of the Caux Region, the colourful Bray Region not to mention the green meadows where the famous Normandy cows graze.
Add to this wealth of natural beauty the attraction of famous abbeys, towns renowned for their artistic treasures, historic castles and well-known seaside resorts.

In order to give our readers the most up to date information the **times and charges** *for admission to sights described in the guide are listed at the end of the guide.*

The sights are listed alphabetically in this section either under the place – town, village or area – in which they are situated or under their proper name.

Every sight for which there are times and charges is indicated by the symbol ⊘ *in the margin in the main part of the guide.*

APPEARANCE OF THE COUNTRY

Normandy is not a single geographical unit. The former province of France stretches over two large regions with different geological structures; that located northwest of the Paris Basin and that which looks towards Brittany and consists of an eroded foundation of ancient rocks *(See Michelin Green Guide Normandy Cotentin)*. From west to east the sandstone, granite and primary schists of the Armorican Massif give way to the clay, limestone and chalk soils of the Secondary and Tertiary Eras.

FORMATION OF THE LAND

Primary Era. – Beginning about 600 million years ago. It was towards the end of this era that an upheaval of the earth's crust took place: this upheaval or folding movement, known as the "Hercynian fold", the V-shaped appearance of which is shown by dotted lines on the map, resulted in the emergence of a number of high mountain ranges such as the Armorican Massif. These mountains were formed by impermeable cristalline rocks such as granite, gneiss and mica-schist mixed with volcanic rock such as porphyry and make up two east-west ranges separated by a central furrow.

Secondary era. – It began about 200 million years ago. Since the beginning of this age, the Hercynian relief was levelled by erosion forming the Armorican peneplain. Erosion, or the constant destruction of the soil by alternating rain, sun, frost and the action of running water, wore away rocks as hard as granite or sandstone. It was during this period that the chalk structure of sedimentary Normandy was formed.

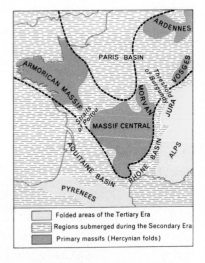

Folded areas of the Tertiary Era

Regions submerged during the Secondary Era

Primary massifs (Hercynian folds)

Tertiary era. – It began some 60 million years ago. The Armorican Massif was raised slightly. On two occasions the Paris Basin was flooded with seas and lakes depositing sand and sediments.

Quaternary era. – It began some 2 million years ago. This is the present age during which the evolution of man has taken place.
The Ice Age brought about the hollowing out of the valleys and for Normandy was the time when superficial alluvium deposits in many places helped to favour agriculture on the chalk plateau. The shoreline underwent significant changes during this period.

Sedimentary Normandy. – The ancient foundation was overlaid in the Secondary Era, at the time of the great marine invasions of the land, by chalk several hundred metres thick. This was soon covered by a flint deposit made up of rocks decomposing in a climate both hotter and wetter than our own. In the Tertiary Era the chalk plateau was shaken by vast undulations which brought about a series of fractures running in the same direction, giving rise to the original relief of the Perche Region.
The plateau, with a mean height of 126m - 413ft bears west, turning into a huge gully walled to the northeast by the Bray Region's volcanic cone and to the southwest by the hills of the Normandy Perche. Erosion attacked the heights and a "button hole" opened up in the Bray Region *(qv)*. The valleys which cut their way down from these large watersheds through the chalk have a striking similarity in their convex shape and wide alluvial covered floors. The alluvial deposits of clay and silex were washed down when the valleys were being hollowed out in the great glaciary periods and have given rise to many different varieties of agricultural land. The cretaceous deposits of the late Secondary Era, however, did not reach the Armorican Massif; when almost in sight of the low wooded hills of the Bocage they fell away, exposing older underlying Jurassic layers. The movements of the original rock foundation, so close and therefore violent, in this hybrid zone, produced many natural divisions – a mosaic of small "regions".

NORMANDY'S LOCAL REGIONS

Upper and Lower Normandy are major divisions within which lie Normandy's local regions. These can be grouped roughly by their vegetation into two totally different types, the open **countryside** and the woodland or **Bocage region** both of which have their counterparts in England.

Open countryside and woodland. – Two types of landscape are to be found in the province, existing without reference to the geological subsoil. In the strictest sense the countryside is open with dry and windswept plains where cereals predominate and the population is concentrated in large villages of houses of solid stone. Gradually local character is being lost as progress takes place in agriculture.
Woodlands are typical of the farmlands of the Armorican Massif; they outrun the original land mass considerably to the east, reaching the Maine, the Perche and the Auge Regions. A network of hedges, each topping an earth bank, encloses fields and meadows, so that from a distance the countryside appears almost wooded. The people in the innumerable hamlets scattered along the low–lying roads continue their traditional self–sufficient lives and raise cattle – a relatively new occupation in the region, but one which suits the "Bocain" temperament.

The open countryside regions. – The **Neubourg Plain** and the **Évreux-St-André Countryside** constitute a flat and monotonous landscape covered with arable crops, typical of large scale farming, with hardly a tree in sight. On the latter a few herds of sheep are still to be seen.

The **Caux Region** is a vast chalk plain bordered, on the Channel side, by cliffs famous for their hanging valleys or *valleuses (qv)*, and to the south by the Seine Valley. Alluvial mud makes it fertile, producing wheat and such industrial crops as flax and sugar beet.
The landscape, however, is not without relief – silex clay deposits retain moisture, enabling trees to grow in occasional clumps on the plateau itself and on the hillsides of the surrounding valleys.

The **Normandy Vexin,** a second chalk plain, a continuation southeast of the Caux Region, ends only where it is cut by the Epte and Andelle Valleys. The particularly thick coating of alluvial mud has made it an intensive arable area, "veritable agricultural factories", primarily of wheat and sugar beet.

The transitional regions. – The **Roumois** and **Lieuvin** plains, divided by the Risle Valley, appear as a transitional belt between the Caux and Auge Regions.
By tradition an area for rotation crop farming, it is transformed at its western end by the appearance of hedges and apple orchards into a woodland landscape.

The **Ouche Region** consists of scenery more sombre than that of the Roumois and Lieuvin, for the land, lacking an alluvial deposit, supports only trees and sparse crops with here and there a hedge or meadow.

The **Normandy Perche** is a country of rolling hills forming a transition between the Paris Basin and the Armorican Massif, noted for the breeding of horses.

The woodland regions. – The Norman part of the **Bray Region** abuts, in the east, on the Caux Region and consists of a vast clay depression, known as the "button hole" (p 47), bordered by two chalk hills. It is a woodland, cattle farming area – its dairy produce and apples destined for the Paris market.

The **Auge Region** spreads into both Upper and Lower Normandy and is different from the others. The chalk strata have been deeply cut by a network of valleys, resulting in the appearance of many non-porous (clay) areas on the valley floors.
Local humidity favours pastureland, hedges and cider orchards. Scattered farmsteads, some still with ancient half timbering, appear part hidden beside the low lying roads. In some ways it is a lush woodland area, the Normandy of "meadowland, brilliant green and glistening dew", of the Norman poet Lucie Delarue-Mardrus *(qv)*.

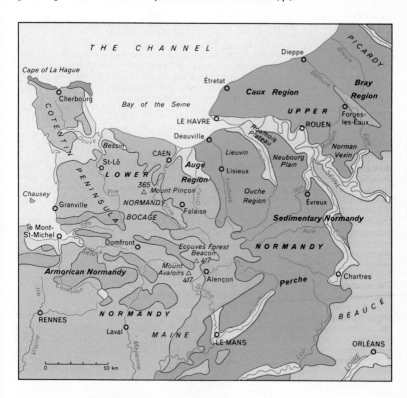

Quaternary Era		Alluvial deposits
Tertiary Era		Sedimentary deposits
Secondary Era		Cretaceous limestones
		Jurassic limestones
Primary Era		Granites
		Crystalline rocks

13

THE COAST

The coast of Normandy from the Valley of the Bresle in the north to that of the Orne is as varied as its hinterland. The Caux Region *(qv)* matches the cliffs of Dover with high chalk cliffs of its own which have won for it the name of the Alabaster Coast. Shingle bottomed creeks break the line of the cliff wall. As rocks are undercut by the sea and fall, hanging valleys can be seen forming in the chalk.

The Calvados Coast is made up of the low Auge and Bessin cliffs and the sand dunes and salt marshes which intersperse them, particularly around Caen. Further east, the Fleurie Coast *(qv)* offers miles of fine sand beaches where there may be a difference on the strand of more than 1/2 mile between high and low water points. It is also an outstandingly sunny region.

The present coastline was drawn after the great upheavals of the Quaternary Era when the sea finally divided the Channel Islands from the Continent. No sooner had the continental shoreline been established than the sea began slowly but endlessly to wear away protruding sectors and to fill more sheltered spots with debris – the sea brought shingle to the Caux beaches; it brings the mud that silts up the Seine Estuary; it has killed more than one port (in Gallo-Roman times Lillebonne was a seaport), and it has raised the level of several of the Calvados beaches.

Lighthouses. – The lighthouses along the Normandy coast make good vantage points for those who do not mind spiral staircases. Both night and day they are precious landmarks for navigators in the Channel. The machinery inside is interesting and can sometimes be visited. The Norman engineer **Augustin Fresnel** (1788-1827) invented a new system for increasing the intensity and range of light when in 1823 he replaced the conventional parabolic reflector by compound lenses – an arrangement known as the Fresnel lens. The result was the outstanding progress made in lighthouse range. Today the nature of light sources has changed and their candle-power has been considerably increased but Fresnel's system is still applied. In the more dangerous coastal areas and inlets several lighthouses can be seen at night, each having its particular characteristics: fixed, revolving or intermittent beam. In addition to lighthouses there are buoys and beacons in channels and on rocks to enable the navigator to determine his position. On the coast other landmarks such as church steeples play the same part.

STOCK RAISING

Cattle. – With 6 million head of cattle, the Normandy breed predominates among the thirty or so to be found in France as a whole. The stock is all-purpose and fertile, and produces more than a quarter of the country's meat, milk and other dairy products.

The Cattle Breeders' Association with its *Normandy Herd Book* is engaged in improving the breed in cooperation with the Testing and Insemination Society.

Productivity is also being studied scientifically by the Milk Control Board which checks the weight and fat content of milk produced by each cow against its food ration. This procedure has been applied particularly in the Orne Department since 1965 where a good cow gives 20 to 30 litres - 4 1/2 to 6 1/2 gallons a day of milk rich in the cream which gives Normandy butter its flavour. Production is entirely absorbed by the local milk and butter cooperatives, cheese makers, dried and condensed milk factories.

The Normandy breed is known by the three colour markings on its hide – white, cream and dark brown. The head is white with brown patches round the eyes – the lack of these "spectacles" bars a beast from entry in the *Herd Book*. Veal calves are sold for slaughter at 6 to 7 weeks when they weigh 130kg - 2 1/2 cwt. The fattening of bullocks and barren heifers is an industry in itself.

Horses. – The centre of Normandy horse breeding is Ste-Mère-Église, although the Cotentin has remained the principal birthplace.

Thoroughbreds, crossbreeds, Bretons and Percherons are magnificently represented in the national studs at St-Lô and Le Pin and in local private studs *(See Michelin Green Guide Normandy Cotentin).*

The **thoroughbred**, descended from Asian stallions and English mares, has been bred in Normandy since the early 18C as a racehorse. This racehorse is a remarkable animal as renowned for its elegance as for its speed. A yearling sale attended by buyers from the region and abroad is held each year in Deauville in August. The sale of brood-mares and young foals takes place at the end of November.

The **trotter** is now also a pure breed with its own stud book.

The **crossbreed,** from a Norman mare and an English thoroughbred or Norfolk crossbreed sire, is used for the increasingly popular pastime of hacking, the occasional star emerging as a racehorse.

There is also another breed: the **cob,** a short-legged and sturdy horse capable of pulling a ton at lively speed.

The **Percheron,** dappled grey or black, is a dray horse of great pulling power, good-natured and strong. Some say the breed goes back to the Crusades; what is certain is that it contains Arab stock. Percherons today are descended from the "great ancestor", the early 19C stallion Jean Le Blanc. Since his day the Percheron Horse Society has kept a stud book jealously marking out the areas where future generations may be bred in the Perche, Mayenne and the Auge.

Percheron

HISTORICAL TABLE AND NOTES

BC   The Celts inhabit parts of France. The Seine becomes the "tin road" *(p 124).*

Roman period

58-51 BC   Roman conquest. New towns appear: Rotomagus (Rouen), Caracotinum (Harfleur), Noviomagus (Lisieux), Juliobona (Lillebonne), Mediolanum (Évreux).

1 C   The main towns develop (Rouen, Évreux...).
2 C   Conversion to Christianity.
260   St Nicaise founds the Bishopric of Rouen.
284   Nordic invasion.
364   Nordic invasion.

Frankish domination

497   Clovis occupies Rouen and Évreux.
511   Clovis's son, Clothaire, inherits Neustria or the Western Kingdom.
6 C   The first monasteries founded *(p 125: The Castles of God).*
7 C   The monasteries flourish: St-Wandrille, Jumièges.

Viking invasions

The Vikings or Northmen who sailed from Scandinavia were of Danish or Norwegian origin. Aboard their *drakkars* carrying from 40 to 70 men they travelled beyond the seas in search of fortune. They harassed Western Europe, parts of Africa and even headed into the Mediterranean.

800   Vikings invade the Channel coast.
820   The Vikings lay waste the Seine Valley *(p 125).*
875   Further persecution in the West.
885   The Vikings besiege Paris.
911   Treaty of St-Clair-sur-Epte; Rollo first Duke of Normandy *(p 17).*

The independent dukedom

10-11 C   Consolidation of ducal powers. Restoration of the abbeys. Creation of new monasteries.

1027   Birth of William, future conqueror of Britain, at Falaise *(See Michelin Green Guide Normandy Cotentin).*

1066   The invasion of Britain *(p 17).* The Duke of Normandy, now also King of England, becomes a threatening vassal to the King of France.

1087   Death of William the Conqueror.
1087-1135   William's heirs are divided. Henry I Beauclerc restores ducal authority (King of England 1100-1135).

1152   Henry II Plantagenet, Count of Anjou, marries Eleanor of Aquitaine at Lisieux.

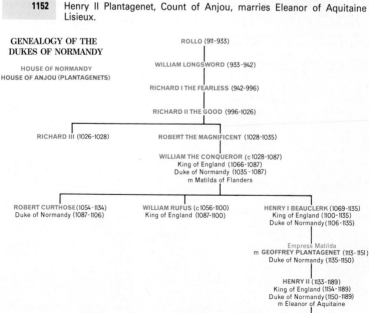

GENEALOGY OF THE
DUKES OF NORMANDY

HOUSE OF NORMANDY
HOUSE OF ANJOU (PLANTAGENETS)

ROLLO (911-933)

WILLIAM LONGSWORD (933-942)

RICHARD I THE FEARLESS (942-996)

RICHARD II THE GOOD (996-1026)

RICHARD III (1026-1028)

ROBERT THE MAGNIFICENT (1028-1035)

WILLIAM THE CONQUEROR (c 1028-1087)
King of England (1066-1087)
Duke of Normandy (1035-1087)
m Matilda of Flanders

ROBERT CURTHOSE (1054-1134)
Duke of Normandy (1087-1106)

WILLIAM RUFUS (c 1056-1100)
King of England (1087-1100)

HENRY I BEAUCLERK (1069-1135)
King of England (1100-1135)
Duke of Normandy (1106-1135)

Empress Matilda
m GEOFFREY PLANTAGENET (1113-1151)
Duke of Normandy (1135-1150)

HENRY II (1133-1189)
King of England (1154-1189)
Duke of Normandy (1150-1189)
m Eleanor of Aquitaine

RICHARD LIONHEART (1157-1199)
King of England (1189-1199)

JOHN LACKLAND (1167-1216)
King of England (1199-1216)

1154-1189	Henry II King of England.
1195	Richard Lionheart builds Gaillard Castle.
1202	John Lackland loses his Norman possessions.
1204	Normandy is reunited to the French Crown.

The French dukedom

1315	The Norman Charter, the symbol of provincial status, is granted and will remain in being until the Revolution.
1346	Edward III of England invades Normandy.
1364-84	The Battle of Cocherel: start of Du Guesclin's victorious campaigns.
1417	Henry V of England invades Normandy. Siege of Rouen *(p 109)*.
1431	Trial and torture of Joan of Arc at Rouen *(qv)*.
1469	The ducal seal is broken as Charles of France, last Duke of Normandy, is dispossessed of his dukedom.

The province of Normandy

1514	The Rouen Exchequer becomes the Parliament of Normandy.
1517	Le Havre is founded *(qv)*.
1542	Rouen is created as a self-governing city.
1589	Henri of Navarre is victorious at Arques *(qv)* and the following year at Ivry-la-Bataille *(qv)*.
1771-1775	Suppression of the Parliament at Rouen.

Contemporary Normandy

1795-1800	Insurrection of the Norman royalists, the Chouans.
1843	Inauguration of Paris-Rouen railway.
1845	Paris-Rouen electric telegraph system.
1870-1871	Franco-Prussian War. Occupation of Upper Normandy and Le Mans.
1928	The Lower Seine becomes the River of Petrol *(p 126)*.
June 1940	Piercing of the Blesle Front. The cities and towns of Upper Normandy are ravaged by fire.
August 1942	Dieppe Commando raid by the Canadian and British troops.
June 1944	Allied landing: heavy bombing.
1954	René Coty, born in Le Havre, is elected President of the Republic.
1974	The Brotonne Regional Nature Park is created.
1977	Completion of the Normandy motorway (A 13).
1978	The Place du Vieux-Marché *(p 116)* in Rouen is restored.
1983-1984	Start-up of Paluel nuclear power station.

THE NORMANS AND HISTORY (9-17 C)

Several different kinds of expedition emphasise the "Norman epic": the first of these were warlike reconnaissances led by the Vikings along all the sea routes of the North Atlantic and the Mediterranean. Whenever these Northmen settled down, new States were created such as Normandy. But the map below gives special place to the achievements by Normans of Normandy: the founding of kingdoms in the 11 and 12C, then, after the Hundred Years War, discoveries (or rediscoveries) of lands accompanied by efforts at colonisation which were more or less successful.

The Norman Kingdoms

① **1066** – Conquest of England by William of Normandy.

② **1042-1194** – The descendants of Tancrède de Hauteville found the Norman Kingdom of Sicily.

③ **1099** – During the First Crusade, Bohémond, son of Robert Guiscard, sets up a principality near Antioch. His descendants stay there until 1287.

④ **1364** – Men of Dieppe land on the coasts of Guinea (Sierra Leone of today) and found Little Dieppe (Petit Dieppe).

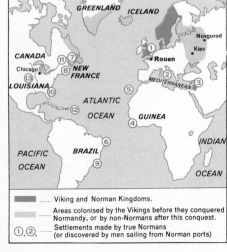

▓▓	Viking and Norman Kingdoms.
░░	Areas colonised by the Vikings before they conquered Normandy, or by non-Normans after this conquest.
①,②	Settlements made by true Normans (or discovered by men sailing from Norman ports)

Norman Discoveries

⑤ **1402** – Jean de Béthencourt, of the Caux Region, goes in search of adventure and becomes King of the Canary Islands but soon cedes the islands to the King of Castile.

⑥ **1503** – Paulmier de Gonneville, gentleman of Honfleur, reaches Brazil in his vessel the *Espoir*.

⑦ **1506** – Jean Denis, sailor from Honfleur, explores the mouth of the St Lawrence, preparing the way for Jacques Cartier of Saint-Malo.

⑧ **1524** – Leaving Dieppe, in the caravel *La Dauphine*, the French Florentine Verrazano, Navigator to François I, reconnoitres New France and discovers the site of New York, to which he gives the name Land of Angoulême.

⑨ **1555** – Admiral de Villegaignon sets up a colony of Huguenots from Le Havre on an island in the bay of Rio de Janeiro but they are driven away by the Portuguese.

⑩ **1563** – Led by René de la Laudonnière, colonies of Protestants from Le Havre and Dieppe settle in Florida and found Fort Caroline but are massacred by the Spaniards.

⑪ **1608** – Samuel Champlain, Dieppe ship-builder, sets sail from Honfleur to found Quebec.

⑫ **1635** – Pierre Belain of Esnambuc takes possession of Martinique in the name of the King of France. The colonisation of Guadeloupe follows soon after.

⑬ **1682** – Cavelier de la Salle, of Rouen, after reconnoitring the site of Chicago, sails down the Mississippi and takes possession of Louisiana.

The formation of the dukedom of Normandy. – Charles the Simple – a name meaning sincere and honest and by no means pejorative – met Rollo, the Viking chief, at **St-Clair-sur-Epte** in the year 911. The Vikings pitched camp on the right bank of the Epte, the French on the left. According to Dudon de St-Quentin, the first historian of Normandy, the Viking placed his hands between those of the French king to ratify the agreement creating the dukedom of Normandy. This "businessman's handshake" was worth a solemn exchange of seals and signatures for no written treaty was ever drafted. The Epte formed the boundary north of the Seine and the Avre to the south. The Norman fronteer was the object of time-honoured battles between the kings of France and the dukes of Normandy who became kings of England at the end of the 11C.

The conquest of England.

– This masterpiece of diplomacy and one of the most astonishing expeditions of the Middle Ages was prepared at the one-time important port of Dives-sur-Mer in 1066.

William the diplomat. – When **William of Normandy** heard of **Harold's** accession to the English throne in January 1066 he sent a diplomatic mission to remind him of his promises. Harold rudely rejected William's claim. The Duke of Normandy then appealed to the Pope who ordered him to punish England. Harold was subsequently excommunicated.

At an extraordinary assembly held at Lillebonne the barons sided with William, who ensured French neutrality and envisaged an alliance with Norway. The fleet was prepared, the troups' pay being assured by the treasures of Rouen and Caen. At Easter the appearance of Haley's comet "whose tail illuminated almost half the firmament" created a fright in England. The duke's astrologer saw in this an omen for the future king.

William the Conqueror. – William lived in Bonneville Castle above Touques. In less than seven months he realised all his political and military plans.

The major part of the fleet was centred at Dives. On the 12 September, protected by the Pope's ensign, about 500 000 knights and soldiers embarked upon 696 ships followed by smaller boats and skiffs bringing the total number of vessels to 3 000. The fleet set sail for St-Valéry-sur-Somme where reinforcements were waiting. In the meantime Harold destroyed Norwegian troops at York but the decoy effect had worked.

The great day came on September 27th. On the 28th at low tide the Normans landed at Pevensey, Sussex. William was last to disembark but he stumbled and fell full length. The superstitious Normans were alarmed, but William laughed and, according to the records, retorted: "My Lords, by the glory of God have I seized this land with my own two hands. As long as it exists it is ours alone."

The Normans occupied Hastings. Harold rushed to the scene and pitched camp on a hill. On October 14th William attacked, and by evening the Normans were victorious thanks to a war strategem. Harold died in combat. William founded an abbey on the site. The history of the invasion is recounted in the embroidery of the famous Bayeux Tapestry.

William, Duke and King. – After his victory William occupied Dover then stopped at Canterbury. Worried by threats of civil war the rich London merchants requested confirmation of their privileges in return for their support. Bishops and army submitted in turn. With Norman assent William accepted the royal crown offered him. The Coronation took place December 25th at Westminster, the new king swearing to maintain the laws and customs of the land. The Conqueror reserved for himself 1422 manors, fortresses and forests whereas his companions were given land.

The following year William returned to Normandy at Easter, the apotheosis for the new king.

Tapestry of Queen Mathilde. Channel crossing by the Norman army

ABC OF ARCHITECTURE

To assist readers unfamiliar with the terminology employed in architecture, we describe below the most commonly used terms, which we hope will make their visits to ecclesiastical, military and civil buildings more interesting.

Ecclesiastical architecture

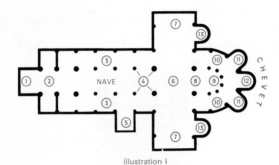

illustration I

Ground plan. – The more usual Catholic form is based on the outline of a cross with the two arms of the cross forming the transept: ① Porch – ② Narthex – ③ Side aisles (sometimes double) – ④ Bay (transverse section of the nave between 2 pillars) – ⑤ Side chapel (often predates the church) – ⑥ Transept crossing – ⑦ Arms of the transept, sometimes with a side doorway – ⑧ Chancel, nearly always facing east towards Jerusalem; the chancel often vast in size was reserved for the monks in abbatial churches – ⑨ High altar – ⑩ Ambulatory: in pilgrimage churches the aisles were extended round the chancel, forming the ambulatory, to allow the faithful to file past the relics – ⑪ Radiating or apsidal chapel – ⑫ Axial chapel. In churches which are not dedicated to the Virgin this chapel, in the main axis of the building is often consecrated to the Virgin (Lady Chapel) – ⑬ Transept chapel.

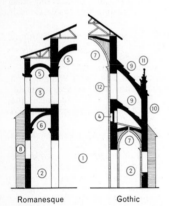

Romanesque   Gothic

◀ illustration II

Cross-section: ① Nave – ② Aisle – ③ Tribune or Gallery – ④ Triforium – ⑤ Barrel vault – ⑥ Half-barrel vault – ⑦ Pointed vault – ⑧ Buttress – ⑨ Flying buttress – ⑩ Pier of a flying buttress – ⑪ Pinnacle – ⑫ Clerestory window.

illustration III ▶

Gothic cathedral: ① Porch – ② Gallery – ③ Rose window – ④ Belfry (sometimes with a spire) – ⑤ Gargoyle acting as a waterspout for the roof gutter – ⑥ Buttress – ⑦ Pier of a flying buttress (abutment) – ⑧ Flight or span of flying buttress – ⑨ Double-course flying buttress – ⑩ Pinnacle – ⑪ Side chapel – ⑫ Radiating or apsidal chapel – ⑬ Clerestory windows – ⑭ Side doorway – ⑮ Gable – ⑯ Pinnacle – ⑰ Spire over the transept crossing.

illustration IV

Groined vaulting:
① Main arch – ② Groin
③ Transverse arch

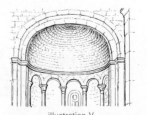

illustration V

Oven vault:
termination of a barrel
vaulted nave

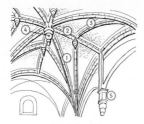

illustration VI

Lierne and tierceron vaulting:
① Diagonal – ② Lierne
③ Tierceron – ④ Pendant
⑤ Corbel

illustration VII

Quadripartite vaulting:
① Diagonal – ② Transverse
③ Stringer – ④ Flying buttress
⑤ Keystone

▼ illustration VIII

Doorway: ① Archivolt. Depending on the architectural style of the building this can be rounded, pointed, basket-handled, ogee or even adorned by a gable – ② Arching, covings (with string courses, mouldings, carvings or adorned with statues). Recessed arches or orders form the archivolt – ③ Tympanum – ④ Lintel – ⑤ Archshafts – ⑥ Embrasures. Arch shafts, splaying sometimes adorned with statues or columns – ⑦ Pier (often adorned by a statue) – ⑧ Hinges and other ironwork.

illustration IX ▶

Arches and pillars: ① Ribs or ribbed vaulting – ② Abacus – ③ Capital – ④ Shaft – ⑤ Base – ⑥ Engaged column – ⑦ Pier of arch wall – ⑧ Lintel – ⑨ Discharging or relieving arch – ⑩ Frieze.

Military architecture

illustration X

illustration XI

Fortified enclosure: ① Hoarding (projecting timber gallery) – ② Machicolations (corbelled crenellations) – ③ Barbican – ④ Keep or donjon – ⑤ Covered watchpath – ⑥ Curtain wall – ⑦ Outer curtain wall – ⑧ Postern.

Towers and curtain walls: ① Hoarding – ② Crenellations – ③ Merlon – ④ Loophole or arrow slit – ⑤ Curtain wall – ⑥ Bridge or drawbridge.

◀ illustration XII

Fortified gatehouse: ① Machicolations – ② Watch turrets or bartizan – ③ Slots for the arms of the drawbridge – ④ Postern.

illustration XIII ▶

Star fortress: ① Entrance – ② Drawbridge – ③ Glacis – ④ Ravelin or half-moon – ⑤ Moat – ⑥ Bastion – ⑦ Watch turret – ⑧ Town – ⑨ Assembly area.

ARCHITECTURAL TERMS USED IN THE GUIDE

Aisle: illustration I.
Altarpiece or **retable:** illustration XIX.
Ambulatory: illustration I.
Apsidal or **radiating chapel:** illustration I.
Arcade: succession of small arches; when attached to a wall they are known as blind arcades.
Archivolt: illustration VIII.
Arms of the transept: illustration I.

Baldachin or **baldaquin:** canopy supported by columns, usually over the high altar.
Barrel vaulting: illustration II.
Basket handled arch: depressed arch common to late medieval and Renaissance architecture.
Bay: illustration I.
Bond: an arrangement of stones or bricks.
Buttress: illustration II.

Capital: illustration IX.
Caryatid: support in the form of carved female figure.
Cheek-piece: illustration XVII.
Chevet: French term for the east end of a church; illustration I.
Ciborium: canopy over the high altar or a receptacle for the Eucharist.
Coffered ceiling: vault or ceiling decorated with sunken panels.
Crypt: underground chamber or chapel.

Depressed arch: three centred arch sometimes called a basket handled arch .
Diagonal arch: arch supporting a vault; illustrations VI and VII.
Discharging or **relieving arch:** illustration IX.
Dome or **cupola:** illustrations XIV and XV.

Elbow rest: illustration XVII.
Entombment: painting or carved group depicting the burial of the crucified Christ.

Flamboyant: latest phase (15C) of French Gothic architecture; name taken from the undulating (flame-like) lines of the window tracery.
Fresco: mural paintings executed on wet plaster.

Gable: triangular part of an end wall carrying a sloping roof; the term is also applied to the steeply pitched ornamental pediments of Gothic architecture; illustration III.
Gallery: illustration II.
Gargoyle: illustration III.
Glory: luminous nimbus surrounding the body; mandorla an almond shaped glory from the Italian *mandorla* meaning almond.
Groined vaulting: illustration IV.

Half-timbered: timber-framed construction.
High relief: haut-relief.
Historiated: decorated with figures of people or animals.
Hoarding: illustration X.

Key or fret pattern: geometrical pattern of straight lines intersecting at right angles.
Keystone: illustration VII.

Lancet window: narrow pointed-arched window.
Lierne: illustration VI.
Lintel: illustration VIII.
Loophole or **arrow slit:** illustration XI.
Low relief: bas-relief.

Machicolations: illustration X.
Misericord: illustration XVII.
Moat: ditch, generally water-filled.
Modillion: small console supporting a cornice.
Mullion: a vertical post dividing a window.

Organ case: illustration XX.
Oven vaulting: illustration V.
Overhang or **jetty:** overhanging upper storey.

Half-timbered house
1 Wall plate 2 Brace
3 Post

Parclose screen: screen separating a chapel or the choir from the rest of the church.
Pepperpot roof: conical roof.
Peristyle: a range of columns surrounding or on the façade of a building.
Pier: illustration VIII.
Pietà: Italian term designating the Virgin Mary with the dead Christ on her knees.
Pilaster: engaged rectangular column.
Pinnacle: illustrations II and III.
Postern: illustrations X and XII.

Quadripartite vaulting: illustration VII.

◄ illustration XIV

Dome on squinches:
① Octagonal dome –
② Squinch – ③ Arches of
transept crossing.

illustration XV ►

Dome on pendentives:
① Circular dome –
② Pendentive – ③ Arches
of transept crossing.

illustration XVI ►

Rood-beam or tref: This supports the triumphal (chancel or rood) arch at the entrance to the chancel. The rood carries a Crucifix flanked by statues of the Virgin and St John and sometimes other personages from the Calvary.

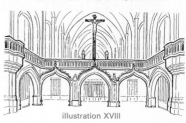

illustration XVII

Stalls: ① High back – ② Elbow rest –
③ Cheek-piece – ④ Misericord.

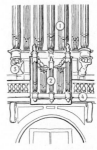

illustration XVIII

Rood-screen: This replaces the rood-beam in larger churches, and may be used for preaching and reading of the Epistles and Gospel. Many disappeared from the 17C onwards as they tended to hide the altar.

illustration XIX

Altar with retable or altarpiece: ① Retable
or altarpiece – ② Predella – ③ Crowning
piece – ④ Altar table – ⑤ Altar front.

illustration XX

Organ: ① Great organ case – ② Little
organ case – ③ Caryatids – ④ Loft.

Recessed arches or **orders:** illustration VIII.

Reliquary: casket to hold a relic or relics of a saint; it sometimes takes the form of the relic ie arm reliquary.

Retable: see altarpiece.

Roodbeam or **tref:** illustration XVI.

Rood screen: illustration XVIII.

Rose or **wheel window:** illustration III.

Saddleback roof: usually of tower where two gable ends are connected by a ridge roof.

Semicircular arch: roundheaded arch.

Spire: illustration III.

Stained glass

Stalls: illustration XVII.

Stringer: illustration VII.

Tierceron: illustration VI.

Timber-framed: see half-timbered.

Transept: illustration I.

Tracery: intersecting stone ribwork in the upper part of a window.

Triforium: illustration II.

Triptych: three panels hinged together, chiefly used as an altarpiece.

Twinned or **paired:** columns or pilasters grouped in twos.

Voussoirs: one of the stones forming an arch.

Watchpath or **wall walk:** illustration X.

ART IN NORMANDY

Norman building materials. – The stone is often quarried from the very land which it later embellishes. Rouen and the towns of the Seine are built with chalky limestone from the valley sides. A similar affinity exists between the local materials and the buildings in the Caux region, where pebbles are set in flowing mortar. Clay, in plentiful supply locally and cheap, was used for the cob or pisé of the timber-framed thatched cottages and for making bricks, which were often ingeniously used to achieve decorative patterns.

Half-timbering

Romanesque Art (11C - early 12C)

The Benedictines and Romanesque Design. – In the 11C the Benedictines returned to their task of clearing the land and building churches and other monastic buildings. These monk architects employed the barrel vault – the same that the Romans had used for their bridges and their triumphal arches or, sometimes, as an alternative, erected domes, using, however, not the original Oriental but the more robust Carolingian methods of construction. Thus the Benedictines created a new architectural style named "Romanesque" by a 19C Norman archaeologist, Arcisse de Caumont, who, in 1840, outlined the theory of regional schools of architecture. Despite its apparent simplicity Romanesque architecture is wonderfully diverse. In England, the style has remained known as "Norman".

The Norman School and its abbey churches. – The Benedictines, supported by the dukes of Normandy, played an immensely important part in the whole life of the province; only their work as architects and creators of the Norman school is described below. The first religious buildings of importance in Normandy were the churches of the rich abbacies. Early monastic buildings may have disappeared or been modified, particularly after the Maurian Reform *(p 24)*, but there remain, as evidence of the "Benedictine flowering", such fine abbey ruins as Jumièges and the church at St-Martin-de-Boscherville.

The Norman school is characterised by pure lines, bold proportions, sober decoration and beautiful ashlared stonework. The style spread to England after the Norman Conquest – it was in Durham Cathedral that quadripartite or rib vaulting officially first appeared, and certainly on such a scale, at the beginning of the 12C. Other fine examples include Westminster Abbey as rebuilt by Edward the Confessor, the two west front towers and square crossing tower at Canterbury and Southwell, Winchester and Ely.

The abbeys are characterised by robust towers on either side of the west front, giving the west face an H-like appearance, and a square lantern tower above the transept crossing. The towers, bare or decorated only with blind arcades below, get lighter with multiple pierced bays the higher they rise (many were crowned by spires quartered by pinnacles in the 13C). Romanesque belfries often surmount delightful country churches – their saddleback roofs rising like a circumflex accent or four-sided wood or squat stone pyramid coverings, embryonic Gothic spires, marking them from afar.

The interior light and size of Norman abbeys is very striking. The naves are wide with an elevation consisting of two series of openings above great semicircular arches – an amazingly bold concept for a Romanesque construction. The explanation lies in the fact that the design was not intended to support a heavy barrel vault: the Norman monks deliberately rejected this style of covering in favour of a beamed roof over the nave and galleries, reserving groined stone vaulting (the crossing of two semicircular arches) for the aisles. The vast galleries on the first level open onto the wide bays of the nave and repeat the design of the aisles.

Finally, on a level with the upper windows or clerestory, a gallery or wall passage in the thickness of the wall circles the church. A dome over the transept crossing supports a magnificent lantern tower which lets in the daylight through tall windows.

Norman decoration. – The abbey churches, like all others of Romanesque design, were illuminated on a considerable scale with gilding and bright colours as were the manuscripts of the time. The main themes were those of Byzantine iconography.

Norman sculpture does not rival other Romanesque schools; the decoration is essentially geometric: different motifs stand out, of which the most common is the key or fret pattern (a pattern of straight lines intersecting at right angles to form crenellated or rectangular designs). The decorative motifs are sometimes accompanied by mouldings, human heads or animal masks emphasising recessed arches, archivolts, cornices and mouldings.

Gothic Art (12C-15C)

The style, conceived in the Ile-de-France, apart from quadripartite or rib vaulting which was brought back from Norman England, was known as "French work" or "French style" until the 16C when the Italians of the Renaissance gave it the appellation of Gothic art.

The cathedrals. – Gothic is a style made for cathedrals, symbolising the sweeping religious fervour of the people, the growing prosperity of the towns. In an all-embracing enthusiasm, a whole city would participate in the construction of the house of God: some would bring offerings, others lend their strength and skill. Under the enlightened guidance of bishops and master builders, city corporations contributed to the cathedral's embellishment: stained glass makers, painters, wood and stone carvers went to work. The doors became the illustrated pages of history.

Gothic architecture in Normandy. – In turn the national Gothic style seeped gradually back to Normandy, preceding the seizure of

Caudebec-en-Caux. Notre-Dame Church

the province by Philippe-Auguste. The St Romanus Tower of Rouen Cathedral and particularly Lisieux Cathedral show the degree of French Gothic influence in Normandy by the end of the 12C.

The Flamboyant Style. – By the 14C, the period of great cathedral building had come to an end. The Hundred Years War killed architectural inspiration: bits were added, buildings were touched up, but little created. When the war was over a taste for virtuosity alone remained – and the Flamboyant style was born. Rouen is the true capital of the Flamboyant, which was particularly widespread in Upper Normandy.

In this new style, the tracery of bays and rose windows resembles wavering flames – the derivation of the term "Flamboyant". The Flamboyant style produced such single masterpieces as the Church of St Maclou at Rouen, the Butter Tower on Rouen Cathedral, the belfries of Notre-Dame at Caudebec and the Magdalene at Verneuil-sur-Avre. Civil architecture developed in importance and passed from Flamboyant to Renaissance – a change symbolised in the gables, pinnacles, balustrades of the Law Courts at Rouen.

Feudal architecture. – In medieval Normandy permission to build a castle was granted to the barons by the ruling duke, who, prudent as well as powerful, reserved the right to billet his own garrison inside and forbade all private wars. Over the years the building of castles along the duchy's frontiers was encouraged – Richard Lionheart bolted the Seine with the most formidable fortress of the period, Gaillard Castle.

Castles were sited so as to command the horizon and be invincible to surprise attack. Originally only the austere keeps were inhabited, but from the 14C a courtyard and more pleasing quarters were constructed within the fortifications. This evolution in military architecture can be seen in some of the Perche manor houses and particularly in the 15C Dieppe Castle.

A taste for comfort and adornment appeared in civil architecture: rich merchants and burgesses built tall houses where wide eaves protected half-timbered upper storeys which in turn overhung stone walled ground floors. The results were as capricious as they were picturesque: corner posts, corbels and beams were all vividly carved.

The Renaissance (16C)

Georges I d'Amboise, Archbishop of Rouen and patron of the arts, introduced Italian methods and taste to Normandy.

An Italian style of decoration was applied by Italian artists to the feudal structure of Gaillon Château by Georges d'Amboise. The new motifs – arabesques, foliated scrollwork, medallions, shells, urns, etc. – were combined with Flamboyant art. The outstanding ecclesiastical works of this period are the main doorway of Rouen Cathedral and Gisors Church.

The château at Gaillon

Castles, manor houses and old mansions. – The Renaissance style reached its fullest grace in domestic architecture. At first older buildings were ornamented in the current taste or a new and delicately decorated wing was added; parks and gardens were laid out where fortifications once stood.

The Classicism rediscovered by humanists took hold so that, among others, Philibert Delorme, architect of Anet Château, sought above all correct proportion and the imposition of the three Classical Orders of Antiquity. Imperceptibly the search for symmetry and correctness mortified inspiration: pomposity drowned fantasy.

In Normandy, the Gothic spirit survived, appearing most successfully in small manor houses and innumerable country houses with sham feudal moats, turrets and battlements incorporated in either half timbering or stone and brick.

Norman towns contain many large stone Renaissance mansions. The façade is always plain and one has to enter the inner courtyard to see the architectural design and the rich decoration (Bourgtheroulde Mansion, Rouen).

In the 16C decoration became richer and less impulsive, but the half-timbered architectural style remained the same. Many of these old houses were destroyed during the war, but some, carefully restored, may still be seen in Bernay, Honfleur, Pont-Audemer, Verneuil-sur-Avre and Rouen.

Classical Art (17C-18C)

In this period, French architectural style, now a single concept and no longer an amalgam of individual techniques, imposed its rationalism on many countries beyond its borders.

Louis XIII and the so-called Jesuit Style. – The reign of Henri IV marked an artistic rebirth. An economical method of construction was adopted in which bricks played an important part: it was a time of beautiful châteaux with plain rose and white façades and steep grey-blue slate roofs.

The first decades of the 17C also coincided with a strong Catholic reaction. The Jesuits built many colleges and chapels – cold and formal edifices, their façades characterised by superimposed columns, a pediment and upturned consoles or small wings joining the front of the main building to the sides.

The "Grand Siècle" in Normandy. – The symmetrical façades of the classical style demanded space for their appreciation as in the châteaux at Cany, Beaumesnil, Champ de Bataille and elsewhere. The Benedictine abbeys, which had adopted the **Maurian Reform,** rediscovered their former inspiration. At the beginning of the 18C, the monastery buildings of the Abbaye aux Hommes in Caen and at Le Bec-Hellouin were remodelled by a brother architect and sculptor, **Guillaume de la Tremblaye** *(qv).* The original plan was conserved but the design and decoration were given an austere nobility.

Finally, towns were transformed by the addition of magnificent episcopal palaces, town halls with wide façades and large private houses.

Ceramics and pottery. – In the mid-16C Masséot Abaquesne was making decorated tiles in Rouen which were greatly prized and, simultaneously, potteries in Le Pré-d'Auge and Manerbe (near Lisieux) were also making "earthenware more beautiful than is made elsewhere". In 1644 **Rouen faience** *(p 117)* made its name with blue decoration on a white background and vice versa. By the end of the century production had so increased that when the royal plate had to be sacrificed to replenish the Treasury, "the Court", wrote Saint-Simon, "had changed to chinaware in a week".

The Radiant style, reminiscent of wrought ironwork and embroidery for which the town was well known, was succeeded by Chinoiserie and, in the middle of the 18C by the Rococo with its "quiver" decoration and the famous "Rouen cornucopia" in which flowers, birds and insects flow from a horn of plenty. A trade treaty in 1786, allowing the entry of English chinaware to France, ruined the industry.

Norman domestic furniture. – Norman sideboards, grandfather clocks and wardrobes are the three most characteristic and traditional pieces of furniture in this region. This

elegant, solid and sturdy furniture is sought out by both the antique dealer and the lover of rustic furniture.

In the 13C the wardrobe slowly replaced the medieval chest; the sideboard already existed by the beginning of the 17C and it was in the 18C that grandfather clocks were widely used.

This period was the golden age of furniture making in Normandy; the sideboard or kitchen dresser was well proportioned and delicately carved; the tall pendulum clock with gilt bronze delicately chased, copper, pewter or enamel dials (the "waisted" ones in the Caen area are known as *demoiselles*); the majestic wardrobe in massive oak ornamented with finely worked brass or other metal fittings or medallions, as well as cornices carved with cornucopia of birds nests, ears of corn, flowers, fruit, Cupidon's quiver, etc. The latter with the trousseau constituted a young girl's dowry.

Norman furniture (detail)

Modern Art

Painting took first place among the arts in 19C France. Landscape totally eclipsed historical and stylised painting and Normandy, land blessed with muses, was to become the cradle of Impressionism.

The open air. – While the Romantics were discovering inland Normandy, Eugène Isabey, a lover of seascapes, began to work on the still deserted coast. **Richard Bonington,** 1801-28, an English painter who went to France as a boy, trained there, and caught, in his watercolours, the wetness of sea beaches.

In the second half of the 19C artistic activity was concentrated, with **Eugène Boudin** (1824-98) round the Côte de Grâce. This painter from Honfleur, named "King of the Skies" by Corot, encouraged a young fifteen-year-old from Le Havre, **Claude Monet,** to drop caricature for the joys of real painting and urged his Parisian friends to come and stay in his St-Siméon farmstead.

Trouville at High Tide by Eugène Boudin

Impressionism. – The younger painters, nevertheless, were to outstrip their elders in the search for pictorial light. They wanted to portray the vibration of light, hazes, the trembling of reflections and shadows, the depth and tenderness of the sky, the fading of colours in full sunlight. They – Monet, Sisley, Bazille and their Paris friends, Renoir, Pissarro, Cézanne and Guillaumin especially – were about to form the Impressionist School which gave France a front rank in the history of painting.

From 1862 to 1869 the Impressionists remained faithful to the Normandy coast and the Seine Estuary. After the Franco-Prussian War they returned only occasionally – although it was in Normandy, at Giverny *(qv),* that Claude Monet set up house in 1881 and remained until he died in 1926 in the full glory of his work.

Impressionism, in its turn, gave birth to a new school, **Pointillism,** which divided the tints with little touches of colour, applying the principle of the division of white light into seven basic colours, to get ever closer to a luminous effect. Seurat and Signac, the pioneers of this method, also came to Normandy to study its landscapes.

In the early 20C **Fauvism** was born as a reaction against Impressionism and neo-Impressionism. These brightly coloured linear compositions exploded on the canvas *(see below).*

For half a century, therefore, the Côte de Grâce, the Caux Région, Deauville, Trouville and Rouen were the sources of inspiration of a multitude of paintings *(1).*

A Pléiade of painters. – Numerous artists still came to Normandy in the first half of the 20C, notably Valloton and Gernez, the latter died in Honfleur; Marquet who had worked in Gustave Moreau's studio in Paris; Othon Friesz who particularly enjoyed Honfleur which he portrayed in its many aspects; and Van Dongen, painter of the worldly and the elegant and frequent guest at Deauville.

If Marquet, Friesz and Van Dongen were strongly influenced by Fauvism, Raoul Dufy, a native of Le Havre, soon overthrew the accepted concepts to associate line drawing and richness of colour in compositions which were full of movement.

Contemporary architecture. – Numerous Norman towns and villages have been greatly remodelled and rebuilt particularly after the large-scale destruction of the Second World War and also to meet the requirements of modern precepts of town planning.

Auguste Perret (1874-1954), the architect who pioneered the use of reinforced concrete construction, was appointed Chief Architect for the reconstruction of Le Havre. His works include the modern quarter of Le Havre and the Church of St Joseph *(p 81).*

Normandy is a region of innovation as well: the Brotonne Bridge *(qv),* the Place du Vieux Marché in Rouen *(p 116)* and the Espace Oscar Niemeyer in Le Havre *(p 81).*

---

(1) Important collections of works by contemporary Norman artists and the important precursors of Impressionism are to be seen in Le Havre in the modern setting of the André Malraux Fine Arts Museum.

MONASTICISM

Normandy, like Champagne and Burgundy, was one of the main centres of monasticism during the revival of religious life in the 11C. Today the abbeys, even the fragmented ones, are symbols of the astonishing fervour and faith of the period and the important role played by the religious orders in the life of the time.

Monks. – From the very earliest times men or women have often retired to live a solitary or communal existence in search of God. The Holy Scriptures tell us how Jesus sometimes fled from the crowds to seek solitude in the mountains of Judea or the hills of Galilea and commune with God his father. Monks have followed this example and the abbey constituted his wilderness, where he led a life of peace and silence and communed with his Maker.

The monk's day. – The day was divided between Divine Service, holy reading and manual labour.

Divine Service. – Known also as God's Work *(Opus Dei)* this consisted of "listening" to God, of singing his praise and munificence. In company with his fellow monks, he worshipped and praised the Lord at various times of the day: matins, lauds and vespers.
Another important activity was the reading of a chapter from the Benedictine Law in the chapter house.

Holy reading. – After Divine Service taken together each monk returns to his cell to commune with God, read the Bible or meditate.

Manual labour. – Intellectual work and manual labour were complementary activities in monastic life. The mind was improved by reading the Bible. Manual labour helped the monk to achieve a balanced existence and to earn his keep by working. The monks usually made their own bread, wove the cloth for their tunics and tended the vegetable garden.

Plan of a medieval abbey. – The monastic buildings were arranged around the cloisters.

Cloisters. – Generally four galleries surround a central garth or courtyard often laid out as a garden. Some monasteries made this central area their herb garden. In the south gallery there was the lavatorium where the monks washed their hands, before going for a meal.
The west gallery bordered the lay-brothers' range or the cellars and gave access to the church via the lay-brothers' door. The lay-brothers were those who did the manual and domestic work.
The north gallery also led to the church through the monks' doorway and opened on to the chapter house.

Chapter House. – The monks assembled daily for monastic business, where they prayed before they started the work of the day and where they listened to the reading of a chapter from the monastic rule. This was where the abbot imposed penance on those who had transgressed the rule.

Refectory. – With its often austere decoration, the refectory has quite astonishing acoustics. The reader from his elevated pulpit read from the Bible at mealtimes.

Dormitories. – There were generally two, one for the choir monks and another on the west side for the lay-brothers. In the Cistercian order seven hours were set aside for repose. The monks slept fully dressed in one communal dormitory. The Maurists, Augustinians and Premonstratensians had individual cells which were later to become bedrooms.

Abbey Church. – The monks spent the better part of their day in the church for mass or other day or nightime services. The abbey church was often characterised by a very long nave. In the Cistercian churches a screen or pulpitum separated the monks' choir with the altar from the lay-brothers' one.

Outbuildings. – These included the barns and the porter's lodge or gatehouse, often a monumental building. The gateway usually combined two entrances, one for vehicles and the other for people. The porter's lodge had living quarters on the first floor. It was here that alms were distributed and justice was dispensed to resolve conflicts and punish crime.

1 Monks Choir
2 Sacristy
3 Chapter House
4 Warming House
5 Day Room
6 Lavatorium
7 Monks' Doorway
8 Lay-Brothers' Doorway
9 Refectory
10 Reader's Pulpit
11 Kitchen
12 Lay-Brothers' Range
      or cellars
13 Guesthouse

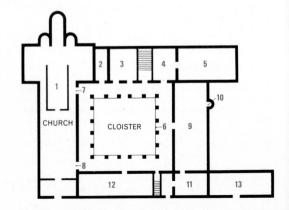

LITERATURE AND MUSIC

LITERATURE

Literature and architecture both sprang from the monasteries. It is therefore hardly surprising that Normandy and its abbeys became rich in literary activity as from the 13C. Monks and clergymen with a good knowledge of history and legend, together with travellers and pilgrims, provided the poets with the inspiration needed to create those marvellous Christian epics known as the *chansons de geste.* Such verse appeared chronologically after the early hagiographical literature (lives of saints) but remains one of the first examples of the use of French as a literary mode.

The most famous, the *Song of Roland,* most probably originated in this way.

17C. – Born in Rouen, **Corneille** (1606-1684) remains the great writer of the classical period. On stage, passion and emotion were almost always overcome by the voice of reason, his taste for grandeur and truth allied to a solid sense of proportion.

18C. – **Fontenelle** (1657-1757) was also from Rouen. His naturally positive outlook expresses the Norman temperament. Clear and direct in his thinking, he preferred philosophy to literature.

Born in Le Havre, **Bernadin de St-Pierre** (1737-1814) embarked on many a journey, driven on by his dreams (Malta, Russia, Poland etc). For a long time he lived in Mauritius and on his return to Paris he became the disciple of Jean-Jacques Rousseau. He is famous for his works *Paul and Virginie* (1787) and *Studies of Nature* (1784).

19C. Born in Le Havre, **Casimir Delavigne** (1793-1843), poet and dramatist, opened his Romantic theatre. **Armand Carrel** (1800-1936), born in Rouen, was an officer by career until the Spanish expedition of 1823. In 1830 with Thiers and the historian Miguet he founded the *National* newspaper favouring the Bourbons. He subsequently separated from Thiers and, once with the Republicans in opposition, he violently attacked the régime of Louis-Philippe, the July monarchy (1830-1848). He was killed during a duel resulting from a press incident. His political and literary works were published from 1854 to 1858.

As in painting *(p 25)* the literary revolution of the 19C was realist movement. **Gustave Flaubert** (1821-1880), a former Romantic from Rouen, considered the art as a means to knowledge. In spite of his Norman character he loved lyricism, yet strove to seek out the truth whenever and wherever he could.

With his novel *Madame Bovary,* one of the masterpieces of modern writing, Emma and M. Homais were immortalised.

Born in Honfleur **Alphonse Allais** (1854-1905) made his début at the Black Cat Cabaret in Paris. His works are noted for a particularly well developed sense of humour.

Subjected to the strict stylistic discipline of his master Flaubert, **Guy de Maupassant** (1850-1893) is an equally attentive observer popular both in and out of France. In his work *Contes de la Bécasse* (1883) made up of some three hundred short stories he evokes the class structure of Normandy, sometimes animated by bitter sarcasm.

20C. – **Lucie Delarue-Mardrus** (1880-1945), loyal to Honfleur until her dying day, sang of her country and was a Romantic poetess and novelist. Born in Mortagne-au-Perche *(qv)* **Alain** (1868-1951) his real name being Emile Chartier, made himself known by his comments in a Rouen newspaper. Professeur of Philosophy and essay writer he revolted against all forms of tyranny. His works *Remarks on Happiness* (1928) *and on Education* (1932) are noteworthy.

André Maurois (1865-1967) was known for his war memories, novels, biographies *(The Life of Disraeli,* 1927) and historical works *(History of England* 1937).

Jean de la Varende (1887-1959) from the Ouche Region evokes in his novels the Normandy of yesteryear. His work *Par Monts et Merveilles de Normandie* is a description of all he saw and admired in the region.

Armand Salacrou, born in 1899 in Rouen, considered dramatic works as a "meditation on the human condition". All genres are to be found in his theatrical works, for example *Un homme comme les autres* (1926) and *Boulevard Durand* (1961).

MUSIC

François Adrien-Boieldieu (1775-1834). – Born in Rouen, he composed operas and comic operas. His work. The *Caliph of Baghdad* (1800) earned him his reputation throughout Europe. From 1803 to 1810 he was Director of Music at the Imperial Opera of Saint Petersburg at the request of Czar Alexander I. His talent was universally recognised with his opera *La Dame Blanche* in 1825.

Camille Saint-Saëns (1835-1921). – He was born in Paris, but his father was from Normandy. A brilliant pianist, he composed symphonies, operas, concertos and religious works. His most famous works include the *Danse Macabre* (1875) and *Samson and Dalila* (1877).

Arthur Honegger (1892-1955). – Born in Le Havre, of Swiss origin. At first he composed melodies to poems by Cocteau, Apollinaire and Paul Fort, then *Pacific 231* (1923) and *King David* (1924). *Joan at the Stake* (1935) and *The Dance of the Dead* (1938) have texts by Paul Claudel.

Erik Satie (1866-1925). – Born in Honfleur he began as a pianist in the cabarets of Montmartre (The Black Cat) where he met Debussy. Sarcasm and irony are dissimulated in his works, his greatest being the symphonic drama *Socrates* (1918) for voice and orchestra based on texts by Plato.

Satie exerted an undeniable influence both on his time and on musicians such as Ravel, Debussy and Stravinski.

THE DOVECOT

A familiar figure in the Normandy countryside and especially in the Caux Region, the dovecot dates back to Roman times. No laws governed its construction until the Middle Ages.

In Normandy only the owner of a fief could possess a dovecot. The number of pigeons was unlimited and hunting them was forbidden. This right was abolished under the Revolution.

Description. – It can be square, polygonal or round, although the last type is the most common. The rectangular door is at ground level, sometimes rounded at the top and very often surmounted by the arms of the owner. Half-way up a stone rat ledge juts out in order to stop the progression of rodents. Pigeons pass through openings all around the building. A cornice ensures the transition between the walls and the roof, conical on circular dovecots, with sidewalls on square or polygonal dovecots, and often covered with slate. The crest finial in lead often has the form of a pigeon, sometimes a weather-cock. Inside the walls are covered with pigeon-holes. Each couple of pigeons has its own hole, the number varying according to the wealth of the owner. They are reached by a spiral staircase fixed to a central post standing on hard stone.

A dovecot may be reserved exclusively for pigeons or may be divided into two parts, the upper part for pigeons but the lower part serving as a hen-house or sheep run. If the two floors are separated by a wooden floor,

Dovecot in the Caux Region

access to the upper part is by way of a mobile ladder through a door on the outside, level with the stone rat ledge.

Varieties of dovecots. – In the so-called classical dovecot range we can distinguish: the freestone dovecot (uncommon), the dovecot in black flint and white stone, the contrast giving it a distinctive style (north and northeast of Le Havre), the brick, black flint and freestone dovecot, with brick making its appearance in the 17C and tending to replace black flint, and the common brick and stone dovecot. The so-called secondary dovecots comprise: the light flint dovecot, the colour reminiscent of freestone, the flint and stone dovecot and the flint, brick and stone dovecot.

TRADITIONS

For the table of principal festivals (date and place) see the chapter Practical Information at the end of the guide.

The Brothers of Charity. – In rural Norman churches one often notices in the chancel lines of delicately finished *torchères* characteristic of the Brothers of Charity, whose essential mission was to provide the dead with a Christian burial. Their origins go back to the 12C when the plague ravaged the countryside and caused the death of many of the inhabitants. In the processions the Brothers, preceded by bell-ringers who rang their hand-bells with monotonous regularity, moved forward with banners and *torchères* and wearing the *chaperon,* a velvet scarf embroidered with silver or gold.

Each Brotherhood has its hierarchy. At the highest level stands the Master or Provost assisted by a magistrate. The Brotherhoods possess their own patron saint, emblems, crosses, banners and staffs.

The Bonfire of Saint Clair. – The bonfire takes place each year on July 16 at la Haye-de-Routot *(qv)* in honour of the patron saint of the parish. A few weeks before the Brothers of Charity cut down a poplar tree. It is sawn into logs at Corpus Christi and left to dry. Once dry it is cut into smaller logs and on the morning of July 16 they are piled up around a mast of pine. A cross is placed on the top. A religious service takes place before the 15m - 49feet high fire is lit. Around 11pm the fire is blessed and set ablaze. The fire-brands picked up by the local population helped protect the houses from lightning. The day is enlivened by the presence of a travelling fair and the organisation of processions and an evening dance.

FOOD AND DRINK

The variety and quality of Normandy's copious products have given rise to good cooking characterised by the widespread use of cream.

Cream and Normandy Sauce. – Cream is the mainstay of the Normandy kitchen: ivory in colour, velvety in texture and mellow in taste, it goes as well with eggs and fish as with chicken, white meat, vegetables and even game. This delicious cream is at its best in the so called Normandy Sauce – *Sauce Normande* – which elsewhere is nothing but a plain white sauce, but in Normandy both looks and tastes quite different.

Cheeses. – If cream is the queen of Normandy cooking, cheese is the king of all fares. *Pont-l'Évêque* has reigned since the 13C; *Livarot* is quoted in texts of the same period; the world renowned *Camembert* first appeared early in the 19C *(details p 139).*
To be really creamy and soft, a *Pont-l'Évêque* should be made on a farm in the Auge Region when the milk is still warm from the cow. *Livarot,* whose strong odour alarms the uninitiated, is made from milk which has stood. Although *Camembert* is now made in factories all over France, only Normandy *Camembert* is authentic.
Finally there are the fresh cheeses from the Bray Region – the *Suisses, demi-sel* double cream – whose repute is more recent but none the less firmly established.
Neufchâtel in its various forms is also a much appreciated farmhouse cheese. It can be eaten within only 12 days of being made, although a mature *Neufchâtel* takes up to 3 months.

How Camembert is made. – There are nine operations in all.

Standardisation. – The raw material is milk containing 30 % fat, obtained from a mixture of whole fat and skimmed milk.

Coagulation. – The milk must coagulate in 100 litres - 22 gallons containers, helped by the curdling agent rennet. This operation lasts 1 1/2 hours and is delicate in that important factors intervene: the milk temperature (30 to 32°) and acidity (24 to 28°). The acidification rate will depend on atmospheric conditions and on the animals yielding the milk.

Moulding. – A temperature of 20 to 30° is needed. Each mould receives 200cl poured with specially designed ladles. The average yield is 1 500 litres - 330 gallons of milk in 8 hours.

Spreading. – The coagulated milk tends to settle towards the middle. In order to even out the surface this operation is repeated three times.

Turning. – After settling the cheese is turned over. By this time it occupies 1/3 of the mould. The operation takes place between 6.30 and 9.30pm.

These five operations take up the whole of the first day.

Withdrawing. – The soft cheese is withdrawn from the moulds and placed on planks which are then wheeled to the drying room to finish the draining process at a temperature of 18 to 20°.

Salting. – The first stage is to salt one side of the cheese and its circumference. The aim of this operation is to obtain the characteristic Camembert flavour by developing the ferment penicillium candidum. The temperature is 14 to 15°. Around 6.30pm the cheeses are turned over and next morning the other side is salted. We are now in day three.

Drying. – On the fourth day the cheese is placed on a trellis and taken to the drying rooms where a system of ventilation ensures a temperature of 10 to 14°. Mold begins to form after the fifth day. On the fourteenth day of the manufacturing process (10 days in the drying room), some of the cheese is put aside to mature whereas the rest is sold as fresh Camembert. The latter needs one to two days' extra drying after leaving the drying room proper. This is achieved by leaving the cheese in a draught.
In the maturing process the cheese is left to rest on planks located in cellars where the humidity rate is constant. It is turned over every day.
The cheese is dispatched 1/3 mature after 20 days (the most common case), 1/2 mature after 25 days and mature after 30 days.

Packing. – The cheese is packed for dispatch when dry. Beforehand it is sorted according to quality.

Gastronomic Specialities. – Normandy tradition has it that one eats duck in Rouen, tripe in Caen and at La Ferté-Macé, an omelette at Mont-St-Michel and that at some point one should also taste Dieppe sole, Duclair duckling, Auge Valley chicken garnished with tiny onions, Vire chitterlings, Mortagne-au-Perche black pudding and Avranchin white pudding.
The only problem for the lover of sea food is the one of choice between the shrimps and cockles of Honfleur, the mussels of Villerville and Isigny, the oysters of Courseulles and St-Vaast and the lobsters of La Hague and Barfleur.
Finally for those with a sweet tooth there are Rouen sugar apples and Caen *chiques* or caramels. Local specialities include cakes and pastries made with locally produced butter.

Cider, Calvados and Pommeau. – In Normandy the most fastidious gourmet will drink cider with shrimps, mussels, chicken from the Auge Valley, tripe or leg of lamb from the salt meadows. True cider, *bon bère,* is pure apple juice fermented. When the cork is drawn, *bon bère* should remain still in the bottle, only sparkling and then without froth when poured into the glass. For daily needs, the Norman dilutes his cider with water.
Auge Valley cider is famous but other local ciders are also good.
Calvados is to the apple what cognac is to the grape. This cider spirit, or apple jack, more than any other, needs to mature – twelve to fifteen years bring it to perfection. In the middle of his copious meal, the Norman breathes deeply for a moment and then swallows a small glass of *Calvados:* this is the famous "Norman hole" or *trou Normand;* at the end of the meal come cups of black coffee accompanied by further small glasses of *Calvados.*
Nowadays however restaurants tend to replace the traditional *trou Normand* by an apple sorbet sprinkled with *Calvados*
Pommeau is drunk as a chilled apéritif. It consists of two thirds apple juice and one third *Calvados.*

Key

Sights

★★★ **Worth a journey**
★★ **Worth a detour**
★ **Interesting**

Sightseeing route with departure point indicated
on the road   in town

✕ ⁂	Castle, Château – Ruins	🏛 ‡ 🏛 ‡ Ecclesiastical building: Catholic – Protestant
⊥ ◉	Wayside cross or calvary – Fountain	⬡ Building with main entrance
⁂ ♈	Panorama – View	⬤—● Ramparts – Tower
⚲ ✕	Lighthouse – Windmill	—•— Gateway
⌣ ✿	Dam – Factory or power station	▪ Statue or small building
✩ ∪	Fort – Quarry	Gardens, parks, woods
▲	Miscellaneous sights	**B** Letters giving the location of a place on the town plan

Other symbols

▬▬▬	Motorway (unclassified)	⊡ Public building
◂▸ ▸ ❶ ❷	Interchange complete, limited, number	✚ ⊠ Hospital – Covered market
▬▬	Major through road	⛨ ⚔ Police station – Barracks
═══	Dual carriageway	† † † † Cemetery
▭▭▭ - - -	Stepped street – Footpath	✡ Synagogue
⊢══⊣	Pedestrian street	🏇 ⚑ Racecourse – Golf course
⊤⊤	Unsuitable for traffic	⩰ ⊡ Outdoor or indoor swimming pool
→^1429←	Pass – Altitude	⍟ ⊤ Skating rink – Viewing table
🚆 🚌	Station – Coach station	⚓ Pleasure boat harbour
	Ferry services:	⍦ Telecommunications tower or mast
⛴	Passengers and cars	⬭ ⊼ Stadium – Water tower
⛵	Passengers only	**B** Ferry (river and lake crossings)
✈	Airport	△ Swing bridge
③	Reference number common to town plans and MICHELIN maps	✉ Main post office (with poste restante)
		❔ Tourist information centre
		▣ Car park

MICHELIN maps and town plans are north orientated.

Main shopping streets are printed in a different colour in the list of streets.

Town plans: roads most used by traffic and those on which guide listed sights stand are fully drawn; the beginning only of lesser roads is indicated.
Local maps: only the primary and sightseeing routes are indicated.

Abbreviations

A	Local agricultural office (Chambre d'Agriculture)	J Law Courts (Palais de Justice)	POL. Police station
C	Chamber of Commerce (Chambre de Commerce)	M Museum	T Theatre
H	Town Hall (Hôtel de ville)	P Préfecture Sous-préfecture	U University

🕐 **Times and charges for admission are listed at the end of the guide**

*When looking for a pleasant, quiet and well situated hotel consult the current **Michelin Red Guide**.*

Normandy
Seine Valley

L'AIGLE

Michelin map 60 fold 5 or 231 fold 45. Town plan in Michelin Red Guide France

L'Aigle, between the Ouche and the Perche Regions, is one of the main towns in the Upper Risle Valley and maintains its metalwork tradition with steel drawing mills producing pins, needles, staples etc.

SIGHTS

St-Martin's Church (Église St-Martin). – The building, though lacking unity, is attractive. An elaborate late 15C square tower contrasts with a small 12C one built of red iron agglomerate known as *grison (qv)* and surmounted by a more recent spire. Beautiful modern statues stand in niches between the windows of the south nave added in the 16C. Inside, two 16C stained glass windows (right of the chancel and first window, south aisle) complement a fine contemporary series, while a Renaissance aisle is decorated with graceful hanging keystones.

Château. – Now the town hall, the château was built in 1690 on the site of an 11C fortress, by Fulbert de Beina, Lord of l'Aigle, and vassal of the dukes of Normandy. He is said to have discovered on the site an eagle's nest, hence the name of the town. The plans are the work of Mansart.

⊙ **Marcel Angot Museum** (Musée Marcel Angot). – A staircase leads to the first floor. Go through the local council chamber to a room containing various musical instruments: string, wind, and a *serpent,* a snake-like wind instrument used in military music. Exotic instruments complete the collection, a donation from a former bandmaster of the town.

⊙ **"June 1944: Battle of Normandy" Museum.** – The museum, located beside the castle, contains wax figures of leading personalities (de Gaulle, Churchill, Leclerc, Roosevelt, Stalin etc.). Their voices may also be heard on recordings. The Battle of Normandy can be followed by means of a relief map and dioramas to retrace the outstanding events.

EXCURSIONS

St-Sulpice-sur-Risle. – Pop 1287. *3km - 2 miles to the northeast on the D 930.*
⊙ The **church** adjoining an old 13C priory, which was partially rebuilt in the 16C, contains a 16C tapestry, a 17C canvas of St Cecilia, a statue of St Anne and two stained glass windows from the 13 and 14C.

Aube. – Pop 1841. *7km - 4 1/2 miles to the southwest. Leave l'Aigle by the N 26.*

Nouettes Château, situated at the entrance to the town and now a medico-pedagogical institute, was the residence of Countess Eugène de Ségur.
⊙ The **Ségur-Rostopchine Museum** is located at number 3, Rue de L'Église and contains mementoes of the countess – née Rostopchine – and of her family (letters, portraits). The characters figuring in the writer's works are represented by a collection of dolls and miscellaneous objects (books, furniture...).

★ AMFREVILLE Locks (Écluses d'AMFREVILLE)

Michelin map 55 fold 7 or 231 fold 23

The locks, which lie just upstream from the Andelle Valley and below the Deux Amants Hill *(qv),* constitute, together with the Poses Dam, the main water flow control of the Lower Seine, dividing the canalised stretch downstream from Paris from the section which flows into the Channel and is subject to tidal variations.

TOUR time: about 1/2 hour

The main lock is 220m - 722ft long by 17m - 56ft wide and can accommodate fifteen boats 38m - 125ft in length. The second lock can accommodate seven of the same length. They are operated by a central control station fitted with a television circuit. Take the footbridge across the Amfreville Locks before walking over the Poses Dam and reaching the left bank from where the full force of the water can be seen.

Green Tourist Guides

Scenery,
Buildings,
Scenic routes,
Geography,
History, Art,
Touring programmes
Plans of towns and buildings

Guides for your holidays

The ANDELLE Valley

Michelin map **55** folds 7, 8 or **231** folds 11, 12, 23, 24

The pretty, swift running Adelle river rises in the Bray Region depression. Although industrialised, particularly downstream, it retains a rural character even more notable on the banks of its tributaries the Héron and the Crevon.

FROM FORGES-LES-EAUX TO AMFREVILLE LOCKS

55km - 34 miles – about 2 hours

Forges-les-Eaux. – *Description p 78.*

> *Leave Forges to the southwest on the D 919 and the D 13.*

Sigy-en-Bray. – Pop 553. On the banks of the Andelle the village boasts a good example of medieval architecture. The **abbey church** is all that remains of the former Sigy Abbey, founded in the 11C by Hugh 1. It has retained the 12C chancel and its seven-sided apse, a 13C portal, and in the nave vaulting restored in the 18C. The 15C bell tower overlooks a cemetery with a late 15C sandstone calvary.

> *Take the D 41 east towards Argueil, then the D 921 south.*

Le Héron. – Pop 242. A pleasant setting shaded by the park of the old castle.

Vascœuil. – *Description p 134.*

The valley beyond Vascœuil is industralised although beautiful houses standing in their own grounds help to maintain the country atmosphere.

★ **Fontaine-Guérard Abbey.** – *Description p 77.*

The road continues past the surprising ruins of a spinning mill built at the turn of the century in "Troubadour" style – a superficial imitation of medieval and Gothic.

Pont-St-Pierre. – Pop 1 059. The town which stretches across the Andelle Valley owes much to its nearby 12-18C château and surrounding park which can be seen through a gap in the main street.
The 11 and 12C church is decorated with **woodwork★**, complemented by Henri II stalls and a 17C altarpiece from nearby Fontaine-Guérard. A 14C Virgin in the chancel has a dress encrusted with cabuchon stones. The great Crucifix between the Virgin and St John in the porch is 15C. It stands on the right on entering.

> *Take the first road to the right after Romilly station and follow the D 19 which crosses the D 20. After the Sabla Factory, turn left along the Seine.*

★ **Amfreville Locks** (Écluses d'Amfreville). – *Description p 32.*

★★ Les ANDELYS
Pop 8 214

Michelin map **55** fold 17 or **231** fold 24 – Local map p 127 – Facilities

Les Andelys, dominated by the impressive ruins of Gaillard Castle, is in one of the loveliest settings along the Seine. It once consisted of two distinct areas, le Petit Andely to the west and le Grand Andely to the east. The latter was the site of a monastery founded by Clotilde, wife of Clovis, in the sixth century. The name of St-Clotilde remains closely associated with the town. The street bearing her name has a fountain (B 29) where she is said to have turned water into wine for the workmen building the monastery chapel.

HISTORICAL NOTES

The King of England's Fortress. – **Richard Lionheart,** King of England and Duke of Normandy, decided, in 1196, to bar the King of France's way to Rouen along the Seine Valley by building a massive fortress on the cliff commanding the river at Andely. Work progressed rapidly so that within the year Gaillard Castle was erected and Richard able to cry aloud "See my fine yearling!"

Philippe-Auguste, though bold, did not at first dare to attack so formidable a redoubt. But when Richard I was succeeded by King John he decided to try and starve it into surrender. By the end of 1203 the castle had been isolated by a double moat reinforced by wooden watch towers. In February, however, the French King learned that the defenders had commons for another year and he decided, therefore, to take the castle by storm.

The only possible access was a narrow isthmus connecting the promontory on which the fortress was built to the hills where the King of France had pitched camp. This was where the attack took place.

The King of France's Attack. – The first obstacle was the triangular redoubt guarding the vulnerable approach across the isthmus. The 15m - 45ft deep moat was, therefore, partially filled in and a corner tower mined by the attackers to force the outer strongpoint to fall. On 6 March the French entered the main defences through the latrines and let down the drawbridge to the lower courtyard. The assailants swarmed in. Repeated ramming soon breached the next line, forcing the garrison to surrender, before they had had the time to seek refuge in the keep.

Three months later Rouen, too, had fallen to the French King.

★★ GAILLARD CASTLE (A) *time: 3/4 hour*

Follow the signs from Rue Louis-Pasteur (B 19).

Ⓥ Leave the car in the car park where there is an outstanding **view** of the castle, the Seine and les Andelys. Another car park, further down, makes the walk a little shorter.

The fortress consisted of two parts: the main fort towering above the Seine and the advanced redoubt *(see above).*

The Redoubt (Châtelet). – The redoubt, separated from the main fort by a moat, possessed five towers of which only one, the tallest, remains. It was the one attacked by Philippe-Auguste and is encircled by a narrow slippery path overlooking the perpendicular walls of the moat.

The Main Fort. – Enter the courtyard between the redoubt and main defences and follow the wall round to the left, passing before the keep foundations which were cleverly cut into the rock. The view at the end is sheer and uninterrupted.

Return along the bottom of the moat passing, on your right, casemates dug as food stores out of the rock. Enter the main defence by way of the footbridge which has replaced the drawbridge. The keep, straight before you, has walls 5m - 16ft thick. The inner diameter is 8m - 26ft; formerly it was three storeys high with removable inner wooden ladders.

The ruins, to the right, were the Governor's lodge.

Coming out through the perimeter wall one can continue to the edge of the rock escarpment from where there is a commanding view up and down the Seine Valley.

A one-way road descends to Rue Richard-Cœur-de-Lion back into town.

ADDITIONAL SIGHTS

★ **Notre-Dame Church (Église Notre-Dame) (B).** – A well-balanced façade of twin towers flanked by a square staircase tower fronts this church in which the 16C south side is a good example of the Flamboyant style and the 16 and 17C north side is Renaissance with round arches, Ionic pilasters, balustraded roofs, caryatids and Antique style statues.

Inside, the well proportioned nave is 13C; the delicately ornamented triforium was remodelled in the 16C and the windows enlarged; the **organ★** and loft are Renaissance. The fine **stained glass★** in the south aisle and the tall windows in the south side of the nave date from the 16C. In the north transept and a nearby chapel are two lovely paintings by Quentin Varin.

The Entombment in the south aisle beneath the tower is 16C, the Christ in the Tomb is 14C.

Ⓥ **St-Sauveur Church (Église St-Sauveur).** – St Saviour's is Greek cross in ground plan and Gothic in style; the chancel is late 12C, the nave early 13C. The wooden porch stands on an early 15C stone foundation.

Inside there is an organ dating from 1674.

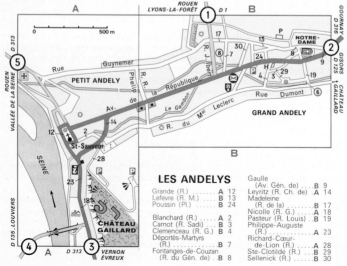

LES ANDELYS

★ ANET Château

Michelin map **55** southeast of fold 17 or **231** fold 36

Of all the French Renaissance châteaux, Anet was reputed the most ornate. The drawing below shows how much of the residence remains and how much was lost, mainly owing to speculation during the Revolution.

Successive owners since 1840 have endeavoured to maintain the original appearance of the buildings which have survived.

HISTORICAL NOTES

A queen without a crown. – Shortly after her arrival at court, **Diane of Poitiers,** widow of Louis de Brézé, Seneschal of Normandy and Lord of Anet, won the admiration of Henri, second son of François I, and 20 years younger than herself. Beautiful and imposing, intelligent and cold, having a taste for the arts, Diane conquered his heart without difficulty, since Henri's wife was merely the daughter of Florentine bankers, "a Medici". Diane was 32 when the dauphin met her and she fascinated him just as much when he became King Henri II. She still had not disappointed him at the age of sixty when, in 1559, Henri was killed by Montgomery during a tournament.

With her constant charm she reigned for twelve years over sovereign, court, artists and royal finances. Anet, which she had rebuilt, was the symbol of both her power and taste. Better still, it was she who brought up the royal children. In 1559 Catherine of Medicis took Chenonceau but left her Anet. Diane retired there and died in 1566 after completing a number of enhancements to the first Henri II style château.

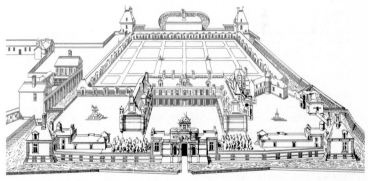

Anet Château in the 16C

Of the original buildings dating from the time of Diane of Poitiers only those in black remain.

TOUR *time: about 1/2 hour*

Work began around 1548 with **Philibert Delorme** as architect. Until then, in François I style, building was carried out according to French architectural tradition with Italian decoration. At Anet architectural design had a strong Italian influence as is seen by the use of pilasters and columns.

In the main courtyard the avant-corps of the main building, taken to the yard of the Fine Arts School (Beaux-Arts) in Paris, was well ahead of its time.

The greatest artists of all time have striven to enhance the château, such as sculptors Goujon, Pilon and Cellini, the enameller Limosin, the Fontainebleau tapestry-makers. Contrary to legend, none of the effigies of the goddess Diane, often depicted at Anet, is a portrait of the duchess.

In the 17C transformations were made by the Duke of Vendôme, grandson of Henri IV and Gabrielle d'Estrées. The duke suppressed the covered walk around the gardens and added an avant-corps and main stairway to the left wing of the main courtyard, the only one surviving today, and had the court of Diane closed to the west by a hemicycle.

Entrance Gate. – The work of Philibert Delorme. Above the central arch, the tympanum consists of a casting of Benvenuto Cellini's bronze low relief now in the Louvre: *Diane recumbent.* Above the door there is a clock dominated by a stag held at bay by four dogs. The statues have been cast and formerly the animals told the time, the dogs barking, the stag stamping its foot. Notice, on either side of the main doorway, chimneys each surmounted by a sarcophagus.

Left wing of the former main courtyard. – The visit begins on the first floor with Diane's bedroom. The main attraction is the Renaissance bed, decorated with the three crescents of Diane. The stained glass windows include fragments of the original *grisailles,* greyish monochrome designs, discretely decorative and recalling Diane's mourning.

The Guards Room with its fine 16C woodwork contains four **tapestries** made in the workshops of Fontainebleau around 1648 depicting scenes from the story of Diane the huntress.

The **main stairway,** added by the Duke of Vendôme in the 17C, affords views of the lake and park.

The vestibule, dating from the same period, leads to the Salon Rouge containing furniture of the French and Italian Renaissance.

The Salle des Faïences, which has conserved part of its original tiling, leads on to the dining room where the huge fireplace is supported by two caryatides by Puget. In the centre note the medallion by Jean Goujon depicting Diane snaring the royal stag.

Chapel. – Built in 1548 by Philibert Delorme, the chapel is in the form of a Greek cross. A dome with skylight window covers the circular nave, one of the first to be built in France. The skilfully executed diamond-shaped drawing on the caissons produces a surprising optical illusion, the whole cupola seeming to be drawn upwards. The design of the floor tiling recalls this geometrical subtlety. The alcoves house the statues of the 12 Apostles by Germain Pilon (mouldings). The low reliefs on the corner stones and arches depicting angelots bearing symbols of the Passion and allegorical characters (Fames) announcing the Resurrection of Christ, are thought to be by Jean Goujon.

⊙ **Funerary Chapel of Diane of Poitiers** (Chapelle funéraire). – *Entrance to the left when looking at the main doorway, place du Château.*
The chapel, built according to the design of Claude de Foucques, architect to the princes of Lorraine, was begun just before the death of Diane in 1566 and completed in 1577. The white marble **statue★** representing Diane kneeling on a tall sarcophagus in black marble, is attributed to Pierre Bontemps, together with the altarpiece. Since the spoiling of the tomb in 1795, Diane's remains have rested against the chevet of Anet parish church, between two buttresses.

★ ARQUES-LA-BATAILLE Pop 2 742

Michelin map 52 fold 4 or 231 fold 11 – 8.5km - 5 miles southeast of Dieppe

Arques, on the junction of the Varenne and Béthune rivers, still reminds us of a famous battle.

The Battle of Arques. – **Henri IV,** when he was still only a king without a kingdom, possessed the fortress of Arques, said to be "capable of withstanding cannon". He gathered within the ramparts every piece of artillery he could find and dug in, with 7 000 men, on the junction of the Eaulne and Béthune rivers, to await the 30 000 soldiers of the League under the Duke of Mayenne.
The battle took place on 21 September 1589. One of the fogs so frequent in the region delayed the artillery's action and Henri's troops were in a very bad position. Fortunately however the fog lifted and the cannons thundered into the ranks of the Leaguers. Mayenne, who had promised to bring back his enemy "tied and bound", beat a hasty retreat.
A monument at the edge of Arques Forest *(p 37)* commemorates this battle.

★ CASTLE time: 1/2 hour

Leave from Place Dexeliers where the town hall (mairie) is located. Take the second road to the right, uphill to the castle entrance. The road is very narrow and winding.

The castle is an interesting feudal ruin built on a rocky promontory with the 12C keep perched on the highest point. Built between 1038 and 1043 and attacked by William, future king of England, in 1053, it was reconstructed by Henry I in 1123. In the 14C it was strengthened by the addition of new towers and equipped to receive artillery at the beginning of the 16C. In 1584 it was taken back from the Leaguers, who had become its masters.
A triple door leads into the castle. On the back of the last one a carved low relief depicts Henri IV at the battle of Arques. At the other end of the courtyard, on the right, stands the mighty square keep with its solid buttresses. Its floors were well separated as a defensive measure.
To walk round, follow the old sentry walk on the side of the moat and enjoy the charming view of the Arques Valley.

ADDITIONAL SIGHT

Notre Dame Church (Église Notre-Dame de l'Assomption). – The church, rebuilt in about 1515, was given the belfry in the 17C.
Look first at the façade with its twin turrets and pierced buttress before walking round the building to see the gallery encircling the nave.
Inside, the nave was roofed in the 16C with wood cradle vaulting on pendentives; the chancel and transept, a fine Flamboyant group, are separated from the nave by a Renaissance rood screen. The apse windows are 16C (restored). A chapel to the right of the chancel with 16C woodwork contains a small bust of Henri IV and an inscription commemorating the battle. Note a 15C *Pietà* in the south chapel.
The Lady Chapel, to the left of the chancel, has 17C woodwork signed (on the right): *"Raudin, ton amy"* (Raudin, your friend).
In the centre are the coats of arms of the donators.

Make up your own itineraries

– The map on pages 4 to 5 gives a general view of tourist regions, the main towns, individual sights and recommended routes in the guide.

– The above are described under their own name in alphabetical order (p 32) or are incorporated in the excursions radiating from a nearby town or tourist centre.

*– In addition the **Michelin Maps** nos 52, 54, 55, 231, 232 and 237 show scenic routes, places of interest, viewpoints, rivers, forests...*

ARQUES Forest

Michelin map 52 fold 4 or 231 fold 11

This beech forest crowns a spur bounded by the Eaulne and Béthune rivers, which join at its foot to form the Arques river, and is the Norman woodland that comes closest to the sea.

ROUND TOUR STARTING FROM ARQUES-LA-BATAILLE

30km - 19 miles – about 1 hour

The Forest roads are sometimes narrow. Please drive carefully.

★ **Arques-la-Bataille**. – *Description p 36.*

Leave Arques to the east on the D 56.

St-Nicolas-d'Aliermont. – Pop 4053. Like other villages on the narrow Aliermont plateau and along the D 56, St-Nicolas is a "street-village", a type which historians associate with 12C and 13C colonisation based around the existing roads. Today, St-Nicolas is an electronic and precision goods centre manufacturing alarm and electric clocks, meters and telephone parts.

After St-Nicolas, turn left into the D 149.

Envermeu. – Pop 1629. The Gothic church, enhanced with Renaissance motifs, is incomplete. It has nevertheless a remarkable **chancel**★ with hanging keystones, and an apse in which the roof ribs are most successfully light and elegant. The spiral columns are the result of skilled craftsmanship. Note the beautifully carved wooden pulpit with dais above.

From Envermeu, the D 920, to the west, then the D 54 lead to Martin-Eglise.

Martin-Eglise. – Pop 1185. The village, on the edge of the forest, is famous for trout.

Take the D1 towards Arques.

Immediately after a lovely timber-framed house and a bridge over the Eaulne, turn left into a narrow road. 600m further on turn right before a house into the forest road which runs by the forest edge providing attractive glimpses of the Arques Valley.

Battle of Arques Monument. – *1/4 hour on foot Rtn.*
Leave the car on the grass on the right of a sharp left bend. A path leads off to the obelisk erected as a tribute to the victory won by Henry IV on this field. Arques-la-Bataille stands on the far side of the valley, dominated by its castle.
The road now enters the forest.

After the Rond Henri IV at the end of a straight stretch of road, turn right into the forest road.

The road crosses another part of the forest with fine beech trees and picnic areas and then winds its way downhill to a crossroads.

The D 56 to the right leads back to Arques.

Each year

*the **Michelin Guide France**
presents a multitude of up-to-date facts in a compact form.
Whether on a business trip, a weekend away from it all
or on holiday take the guide with you.*

★ The AUGE Region

Michelin maps 54 folds 17, 18 or 231 folds 19, 20, 31, 32

The Auge Region provides a wonderful hinterland to the beaches of the Fleurie Coast *(qv)*, with its pasturelands, thatched cottages, manor houses and local products including cider and cheeses.

THE REGION'S RICHES

The Auge has an unusually wooded appearance, greenery largely hiding the variations in relief brought about by the raising, in the west, of the chalk foundation which ends abruptly in an escarpment 30m high overlooking the Dives Valley and the Caen area *(map p 13)*. The escarpment is known to geographers as the Côte d'Auge.
Fame has come through cider, calvados and cheeses: *Camembert, Pont-l'Évêque, Livarot*.

The Manor Houses. – The farms of the Auge Region are as isolated within their orchards as are those of the Caux Region in their farmsteads *(qv)*. The farm buildings, set round the living quarters, contain the oven, the cider press, the apple stores and the stables. The dairy, domain of the farmer's wife, is usually in a choice spot.
One of the great charms of the country lies in the diversity of its many manors which are generally countrified, pleasant to look at, and always perfectly adapted to the rural setting.
Some of the more picturesque can be discovered during a round tour starting from Crèvecœur-en-Auge *(qv)*.

THE CÔTE D'AUGE

1 From Lisieux to Cabourg

26km - 16 miles – about 1 hour – Local map p 39

★★ **Lisieux.** – *Description p 93.*

Leave Lisieux by ⑥, the N 13. At la Boissière take the D 59 on the right.

Former Val Richer Abbey (Ancienne Abbaye du Val Richer). – *(not open to the public)* Following the destruction of the Cistercian abbey, all that remained was the 17C hospice. The minister François Guizot (1787-1874), leader of the conservative constitutional monarchists during the July monarchy, historian and briefly Ambassador to England, retired here after the 1848 revolution until his death in 1874.

The Schlumberger brothers *(p 58)* spent time here working on their inventions. Shortly after there appears the château of Roque-Baignard in its pleasant setting.

Take the D 101 on the left and continue straight ahead on the D 117. Turn left at the crossroads with the D 16 and then right on the D 85.

★ **Clermont-en-Auge.** – *Follow the signs "Chapelle de Clermont Panorama".* Leave the car at the start of the beech-lined avenue leading to the **church** *(1/4 hour Rtn).* From the east end there is an extensive **panorama★** of the Dives and Vie Valleys while in the distance the Caen countryside can be seen, bounded by the dark line of the Bocage Hills. The church contains a number of statues. St Marcouf and St Thibeault in polychrome stone stand in the chancel and on either side of the altar St John the Baptist and St Michael.

On the way down from Clermont-en-Auge to Beuvron-en-Auge there are several delightful views of the Dives Valley and the Caen countryside.

★ **Beuvron-en-Auge.** – Pop 276. This charming village has kept its lovely old timber-framed houses around the central square and the former covered market, now a shopping centre adds an extra picturesque note. There is a very pretty manor at the south exit of the village, decorated with wood carvings.

Manor at Beuvron-en-Auge

Take the D 49 towards Putot-en-Auge. The road crosses the N 175 and passes under the motorway. Fork right to Cricqueville.

Criqueville-en-Auge. – Pop 102. The **château** *(not open to the public),* completed in 1584, and its three main buildings with vast roofs, remains typically medieval while its chequered stone and brick decoration makes it characteristically Norman.

Driving down from Sarlabot to Dives there is a beautiful panorama over the Calvados coast on either side of the mouth of the Orne.

★ **Dives-sur-Mer.** – *Description p 63.*

★★ **Cabourg.** – *Description p 50.*

TRADITIONAL NORMANDY

2 From Villers-sur-Mer to Lisieux

36km - 22 miles – about 1 1/4 hours – Local map p 39

On this drive there are extensive views over the Lower Touques Valley.

★★ **Villers-sur-Mer.** – *Description p 60.*

Leave Villers to the southeast on the D 118.

Beaumont-en-Auge. – Pop 397. This small town, remarkably situated on a spur commanding the Touques Valley, was the birthplace of the mathematician and physicist **Laplace** (1749-1827). His house and statue can be seen on the place de Verdun.

Go south on the D 58, then left on the N 175 as far as the crossroads with the D 280. Turn right. The road passes under the motorway.

St-Hymer. – Pop 502. Pleasantly set in a valley, the village has a 14C **church** with traces of Romanesque in its style. It belonged to the priory and was one of the last Jansenist centres of activity in the 18C. Its belfry is a replica of that of Port-Royal-des-Champs, the famous abbey southwest of Paris.

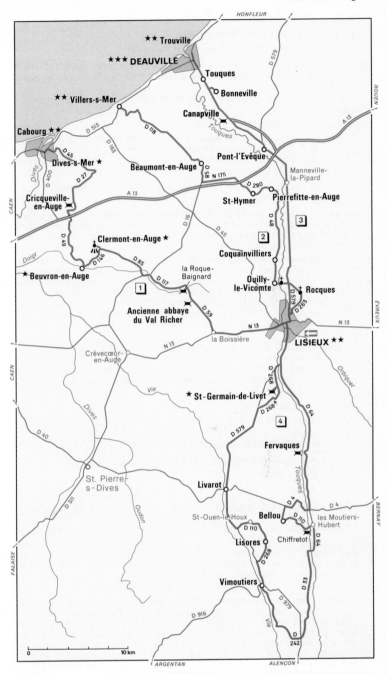

HONFLEUR

★★ Trouville

★★★ **DEAUVILLE**

Touques

Bonneville

★★ Villers-s-Mer

Canapville

Cabourg ★★

Pont-l'Evêque

Beaumont-en-Auge

Dives-s-Mer ★

Manneville-la-Pipard

Cricqueville-en-Auge

St-Hymer

Pierrefitte-en-Auge

3

Clermont-en-Auge ★

2

Coquainvilliers

★ Beuvron-en-Auge

la Roque-Baignard

Quilly-le-Vicomte

† Rocques

1

Ancienne abbaye du Val Richer

la Boissière

N 13

LISIEUX ★★

Crèvecœur-en-Auge

★ St-Germain-de-Livet

4

Fervaques

St. Pierre-s-Dives

Livarot

St-Ouen-le-Houx

Bellou

les Moutiers-Hubert

Chiffretot

Lisores

Vimoutiers

CAEN *FALAISE* *ARGENTAN* *ALENCON* *BERNAY* *EVREUX* *ROUEN*

0   10 km

Inside there is some fine 17 and 18C woodwork, 14C stained glass windows and canvases by the Rouen painter Jean Restout.

The sometimes winding road from St-Hymer to Quilly-le-Vicomte is particularly pleasant in the spring when the tall hedges are in flower and the orchards in blossom. Several attractive half-timbered farms are visible from the road.

Pierrefitte-en-Auge. – Pop 136. In the 13C **church** the panelled arches of the nave are decorated with cameo paintings of landscapes. There is a fine 16C rood beam.

Coquainvilliers. – Pop 669. Located in the very heart of the Auge Region, this small village is the home of the **Moulin de la Foulonnerie Distillery** where the making of the renowned *calvados* is explained. We see the stills, the storehouses where the precious drink matures in oak casks and an audio-visual explanation of cider distillation leading to our "calva". The visitor may sample the product at the end of the tour.

Quilly-le-Vicomte. – Pop 907. The **church**, standing on the road linking the two banks of the Touques, is one of the oldest in Normandy with remains of the 10 and 11C. It has a Renaissance altar in carved wood, a lectern of the same period, modern stained glass windows by Grüber and a 17C Crucifixion (3 statues).

Continue to Lisieux on the D 159 and D 579.

★★ **Lisieux.** – *Description p 93.*

THE TOUQUES VALLEY

③ From Lisieux to Trouville

28km - 17 miles – about 1 hour – Local map p 39

During the holiday season there is heavy traffic on the D 579 and N 177. The D 579 offers glimpses of the Touques Valley and the fertile east bank with its alternating orchards and pastures.

Most of the town names recall the time of the early invasions of Normandy.

★★ **Lisieux.** – *Description p 93.*

Leave Lisieux by ① D 579, then take the D 263 to the right.

Rocques. – Pop 209. The village **church** in the centre of its old burial ground has two wooden porches. The chancel and the tower date from the 13C. Inside note the torches and painting of the Brothers of Charity and several polychrome wooden statues.

Join the D 579 by the D 262.

On leaving Manneville-la Pipard there is a good view from the hilltop.

Pont-L'Évêque. – *Description p 107.*

ⓒ **Canapville.** – Pop 188. The 13-15C **Manor of the Bishops of Lisieux** (manoir des Évêques de Lisieux) is one of the most charming in the Auge Region. It consists of the large manor, main building grouping around the stairway tower three monumental stone chimneys, and the small manor with a bishop's head carved on the entrance post.

ⓒ **Bonneville-sur-Touques.** – Pop 342. The **castle** of William the Conqueror, of which only the moat and fortified enclosure remain, stands in a beautiful setting. From the top of the Jean-sans-Terre tower there is a fine **panorama** of the sea and Deauville to the north, the Touques Valley and surrounding countryside to the south. From under this tower an underground passage led to the port of Touques. The origin of the castle goes back to the 11C, its position enabling the occupiers to watch over the port. Between 1203 and 1449 it belonged in turn to the English and the French. Only in 1451 did it become French for good.

Touques. – Pop 2 237. On the mouth of the river which gave the town its name, former port of William the Conqueror, Touques retains some old houses along the Ouies Stream (ruisseau des Ouies), the 12C church of St Thomas (so named after Thomas ⓒ Becket's visit) and the 11C **church** of St Peter, now an exhibition centre.

The N 177 leads to Deauville then Trouville.

★★★ **Deauville.** – *Description p 59.*

★★ **Trouville.** – *Description p 132.*

UPPER TOUQUES VALLEY

④ Round tour of 75km – 47 miles starting from Lisieux –

description p 94

BAILLEUL Château

Michelin map 🗺 fold 12 or 🗺 folds 8, 9 – 10km - 6 miles southeast of Fécamp

ⓒ Built mid-way through the 16C by Bertrand de Bailleul, the château is square with a quadrangular building on each corner crowned by a statue representing one of the four cardinal virtues. The main façade reflects the three Greek Orders: Doric on the ground floor, Ionic on the first floor, Corinthian on the second. The lateral façades, almost without windows or any other openings, remain medieval.

Inside. – The imposing kitchen houses a fine collection of utensils (saucepans, braising pans, frying pans). In the adjoining room there are some interesting 19C crystal perfume bottles and salt cellars. Upstairs the *grand salon* is decorated with 17C tapestries from Brussels. A wooden balustrade runs all the way round the room.

Also to be visited is the bedroom where Mary Queen of Scots stayed on returning from Scotland in 1561. The Balliols, a derived form of Bailleul, descendants of a companion of William the Conqueror, acceded to the Scottish throne in 1292. Note also the chapel in which a 15C carved relief depicts the Adoration of the Magi.

Outside. – End the visit with the chapel and the park's century-old trees.

BARENTIN   Pop 12 776

Michelin map 🗺 fold 6 or 🗺 fold 22 – 17km - 11 miles northwest of Rouen

An industrial town specialising in textiles and electrical goods. Barentin is noted for its brick viaduct, 505m - 1 657ft long, which carries the Paris - Le Havre railway line across the Austreberthe Valley. When arriving from Rouen the visitor will be surprised to see the Statue of Liberty next to a vast shopping centre. It was made out of polystyrene for the French film *Le Cerveau* and has finished its career here in Barentin as the symbol of free trade: 13.5m - 44ft tall, it weighs 3 tons. The town boasts a large number of works by contemporary sculptors such as Rodin, Janniot, Bourdelle and Gromaire, whose monumental fresco represents peace under the skies of France.

There is a pretty 17C fountain by Nicolas Coustou on the Place de la Libération.

ⓒ **Church (Église).** – Built in the 19C, it has a number of modern windows of graceful design relating the lives of St-Martin, St-Hélier and St-Austreberthe.

ⓒ **Local history museum (Musée d'histoire locale).** – Housed in the town hall (hôtel de ville) the museum has a collection of objects and documents on the history of the region.

Michelin map **54** fold 19 or **231** fold 21 – Facilities

The importance of Le Bec-Hellouin Abbey as a medieval religious and cultural centre can still be seen, in spite of mutilation to the building. Two great Archbishops of Canterbury came from it.

HISTORICAL NOTES

The Anchorite Knight. – In 1034 the knight **Herluin** abandoned his charger for a donkey and vowed to devote himself to God. Others, inspired by a similar calling, followed his example and by 1041 there were thirty-two monks in the "Bec" community.

Lanfranc the Illustrious. – One day in 1042 as Herluin was mending the bread oven a stranger appeared. It was the Italian clerk, Lanfranc, who had been teaching at Avranches, and, tired of his success, had left and come to Bec, drawn by the monastery's obscurity.
He stayed for three years before Herluin persuaded him once more to take up his teaching.

The Faithful Counsellor. – It was during his siege of Brionne from 1047 to 1050 *(p 48)* that the young Duke William got to know Lanfranc who subsequently became his most trusted adviser – Lanfranc was the monk sent as emissary to Rome to get the interdict raised which had weighed on Normandy since William's marriage to Matilda *(see Michelin Green Guide Normandy Cotentin, under Caen)*.
In about 1060 Herluin moved the community further up the valley. Some years later William asked Lanfranc to be responsible for the building of the Abbaye aux Hommes in Caen.
Then Pope Alexander II, who had been one of Lanfranc's students at Bec, appointed his former teacher Archbishop of Canterbury, a position which made him virtual Regent of England whenever William returned to Normandy. On Lanfranc's death in 1093, Anselm, the philosopher and theologian who had come from Aosta and was by now Abbot of Bec, was transferred to Canterbury. Bec Abbey long continued as a major intellectual centre.

The Maurists. – In the 17C, Bec accepted the reform of St-Maur and found a new lustre with Guillaume de la Tremblaye (1644-1715). The great master builder of the congregation and one of the greatest sculptors and architects of his period made his profession of faith there in 1699.
The monks were driven out during the Revolution and the abbey church, one of the largest in Christendom, demolished under the Empire. In 1948 the site was restored to the Benedictine Order. The tradition had thus been renewed and on 29 September of that year Mass was celebrated once more.

★★THE ABBEY *time: 1/2 hour*

⊙ **New Abbey.** – The New Abbey is in what was the former Maurist refectory. At the entrance is a 14C statue of the Virgin, the Fathers of the Church are 15C; the altar was presented in 1959 by Aosta, birthplace of Bishop Anselm; before the high altar lies the 11C sarcophagus of Herluin, founder of Bec (1).
On going out on the left, the conventual buildings are characteristic of the Maurian style and enhanced by the surrounding greenery.

Old Abbey. – Only the column foundations and fragments of the south transept remain.

Cloister. – A monumental 18C grand staircase (2) (modern banister) leads to the cloister. Built between 1640 and 1660, the cloister was modelled after the cloister of Mont Cassin (Italy), the work of Bramante. A good 14C Gothic doorway in the north-east corner (3) has a tympanum with a Virgin in Majesty.

St Nicholas' Tower. – The 15C tower is the most important remainder of the Old Abbey Church, although it stood apart from it. A plaque recalls the Abbey's ties with England in the 11 and 12C. The **view★** from the tower summit *(201 steps)* includes the Bec Valley and the old abbey lodgings.

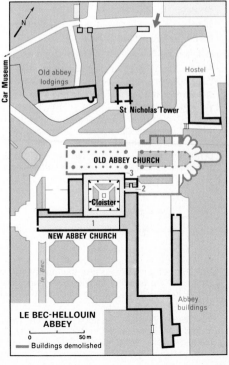

LE BEC-HELLOUIN ABBEY
0 ——— 50 m
▬ Buildings demolished

ADDITIONAL SIGHT

⊙ **Car Museum.** – The museum contains a collection of fifty cars from 1920 to the present; all are in working order, including six Bugattis.

THE NEUBOURG AND ROUMOIS REGIONS

The open **Neubourg** Plain, the best cultivated land south of the Seine, and the **Roumois** area which adjoins it to the northwest *(map p 13)* are reminiscent of the Caux Plateau. Those who enjoy the picturesque will be drawn by small country churches always guarded by a yew tree which, in the Middle Ages, was considered as having power to cleanse the atmosphere and, therefore, had pride of place among the other trees in the burial ground.
There are several noble castles upon the plain.

⊙ **Bouquetot.** – Pop 645. The 11 and 12C **church** contains fine statues in wood and stone and three restored 18C paintings. The giant hawthorn beside the church, protected by railings, is 700 years old. Note the beautiful yew trees in the burial ground.

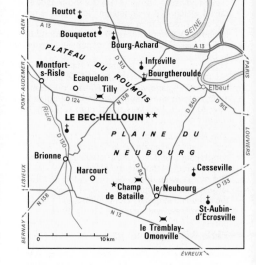

Bourg-Achard – Pop 2 022. The church has some beautiful 16C glass in the chancel and north transept and outstanding 15 and 16C woodwork which includes, in addition to the stalls, an imaginatively carved celebrant's chair.
In the south transept four panels illustrate the lives of St Eustace and St Placid. The central altar has been restored and is in harmony with the rest of the decor. At the chancel entrance, note a 15C stone polychrome Virgin.

Bourgtheroulde. – Pop 2 555. Renaissance stained glass windows in the chancel of the church.

Brionne. – *Description p 48.*

Cesseville. – Pop 252. The church has a 16C façade.

★ **Champ de Bataille** (Château). – *Description p 56.*

⊙ **Ecaquelon.** – Pop 357. A pretty village on the edge of the forest of Montfort. The **church** contains some lovely 16C woodwork.

Harcourt. – *Description p 80.*

Infreville. – A large Rococo altarpiece can be seen inside the church.

Montfort-sur-Risle. – *Description p 108.*

Le Neubourg. – Pop 3 669. Main town of the region with a 16C church.

Routot. – Pop 1079. The church has a Romanesque belfry with intersecting arches in its blind arcade.

St-Aubin d'Écrosville. – Pop 508. Note the west face of the church.

Tilly Château. – The château was built by Guillaume le Roux, Lord of Bourgtheroulde, around 1500. He also had the *hôtel* of the same name built in Rouen. The front is faced with a lozenge design in stone and glazed brick. The perimeter wall, which is still standing, is quartered by pointed turrets.

Le Tremblay-Omonville. – Pop 199. The castle is characterised by a curious front (mid – 18C) and boasts terraces and impressive outbuildings.

BELLÊME
Pop 1 849

Michelin map **60** north of folds 14 and 15 or **231** south of fold 45 – Local map p 104

Bellême, capital of the Perche Region, a title long disputed with neighbouring Mortagne, groups its houses at the top of small spur of 225m - 738ft overlooking the forest and the beautiful Perche countryside. The town had a particularly turbulent history in the Middles Ages when Blanche of Castile and the future St Louis took the fortress by assault in 1229.

The Walled Town. – The porch, flanked by two reconstructed towers, together with towers now incorporated in domestic buildings, are the only remains of the 15C ramparts which were, in turn, built upon 11C fortress foundations. When going through, note the portcullis grooves.

The Rue Ville-Close (**9**), on the site of the former citadel, is lined with fine 17 and 18C Classical style houses most of which have retained their exterior decoration: well-proportioned balconies, wrought iron railings and a huge gate. Outstanding are no 24, the Governor's house, and especially no 26, the **Bansard des Bois Mansion** (**B**) (Hôtel de Bansard des Bois). Its elegant façade can be seen from beside a stretch of water, once the castle moat.

St-Sauveur Church (**Église St-Sauveur**). – This late 17C church has a richly decorated

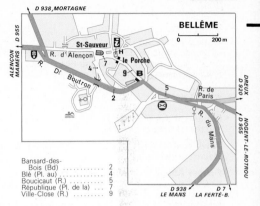

Bansard-des-
Bois (Bd) 2
Blé (Pl. au) 4
Boucicaut (R.) 5
République (Pl. de la) ... 7
Ville-Close (R.) 9

interior. Note in particular the imposing high altar and canopy (1712) made of stone and marble, the chancel woodwork from the former abbey of Valdieu and the windows, each composed of six scenes from the life of Jesus. The baptismal font, decorated with garlands, stands against a three-panelled altarpiece.

*The layout diagram on page 3 shows the **Michelin Maps** covering the region.
In the text, reference is made to the map which is the most suitable from a point of view of scale and practicality.*

★ BELLÊME Forest

Michelin map 60 folds 4, 5, 14, 15 or 231 folds 44, 45

This National Forest of 2 400 ha - 5 930 acres is one of the most beautiful in the Perche Region with its majestic oaks and its beautiful and varied site.

ROUND TOUR STARTING FROM BELLÊME

27km - 17 miles – about 1 1/2 hours

Bellême. – *Description p 42.*

> *Leave Bellême to the northwest by the D 938.*

From the road there is a very pretty view of the town. It then crosses some remarkable woodland before reaching La Herse Pool.

La Herse Pool (Étang de la Herse). – *A path circles the pool – 1/4 hour on foot.* The calm waters of the pool reflect the surrounding greenery and offer freshness much appreciated by tourists.

On the other side of the road, opposite the forester's lodge, is a Roman fountain. Near the fountain are two blocks of stone which bear inscriptions in Latin.

> *Turn round and continue straight ahead; then turn right at the Colbert crossroads.*

The forest road (surfaced) affords lovely views as it leads to the Creux Valley crossroads, where you turn left. Follow the road as it winds along to the edge of the forest.

> *Turn first right and enter the forest once again.*

Before reaching the Montimer crossroads the road crosses a thicket.

> *Descend on the left for 400m - 1/4 mile.*

École Oak Tree (Chêne de l'École). – It stands 40m - 130ft tall and has a circumference of 22m - 66ft. Even after 300 years it is still perfectly straight.

> *Return to the Montimer crossroads and continue to La Perrière.*

La Perrière. – Pop 422. The name cames from the Latin petraria, meaning "stone quarry". Indeed the village is built on a chalk promontory covered by sand. Here and there we can see dark red ferruginous sandstone blocks called *grisons*. Many of the houses have been built with these stones.
The village offers one of the best **panoramas**★ of the Perche countryside, including to the west the Perseigne Forest and, further off, the Écouves Forest, which can be seen from the cemetery path near the church.
To admire the old dwellings (15-17C) and streets of the town, follow the "discovery path" *(sentier de la découverte: plan available locally)*. From La Perrière cycle tours and country walks are organised.

> *Return to the forest road which crosses the Bellême Forest from west to east and passes through the delightful Creux Valley. At the Rendez-vous crossroads take the D 310 on the right.*

St-Martin-du-Vieux-Bellême. – Pop 584. The houses of this picturesque village stand grouped round the 14-15C church.

> *Continue on the road which joins the D 955 and turn left back to Bellême.*

Michelin map 54 fold 19 or 231 fold 33

Bernay developed rapidly round an abbey founded early in the 11C by Judith of Brittany, wife of Duke Richard II. It was at Bernay in the 12C that the trouvère Alexandre of Bernay wrote the long poem, the *Romance of Alexander,* in twelve syllable lines known subsequently as alexandrines. Tucked away in the Charentonne Valley, the town possesses a collection of renovated half-timbered houses.

SIGHTS

★ **Boulevard des Monts** (A). – This lovely hillside road has good views over the town and the Charentonne Valley.

Town Hall (Hôtel de Ville) (B H). – The former Bernay abbey. The 17C buildings are Maurist in style *(p 24).*

⊘ **Former Abbey Church** (Ancienne Église Abbatiale) (B). – The church was begun in 1013 by Guglielmo da Volpiano *(qv)* called from Fécamp by Judith of Brittany. At the time the rôle of such an establishment was religious and intellectual but also political and economic. In the 15C the semi-circular apse was replaced by a polygonal one. Note the carved capitals above the nave and the twin bays in the galleries. The north aisle, rebuilt in the 15C, has diagonal vaulting.

⊘ **Municipal Museum** (Musée municipal) (B M). – The museum is housed in the former Abbot's lodge, a chequered stone and brick construction dating from the end of the 16C. Exhibits include a fine collection of Rouen, Nevers and Moustiers china and old Norman furniture.

Old Dwellings (A). – Some streets are lined with houses typical of old Bernay.

⊘ **Rue Gaston-Follope.** – This is the antique dealers' street. At no 15 there is a **Norman museum** (A M¹) devoted to folk art and traditions (household objects, farming tools, funny carafes portraying Thiers, Victor Hugo, Gambetta etc.).

Rue Thiers and Rue Général-de-Gaulle. – Busy shopping streets.

Rue Gabriel-Vallée. – Access is through the passage du Grand Bourg, rue Général-de-Gaulle. Note the corbelled half-timbered house at number 17.

⊘ **Ste-Croix Church** (Église Ste-Croix) (B). – The church of the Holy Cross, started in the 14C, has been heavily restored and contains fine works of art from Bec-Hellouin. Behind the portal is a 16C low relief in gilded wood: the Bearing of the Cross. There are tombstones of abbots near the organ gallery and in the south transept. The remarkable **tombstone** of Guillaume d'Auvillars, Abbot of Bec (1418) stands at the entrance to the sacristy. Sixteen great statues of apostles and evangelists from the end of the 14C are to be found on the pillars of the nave and choir decorated with the terracotta statues of St Maur and St Benoît (17C). On the high altar stands a sculpture in marble representing the Nativity scene (1683), based on a work by the Anguier brothers for the Val-de-Grâce in Paris (1662). Opposite the church there is lovely old **covered market**.

Notre-Dame-de-la-Couture Basilica (Basilique Notre-Dame-de-la-Couture). – *Access by Rue Kléber-Mercier, south* (A). The interior of this 15C church, established as a basilica in 1950, has a wooden vaulting; the statue Notre-Dame-de-la-Couture (16C), much venerated by pilgrims *(p 143),* is placed on a modern altar in the north transept. The church has some fine windows, skilfully restored, representing the Ascension and Resurrection.

BERNAY

Charentonne (R. de la)	B 5	Le-Prévost-de-Beaumont (R.)	B 33
Alexandre (R.)	B 3	Delamotte (R.)	B 8	Liberge-de-Granchain (Av.)	A 35
Gaulle (R. Gén. de)	A 24	Folloppe (R. G.)	A 20	Morsan (R. de)	A 38
Leclerc (R. Gén.)	B 28	Gambetta (R.)	B 23	Parissot (R. A.)	B 40
Thiers (R.)	AB	Héon (Pl. G.)	B 26	République (Pl. de la)	B 44
Union (R. de l')	B 45	Kléber-Mercier (R.)	A 27	Victoire (R. de la)	B 48
		Lemoing (R. M.)	A 30		

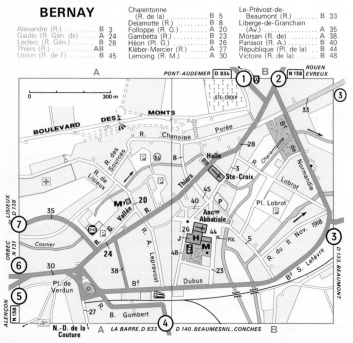

Beaumesnil Château

EXCURSION

★ **Beaumesnil.** – Pop 256. *13km - 8 miles to the southeast by the D 140.*
The **château★**, a masterpiece of the Louis XIII style, stands with its impressive façade mirrored in its moat.
⊙ The château is surrounded by formal gardens.
Inside one can see the saloon with its Louis XV furniture, the library, the chapels and two guardrooms.
In addition there is a **museum** that displays an important collection of bound books.

BEUZEVILLE
Pop 2 536

Michelin map 55 fold 4 or 231 fold 20

Beuzeville is a large market town situated east of the picturesque Morelle Valley.

Church (Église). – The church (13-16C) has 19 stained glass windows (1955-61) by the master glassmaker Decorchemont (1880-1971) who, by applying his own special technique, produced *pâte de verre* (powdered glass fired in a mold) which has the appearance of crystal. The subjects treated in this series of windows include: the Trinity (chancel), the Canticle of Canticles (Lady Chapel) and the Holy Family and the Sacraments (St Joseph's Chapel), as well as several saints (aisles).

★ BIZY Château

Michelin map 55 fold 18 or 231 fold 36 – 4km - 2 1/2 miles west of Vernon

Construction started in 1740 by Coutant d'Ivry for the Marshal of Belle-Isle, grandson of Fouquet. The buildings have since been altered by their successive owners, the Duke of Penthièvre, King Louis Philippe and above all the Baron de Schickler. Only the outbuildings remained unmodified. Today it belongs to the Duke of Albufera and the Marquise de Gramont.
The château, classical in appearance, presents an attractive façade decorated with colonnades and oculi on the park side, whereas on the more austere south side it forms, with the outbuildings and stables – now housing a collection of vintage cars – a well-proportioned court.

⊙ **TOUR** *time: about 1/2 hour*

Inside. – The rooms embellished by beautiful Regency woodwork and 18C tapestries contain Empire style furniture and mementoes reminiscent of the present owners' ancestors, marshals Suchet, Masséna, Davout and of Bonaparte. Note the beautiful carved oak staircase.

Park. – Designed in the 18C by Garnier d'Isle, the park was replanted for King Louis Philippe. It is adorned with 18C basins and statues including the famous sea horses (chevaux marins) which have been successfully restored.

Each year

the Michelin Guide France

revises its selection of hotels and restaurants
in the following categories
– pleasant, quiet, secluded
– with an exceptionally interesting or extensive view
– with gardens tennis courts, swimming pool or equipped beach,

BLAINVILLE
Pop 797

Michelin map **55** fold 7 or **231** fold 23 – 20km - 12 1/2 miles northeast of Rouen

This small village located in the Crevon Valley is the home of the artist **Marcel Duchamp** (1887-1968), forerunner of the New York school of painting *(see Michelin Green Guide: New York City).*

Church (Église). – Founded in 1488 by Jean d'Estouteville, this collegiate church, an attractive building with a chequered sandstone and silex facing, became the parish church in the 19C. Inside the Flamboyant church the north transept chapel contains a 15C group of St Anne and the Virgin and the tombstone of Lord Mouton de Blainville (14C). The 15C stalls have curiously decorated misericords. Above the choir, a sculptured group represents the Compassion of the Father, the dead Christ in the arms of the Eternal. In the sacristy there is a monumental late 15C polychrome wood statue of St Michael slaying the dragon.

Castle (Château). – Excavations since 1968 have uncovered the remains of a medieval castle with an 11C staircase, about a hundred yards of curtain wall around five to eight yards high, the ditches and two well conserved towers, all dating from the 14 and 15C.

BOURY-EN-VEXIN Château

Michelin map **55** northeast of fold 18 or **237** fold 3 – 6km - 4 miles south of Gisors

Located in a small village in the Oise département, the castle was built in the 17C from the plans and drawings of Jules Hardouin-Mansart, and is a good example of well blended Classical architecture.
The main part of the building has two levels lit by high windows and is flanked by two wings at rightangles. The semi-circular windows on the ground floor carry representations of Jupiter and the four seasons.
The façade has a number of twinned pilasters with Ionic capitals.

TOUR *time: about 1/2 hour*

The entrance gallery contains 18C Navarre porcelain. The chapel was added in 1718 and is decorated with windows bearing the arms of the Haubourgs, first marquis of Boury. Notice in the sacristy next door 17C sketches depicting moments in the life of Christ. The visit continues with the Louis XV room, the main room, the *salon bleu* (notice above each door a low-relief illustrating the pleasures of the countryside: hunting, fishing, harvesting and grape-picking, music and games), the dining room and the kitchen. The former contains pastels representing the Marquis and Marquise of Boury. The kitchen once had three fireplaces for heating, grilling and roasting respectively. The copper utensils and blue Caen glass are 18C.

The BRAY Region

Michelin map **52** folds 15 and 16 or **231** folds 12, 24 and **237** fold 3

The Bray Region, a green oasis in the centre of the bare vastness of the Caux Plateau, has a landscape of more clearly defined outlines than any other area in Normandy. It exists because of that geological accident known as the "buttonhole".

THE "BUTTONHOLE" OF THE BRAY REGION AROUND FORGES-LES-EAUX

– – – – probable outline of the Bray "dome"

White chalk: forming the upper edge of the precipice, often crowned with woodland.

Marly chalk: giving the sides of the depression their bare appearance. Ploughed in places. At points of contact with white chalk springs rise with surrounding villages.

Clay and sand: water is retained, giving rise to pastureland.

Sand and ferruginous sandstone: very thick and sometimes forming infertile surface deposits (Bray Forest, Epinay Wood). From these layers spring the ferruginous waters of Forges for which the town is known.

Marl, sandstone and clay: these Jurassic deposits contain permeable chalk layers not thick enough to change significantly the appearance of the pastureland.

The "Buttonhole" of the Bray Region. – The movement of the earth's crust which brought about the raising of the Alps in the Tertiary Era had repercussions as far as the Paris Basin. The shocks which disturbed the ancient shelf formed ridges in the upper layers deposited in the Secondary Era.

Wide and deep undulations were formed in a southeast-northwest direction and subsequently one of these swelled into a large dome with a steep northeast face of some 1 000m - 3 000ft.

Ceaseless erosion wore away and cut into the dome exposing subjacent Jurassic soil in considerable geological variety. This cut, with its clearly defined rim, is known as the "Bray buttonhole" and explains the variations in landscape resulting from the differences in the nature of the soil. Its southwest edge is indented by large gaps made where the Andelle and the Epte flow out of the depression.

The whole area is a watershed: the courses of the Andelle and the Epte are only separated by the width of the town of Forges-les-Eaux, while the sources of the Béthune and the Thérain, though flowing in opposite directions, run parallel with only 5km - 3 miles between them.

Riches of the Bray Region. – Bray is most closely associated with food supplies to the Paris region. Dairy-farming – almost the sole type of farming in the area – is centred on Ferrières, Gournay, Neufchâtel, Serqueux and Aumale. The Neufchâtel cheeses are well-known among connoisseurs. Increased production of dessert apples and the development of industrial cider making are indicative of a nearby large urban market. Recently the region's geological structure has attracted the attention of oil prospectors.

ROUND TOUR STARTING FROM FORGES-LES-EAUX

52km - 32 miles – about 1 1/2 hours

Forges-les-Eaux. – *Description p 78.*

Leave Forges on the D 921 to the south.

La Ferté. – Pop 319. The village is perched just before the main edge of the "buttonhole" of the Bray region *(drawing p 46)* which the Andelle and its affluents have cut up into regularly shaped mounds.

As you walk up to the church there is an extended view of the Bray region depression with its clearly defined rim. On the main square is the gracious 16C **Henri IV's house** (maison de Henri IV), brought in 1968 from the region of Dieppe and rebuilt.

At Fry turn left onto the D 1 before the church.

The road brings you to the southwest Bray escarpment, massive bare mounds crowned with beech trees (Mont Robert).

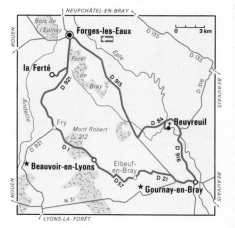

★**Beauvoir-en-Lyons.** – Pop 464. Park the car beyond the town hall and walk up the street on the left to the church. From the east end there is a **view**★ of the green depression of the Bray Valley cutting away in a straight line southeast. In clear weather you can see Beauvais Cathedral.

Return to the car and continue along the D 1. At a crossroads, turn left downhill into the D 57. Then follow the D 21.

★**Gournay-en-Bray.** – *Description p 79.*

Leave Gournay by the D 916 to the north.

⊙ **Beuvreuil.** – The wooden 16C porch of the small 11C country **church** is decorated with enamelled bricks.
Inside the church note the 11C baptismal fonts, a 15C holy water font, the Gothic statues the 15C altarpiece and a 16C lectern.

Return to Forges by the D 84 and D 915, on the right.

ROUND TOUR STARTING FROM NEUFCHATEL-EN-BRAY

49km - 31 miles – about 1/2 hour

Neufchâtel-en-Bray. – *Description p 101.*

Leave Neufchâtel-en-Bray to the north on the D 1314.

From the D 1314, going north through a strangely denuded landscape on the northeast slope of the buttonhole, there are ever more extensive views of the Béthune Valley before you cross the Hellet Forest (D 56) to come out at Croixdalle.
There turn left, D 77, first, to descend into the Béthune Valley and then, beyond Osmoy-St-Valéry, climb out of it, up its southwest slope by what is virtually a pass into the Mesnil-Follemprise Valley, which you leave by a second pass. In front of you lies the Nappes Forest.

The BRAY Region

Once more the view opens out and you see farming country on the chalklands, the Bures-en-Bray belfry, the Hellet Forest and Mesnières Château.

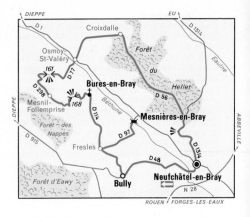

⊙ **Bures-en-Bray**. – Pop 301. The **church**, partly 12C, has a modern brick façade with porch and a bold twisted wooden spire. In the north transept we can see an Entombment, a 16C stone polychrome altarpiece and a 14C Virgin and Child.

Uphill after the church take the first road on the left near the café-tobacconist.

The D 114 follows a terrace along which the villages at the foot of the southwest face have been built.

At Fresle turn left on the D 97.

Before crossing the Béthune there is an attractive view of Mesnières Château.

Mesnières-en-Bray. – *Description p 98.*

Return to Fresles and take the D 114 on the left.

⊙ **Bully**. – Pop 633. The **church** has conserved its fine 13C Gothic chancel. Inside, notice the 16C keystones in the nave and aisles, the 15C stained glass windows, a polychrome stone *Pietà* and 17C statues.

Take the D 48 to return to Neufchâtel-en-Bray.

BRETEUIL
Pop 3415

Michelin map 55 fold 16 or 231 fold 34 – 14km - 9 miles south of Conches-en-Ouche

Backing onto the forest area of the Ouche region, the town is almost surrounded by an arm of the Iton river, forming a pool bordered by the public gardens on the site of the earlier fort.

Church (Église). – The oldest parts of the building date from the 11C. In 1081 Adèle, daughter of William the Conqueror celebrated her marriage with Etienne Count of Blois, on this very spot.

The belfry is a large square tower over the transept crossing.

The inside of the church is striking for the arrangement of the great arcades in the nave, resting on twelve massive pillars built of *grison,* a reddish stone of the area. The pillars in the cross of the transept date from the reign of William the Conqueror. The balustrade of the organ loft is decorated with Italian Renaissance motifs and twelve angel musicians.

BRIONNE
Pop 5038

Michelin map 54 fold 19 or 231 fold 33 – Local map p 42 – Facilities

Brionne in medieval times was a stronghold commanding the Risle Valley and in the 11C had close ties with the monastery in the neighbouring Bec Valley. It was in fact, when William of Normandy was besieging the Duke of Burgundy in Brionne from 1047 to 1050, that he first came in contact with the cultural centre of Bec-Hellouin Abbey which was to have such influence on the organisation of religious life in England *(p 41)*. Brionne is not only an industrial and commercial centre but also a tourist attraction because of its old keep and its park on the banks of the Risle.

SIGHTS

Keep (Donjon). – *1/4 hour on foot Rtn.*
Leave the car in the Place du Chevalier-Herluin or by the church. Take the Rue des Canadiens and 50m further on, to the right, the *Sente du Vieux Château*. This leads steeply up to the ruins of one of the best examples of a square Norman keep (11C), once supported by solid buttresses.
From the base of the keep (viewing table) there is a pleasant view over the town and the Risle Valley.

St-Martin's Church (Église St-Martin). – The nave is 15C and the Gothic wood vaulting above 14C. The marble altar and altarpiece (17C) come from Bec-Hellouin Abbey.

Shaftesbury Garden (Jardin de Shaftesbury). – Take a stroll along the Risle in a small garden bearing the name of Brionne's twin town in England.

⊙ **Normandy House (Maison de Normandie)**. – On the outside it looks like a house typical of the Normandy region: brick and stone chequered walls on the ground floor and half-timbered first-floor. The inside is devoted to local crafts: display and sale of leather, glass and porcelain goods and local products of the land.

BRIONNE

*The main
throughroutes
are clearly indicated
on all town plans*

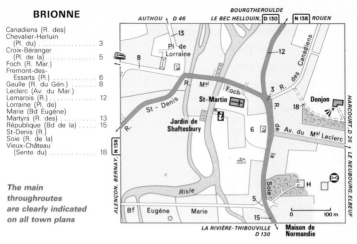

EXCURSIONS

★★ **Le Bec-Hellouin.** – *6km - 4 miles to the north on the N 138 and D 39 on the left. Description p 41.*

Harcourt. – *7km - 4 miles to the southeast on the D 26 and D 137. Description p 80.*

Tour in the Lieuvin. – *28km - 17 miles – about 1 hour.*
The Lieuvin is a plateau covered with silex clay and alluvial mud. It is also a region of pastures and activities include cereal-growing. Together with the Roumois from which it is separated by the Risle Valley, it forms the transition between the Caux and the Auge Regions.

   Leave Brionne to the north on the D 46. At Authun, turn left on the D 38.

The D 38 ascends into the pleasant Livet Valley.

Livet-sur-Authou. – Charming black and white half-timbered houses line the entrance. The castle with its park and church on the other side of the road complete the picturesque scene.

St-Benoît-des-Ombres. – Pop 114. Beyond the miniature town hall look out, on the right, for the chapel hidden in the greenery. Its wooden porch of the 15C is crowned by a great wooden statue of St Benedict. Inside, notice the fine vault and 16C font.

   Go right towards St-Georges-du-Vièvre.

The roof of Launay Château appears as you reach the bottom of a steep hill. Continue up through an archway of beech trees.

Launay Château. – *Turn right and walk along the castle approach.* From the main gate there is a good view of this attractive Regency building with 16C half-timbered outbuildings. There is also a remarkable **dovecot★** with beams carved to depict monsters and generally grotesque characters.
In the park, notice the formal gardens and magnificent weeping beech.

   Return by the D 137 and D 130.

The road offers a pretty view of the Risle Valley.

BROGLIE
                                    Pop 1 126
Michelin map 54 folds 18, 19 or 231 fold 33

The small town of Chambrais, watered by the Charentonne River, took its name from the Piedmontese family whose fief it became in the 18C. The huge buildings of the **château** *(not open to the public),* formerly a medieval fortress rebuilt in the 18C, dominate the area.

Church (Église). – The centre of the church façade and the lower part of the belfry are in *grison (p 107),* the remainder in sandstone. Inside, the massive pillars, also in hard limestone, on the north side and the chancel are Romanesque. The rest is 15 and 16C. Notice the 15C and especially 16C statues in the south aisle.

BROTONNE Forest
Michelin map 55 fold 5 or 231 fold 21

This large massif, enclosed in a bend of the Seine, is responsible for the rustic and sometimes lonely appearance of the left bank of the river. The breaks through the trees made by these forest roads afford some fine vistas of the leafy glades of beeches, oaks or pines.
The creation of the **Brotonne Regional Nature Park** in 1974 and the construction of the Brotonne Bridge *(p 50)* have made the forest easily accessible.
Within the context of the Lower Seine's regional open-air "museum" of crafts and traditions (Écomusée de la Basse Seine) which strives to bring back and revive the professions of our ancestors, the Brotonne Forest has a village on the southern edge where traditions survive, la Haye-de-Routot *(p 50)*. Bordering the forest, the "route of the thatched houses", in effect the D 65, follows the left bank of the Seine and offers views of several thatched houses surrounded by apple trees.

49

BROTONNE Forest

FROM ROUTOT TO CAUDEBEC-EN-CAUX

33km - 21 miles – about 1 hour

Routot – *Description p 42.*

On leaving Routot, bear right on the D 686 towards la Haye-de-Routot.

La Haye-de-Routot. – Pop 197. The cemetery surrounding the little church is surrounded by two **yew trees**★, some thousands of years old, 16 and 14m in circumference – 52 and 46ft. The bonfire of St Clare, on the night of 16-17 July always draws a huge crowd to the village *(p 28).*

In an 18C building the **bread oven** (four à pain) revives the old baking methods and bread is still baked there over a wood fire. Bakers' tools are exhibited.

The **sabot-maker's workshop** (maison du sabotier) presents tools and techniques formerly used and a large collection of sabots.

Follow the D 40 for 4.5 km - 3 miles, then turn left into the narrow forest road.

This very pleasant road named *Mare de la Chèvre* which crosses the plateau before descending into the Seine Valley, passes through several beautiful copses.

3 km - 2 miles after crossing the D 131 there is a beautiful **view** on the left of the Seine and its valley as far as Tancarville Bridge.

5 km - 3 miles further on at Le Quesney, bear right on to La Mailleraye road and right

The bonfire of Saint-Clair at La Haye-de-Routot

again on to the forest road of the St-Maur Chapel which drives through thick forest.

Rond-de-Nagu. – A large clearing in the shape of a star.

By the D 131, bear left and reach Rond-Victor and St-Nicolas-de-Bliquetuit.

Along the road from St-Nicolas-de-Bliquetuit to the Seine, gardens and half-timbered houses can be seen.

★**Brotonne Bridge** (Pont de Brotonne). – *Toll bridge.* Opened to traffic in 1977, the bridge spans the Seine above Caudebec-en-Caux. Some figures: length 1 280 m - 4 200 ft, height above water 50 m - 164 ft, height of the pylons 125 m - 410 ft.

★**Caudebec-en-Caux.** – *Description p 51.*

★★ CABOURG   Pop 3 249

Michelin map 54 folds 16, 17 or 231 fold 19 – Local map p 39 – Facilities

The large seaside resort of Cabourg, created at the time of the Second Empire, has always kept its elegant clientèle. A huge stretch of water has been created as a yachting facility at the mouth of the Dives.

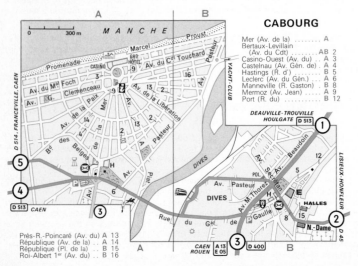

CABOURG

Mer (Av. de la)	A
Bertaux-Levillain (Av. du Cdt)	AB 2
Casino-Ouest (Av. du)	A 3
Castelnau (Av. Gén. de)	A 4
Hastings (R. d')	B 5
Leclerc (Av. du Gén.)	A 6
Manneville (R. Gaston)	B 8
Mermoz (Av. Jean)	A 9
Port (R. du)	B 12
Près-R.-Poincaré (Av. du)	A 13
République (Av. de la)	A 14
République (Pl. de la)	B 15
Roi-Albert 1er (Av. du)	B 16

A Famous guest. – **Marcel Proust** went to Cabourg for the first time in 1881, when he was 10. As he suffered from asthma the coastal climate did him a great deal of good. Attracted by the charm of the place, he often visited the town and stayed at the Grand Hôtel. Cabourg gave him the opportunity of rediscovering his childhood. French literature is indebted to him for *Within a Budding Grove (A l'Ombre des Jeunes Filles en Fleurs)*, a clear picture of life in a seaside resort at the turn of the century and of the customs of Cabourg.

THE RESORT

The town has a geometrical symmetry. The Casino and Grand Hôtel (A) stand together facing the sea and forming the focal point from which streets radiate, linked at their perimeter and two intermediary points by concentric semicircular avenues. The avenues and streets are, in many cases, lined by attractive houses set in shaded gardens.
The Boulevard Marcel-Proust, a terrace running the full length of the immense fine sand beach, makes a magnificent promenade with a view extending from Riva-Bella to Houlgate with Trouville as background and Cape Hève on the horizon.

EXCURSIONS

Merville-Franceville Plage. – Pop 1 309. Facilities. *6km - 4 miles. Leave Cabourg by* ⑤, *the D 514.*
Merville fortifications, captured by the British paratroopers on 5-6 June 1944, consisted of four concrete shelters each containing a 150mm gun with a range of 20km - ⊘ 12 1/2 miles. A **museum** has been installed in one of the shelters.

Ranville. – Pop 1 690. *8km - 5 miles to the south of Merville-Franceville Plage on the D 223.*
The village, the first on French soil to be liberated, was attacked and captured by parachute troops of the 13th Battalion, Lancashire Fusiliers, at 2.30am on 6 June 1944. A cemetery commemorates the event.

★ CAUDEBEC-EN-CAUX   Pop 2 477

Michelin map 団 fold 9 or 團 fold 21. – Local map p 129 – Facilities

Caudebec, which for many years enjoyed the status of being capital of the Caux Region, has been built in the form of an amphitheatre facing the Seine where the Ste-Gertrude Valley runs into the river. It lies at the place where the tidal bore, a phenomenon known as the *mascaret,* driven further upstream by the Seine embankment, was highly spectacular at times.
The Brotonne Bridge, 50m - 165ft above the Seine, provides direct access to the opposite bank of the river and to the Brotonne Forest.
The fine Church of Our Lady was virtually undamaged by the fire which swept the town in June 1940. Also preserved were the three old houses to the left of the church which give an idea of what Caudebec must once have looked like.

HISTORICAL NOTES

The name Caudebec is mentioned for the first time in the 11C on a charter granted to the monks of St-Wandrille Abbey. In the 12C the town was surrounded with fortifications in order to withstand the English who were nevertheless victorious in 1419.
Charles VII visited the town in 1449 after its liberation. Caudebec had a difficult time during the Wars of Religion but after submitting to Henri IV in 1592 it became a flourishing glove and hat making centre. The revocation of the Edict of Nantes in 1685 put an end to this period of prosperity.

★NOTRE-DAME *time: 1/2 hour*

Leave the car on Place du Marché, except on Saturdays when the market, which has been held on the same spot since 1390, is in full swing.
This fine Flamboyant edifice which Henri IV described as "the most beautiful chapel in the kingdom" was built between 1425 and 1539.

Exterior. – The belfry adjoining the south wall, 53m - 174ft high, has a delicately worked upper part surmounted by a stone tiara shaped spire which had to be restored in the 19C after being struck by lightning.
The west face is pierced by three beautiful Flamboyant doorways and, above, a remarkable rose window surrounded by small statues.

Interior. – Immediately noticeable are the general inner proportions, the lack of transept and the triforium and tracery which are the areas most characteristically Flamboyant.
The 17C **font,** on the left, is decorated with intricately carved panels; the great early 16C organ was restored in 1972; its 3 325 pipes of repoussé pewter produce a sound that is distinguished for its fine quality. They are located in a fine carved oak buffet.
The stained glass windows are 16C, the most outstanding being those of St Peter beside Christ Crucified, on the left above the high altar, and, on the right, the Coronation of the Virgin and St Paul.
Some attractive old statues which have been cleaned and now appear in all their original colouring and character may be seen in the side chapels.

CAUDEBEC-
EN-CAUX

Baillage (R. du) 2
Basin (R.) 3

Churchill (Av. W.) 4
Cordonnerie
  (R. de la) 5
Gaulle
  (Pl. Gén. de) 6
Havre (R. du) 7

Letellier (R.) 8
Marché (Pl. du) 9
Poissonnerie
  (R. de la) 10
Rive (R. de la) 12
St-Clair (R.) 13

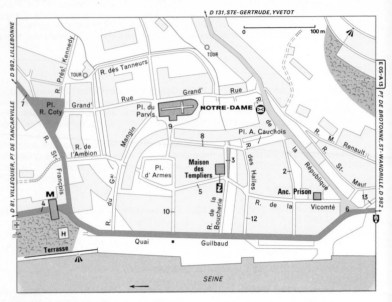

Chapel of the Holy Sepulchre. – The chapel inspired Fragonard to paint a picture of it. Beneath the 16C baldachin a recumbent Christ, carved in incredible detail, faces some very large stone statues – all come from Jumièges Abbey. The *Pietà* between the windows in 15C.

Lady Chapel (axial chapel). – The chapel is famous for its **keystone★**, a 7 ton monolith supported only by the dependent arching and forming a 4.30m - 13ft pendentive. This feat by the architect Guillaume Le Tellier, who lies buried in the chapel, is commemorated in a plaque beneath the right window.
The right window is composed of 16 panels, 12 of which recount the life of St Nicolas. The uppermost tells of the martyrdom of St-Catherine.

ADDITIONAL SIGHTS

⊙ **Templars' House (Maison des Templiers).** – This precious specimen of 13C civil architecture retains its two original gable walls intact. The interior houses the local history museum.

Town Hall Terrace (Terrasse). – Bordering the Seine, this terrace affords a pleasant view over the river.

Former Prison (Ancienne prison). – The former prison is in the 15C ramparts.

⊙ **Seine Maritime Museum (Musée de la Marine de Seine) (M).** – The museum is devoted exclusively to the history of navigation on the Seine; the ports, trade, shipbuilding, fishing. The visit starts with a display of wooden boats, notably a *gribane* of 1886, used for transporting building materials in the Seine-Maritime region.

EXCURSIONS

Round tour of 8km - 5 miles. – *about 1/2 hour – Local map p 129. Leave Caudebec by Rue St-Clair and follow the chemin de Rétival, keeping well to the right.*
The road runs along the top of a small escarpment with beautiful glimpses of the bend in the river.

At the bottom of a steep descent, take the D 37 on the left.

The road goes up a delightful little **valley★** with scattered thatched farmhouses now, in some cases, converted into country houses.

Before Rançon, take the D 33 on the right to St-Wandrille.

★ **St Wandrille.** – *Description p 122.*

Return to Caudebec by the D 22 and the D 982.

Round tour of 21km - 13 miles. – *About 3/4 hour – Local map p 129. Leave Caudebec to the north on the Yvetot road and bear left onto the D 40.*

Ste-Gertrude. – The small church stands in picturesque surroundings. Consecrated in 1519, it is Flamboyant in character. Inside, notice on the right of the high altar a rare 15C stone tabernacle and some interesting statues, including a Christ in stone.

Keep following the D 40, then take the D 30 to the left. Next, take the D 440 towards Anquetierville as far as the crossroads with the D 982. Bear left on the D 982 and then the D 440 on the right on entering St Arnoult. The D 440 leads back to the D 281. Turn left steeply down to Villequier.

★ **Villequier.** – *Description p 139.*

Return to Caudebec on the D 81 (journey described in the opposite direction p 128).

★ The CAUX Region

Michelin map **52** folds 2 to 5 and 11 to 15 or **231** folds 7 to 10.

A massive chalk plateau covered by an impermeable layer of silex clay and alluvial mud, monotonous but prosperous and bordered by the Channel, the Lower Seine and the Bresle Valley. The Caux Region is mainly known for its impressive coastline, where holidaymakers delighting in the region's natural beauty return each year to the beaches below the chalk cliffs.

GEOGRAPHICAL NOTES

The Alabaster Coast or "Côte d'Albâtre". – The chalk cliffs with alternate strata of flint and yellow marl are worn away ceaselessly by the combined action of the tides and the weather. The Etretat needle rocks and underwater shelves a mile from the present shore indicate the former coastline.

At the particularly exposed point of Cap Hève erosion is 2m - 6ft a year; the water is milky with chalk, and flints are pounded endlessly upon the beaches. The cliffs lose annually 3 million cubic meters. The **valleuses** or dry hollows cut into every cliff top as far as the eye can see are dry valleys, which, overcome by the retreating coastline, are now isolated and hang more or less suspended in mid air; only abundant water courses actually reach the sea.

Ports and harbours have been constructed from the natural inlets and seaside resorts use the hanging valleys as means of access to beaches and the sea.

The Caux Farmsteads. – Seen from a distance, the farms appear as green oases but as you approach the plan becomes evident: 2m - 6ft high embankments topped by a double row of oaks, beeches or elms protect the **farmstead** from the wind. This comprises a meadow of some 2 to 3 ha - 5 to 7 acres planted with apple trees in the centre of which stand the half-timbered farmhouse and other buildings. In winter the cattle are gathered here, around the pond. The entrance is often through a monumental gateway. Farms have their own ponds, wells and cisterns although with mains water the latter have now often been replaced by water towers.

Caux cattle raising procedure is nothing if not unusual, including putting cattle and horses out on a tether in spring on the patches of artificial fodder, where each animal delimits his territory in the form of a perfectly geometrical circle. Milk – the chief source of income – is sent to the towns of the Lower Seine or the butter and cheese factories in the valleys.

★ THE ALABASTER COAST

1 From Dieppe to Etretat

104km – 65 miles – about 5 hours – Local map pp 54-55

By many bends and twists, the road serves a whole string of beaches each set either at the mouth of a little coastal river or lying in a deep dry valley. Glimpses of the sea and the cliffs and pleasant views of the pretty setting of some resorts give the drive, which is best done in the morning, its tourist attraction. The monotony of the Caux Plateau is fortunately broken by the islands of dark green formed by the far off farms and villages.

★★ **Dieppe.** – *Description p 61.*

Leave Dieppe by ⑥, the D 75.

Pourville-sur-Mer. – This seaside resort, pleasantly situated near jagged cliffs, has re-arisen from the ruins resulting from the Commando raid of 19 August 1942 *(details p 61)* when the Cameron Highlanders and a Canadian Regiment the South Saskatchewan, landed to the sound of the pipes, inflicted severe damage on the enemy and, under cover of the Navy and through the sacrifice of their own rearguard, re-embarked early in the afternoon.

★ **Varengeville-sur-Mer.** – *Description p 134.*

Ste-Marguerite-sur-Mer. – Pop 465. *Facilities.* The 12C church, which has no transept, was considerably remodelled in the 16C. Inside, four of the original **arches★** remain on the north side; those on the south date from 1528. The second column on the right is twisted and scattered with shells; the high altar dates from 1160 and is one of the very few still extant. Notice on the front and at each end the colonnettes with Romanesque capitals.

At St-Aubin bear left on the D 237.

Bourg-Dun. – Pop 419. *3km - 2 miles by the D 237 starting from St-Aubin.* Notre-Dame Church is a vast composite edifice, outwardly remarkable for its **tower★** built on a massive square 13C base. The hatchet-shaped roof is 17C. Go through the Renaissance door into the south aisle.

Only the base of the rood screen remains to support statues of St Anthony and St Sebastian. Beneath Flamboyant vaulting in the south transept are a Renaissance bay and piscina; the beautiful south aisle through three wide bays off the chancel was added in the 14C. The font in the north aisle is Renaissance.

Return to St-Aubin.

Veules-les-Roses. – Pop 686. The seaside resort lies sheltered in a small valley which is particularly attractive higher up. St Martin's **Church** in the town itself is 16 and 17C with a 13C lantern. Inside are five 16C twisted, carved limestone columns and ancient statues together with two fine paintings. A timber-framed roof covers the nave and aisles.

Turn left on the D 37.

Blosseville Church (Église). – The church, surmounted by a 12C belfry, possesses beautiful Renaissance stained glass windows and some old statues.

St-Valéry-en-Caux. – *Description p 122.*

Paluel Nuclear Power Station (Centrale nucléaire de Paluel). – The station consists of 4 autonomous units each with a capacity of 1 300 MW. Enriched uranium is used to fuel the station and cooling ensured by sea water pumped from the ocean and attaining a maximum temperature of 15 °C. The thermal energy generated by the fuel is transformed into mechanical then electrical energy. The Information Centre has an exhibition on the range of energy sources, the choice of nuclear energy, and the history and operation of the power station. A cartoon show tells the story of energy throughout the ages.

Veulettes-sur-Mer. – Pop 404. Facilities. The 11 and 13C church stands halfway up a hill overlooking the seaside resort in the wide green valley below.

The drive's finest **panorama★★** is to be seen between Senneville *(narrow road)* and Fécamp, near the **Notre-Dame-du-Salut Chapel** (sailors' pilgrimage), from the belvedere with viewing table.

The road quickly loses height. The cliffs to the west of Fécamp stretch as far as Étretat. Fécamp and its harbour appear after a sharp bend to the left.

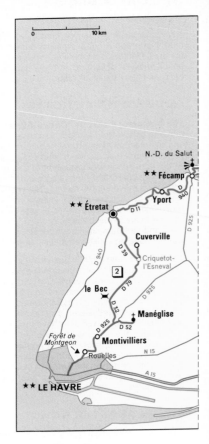

★★ **Fécamp.** – *Description p 75.*

Yport. – Pop 1 122. A seaside resort tucked away in a valley.

★★ **Étretat.** – *Description p 69.*

THE LÉZARDE VALLEY

2 From Étretat to Le Havre

33km - 21 miles – about 1 hour – Local map above

★★ **Étretat.** – *Description p 69.*

Leave Étretat by ③, the D 39.

After leaving Étretat the road passes through a small valley as it heads inland.

At Criquetot – l'Esneval take the D 239 on the left.

Cuverville. – Pop 187. The writer, **André Gide** (1859-1951), is buried beneath a plain concrete slab in the small church cemetery.

The road drops again, along the pleasant Lézarde Valley.

Le Bec Castle (Château du Bec). – *(not open to the public)* The 12-16C castle has an enchanting setting of trees and still waters.

At Épouville take the D 925 left and then the D 52 right.

Manéglise. – Pop 915. The small church is one of the most graceful examples of Romanesque architecture in Normandy. In spite of its minuteness, the 12C nave is flanked by aisles. Notice the geometrical patterns on the portal.

Montivilliers. – *Description p 99.*

The road runs away from the Lézarde Valley through the small valley of Rouelles, a suburb of Le Havre boasting a very pleasant park with a pretty flint dovecot.

The road then runs along the Montgeon Forest and into the Jenner Tunnel leading into the town centre.

★★ **Le Havre.** – *Description p 80.*

THE DURDENT VALLEY

3 From Veulettes-sur-Mer to Fécamp

36km - 23 miles – about 3 hours – Local map above

The Durdent, which flows idly into the sea at Veulettes-sur-Mer, has cut a wide valley across the Caux plateau.

Veulettes-sur-Mer. – *Description above.*

Leave Veulettes to the south on the D 10. Take the D 68 left at Paluel.

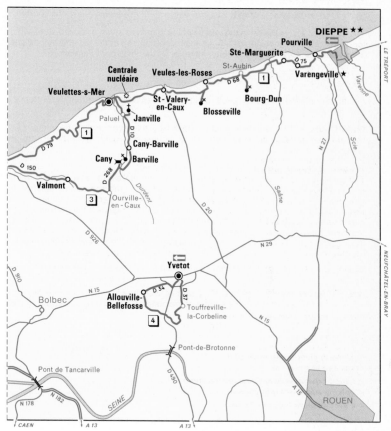

Janville Chapel (Chapelle de Janville). – Continue beyond a sharp right turn along the D 68. At the top of the hill turn left towards the chapel on the edge of the plateau. Inside this old pilgrimage church there is an attractive wrought iron grille in the chancel.

Return to Paluel.

ⓥ **Cany-Barville.** – Pop 3 267. The **church** on the left bank, rebuilt in the 16C in its original pointed arch style, has a 13C belfry. Notice on entering the two 16C **carved panels★** showing the Virgin of the Seven Swords and St-Martin.

Barville. – The small church has a delightful **setting★** between the two arms of the Durdent River.

The drive on the D 268 is particularly pleasant between Cany-Barville and its junction with the D 131 and there is a close view of Cany château.

ⓥ **Cany Château.** – Standing behind a large courtyard lined with two symmetrical outbuildings extended by two pavilions the château is an imposing stone and brick structure built at the end of the Louis XIII era. It is surrounded by moats fed by the Durdent River.

The main building has two projecting wings and is approached at the front by a double stairway in the form a horseshoe. The apartments have retained fine 17 and 18C furnishings. On the second floor the bedrooms are decorated with beautiful Flanders tapestries. The main room, or *salon vert,* contains Regency woodwork.

In the basement the former pantry and kitchen contain utensils, ovens, crockery and manikins.

Take the D 50 to Ourville, then the D 150 to the right along the Valmont Valley.

Valmont. – *Description p 133.*

Return to the D 150 towards Fécamp.

★★ **Fécamp.** – *Description p 75.*

★ THE CAUX PLATEAU

4️⃣ **Round tour starting from Yvetot**

22km - 14 miles – description p 140

*Respect the life of the countryside
Go carefully on country roads
Protect wild life, wild plants and trees.*

★ CHAMP DE BATAILLE Château

Michelin map 54 fold 20 or 231 fold 24 – 4km - 2 1/2 miles northwest of Neubourg

This beautiful 17C mansion in the middle of the woods has twin brick and stone wings, long and low, on either side of a huge main court, joined at the far end by porticoes. It was built by Alexandre de Créquy, inheritor of the Vieuxpont Family.

⏱ TOUR *time: 1 hour*

Bowls were played on the forecourt, an immense esplanade in front of the entrance to the château.

Main Court. – This four-sided court flanked by two symmetrical buildings has a monumental gateway crowned by classical figures representing earth, air, fire and water.

Inside. – *Entrance through the main court on the left.*
The walls of the entrance are covered with imitation marble to recall the real marble on the floor. The main stairway is decorated with wrought iron railings bearing the initials of the Créquy Family, founders of the château. Of particular interest are the Vestibule of the Four Seasons (notice the reliefs of the seasons above the doors), the *grand salon* (18C Gobelins tapestry), the dining room (19C woodwork by a local artist), the guest room (chambre d'hôte) which was reserved for those staying in the château, the archives room with documents on the history of the building, and the chapel where the staff attended on the ground floor and the master on the mezzanine.

Outbuildings. – The large arched room, once a stable, now houses a collection of stuffed animals.

Park. – One can see the "ice house", a sort of watchtower where ice was stored in winter after being taken from the surface of the ponds, the wild rhododendrons, the old oak, the purple beech and the gardens.

The practical information chapter, at the end of the guide, regroups

– a list of the local or national organizations supplying additional information

– a section on times and charges.

The CHARENTONNE Valley

Michelin map 55 folds 14, 15 and 60 fold 4 or 231 folds 32, 33

This swift running river, tributary of the Risle and full of fish, winds through the sometimes solitary damp valley grasslands.

FROM SERQUIGNY
TO ST-EVROULT-NOTRE-DAME-DU-BOIS

65km - 41 miles – about 2 hours

Serquigny. – Pop 2 320. The church, with a chequered façade of black flint and white stone, has a Romanesque doorway. Inside, on the left, are a Renaissance chapel and stained glass windows of the same period. Four massive round pillars support the belfry. Note also: the small pulpit with its carved panels, modern stained glass windows in the south chapel and chapel off the chancel and the old wooden statues in the nave.

The D 133 runs along the Charentonne River. Take the D 133 southeast.

The road from Serquigny to Anceins often approaches the river. Châteaux and pointed belfries of country churches can be seen from time to time through clearings in the trees.

⏱ **Fontaine-l'Abbé.** – Pop 510. A pretty Norman village with a **church,** next to the Louis XIII château. Note the colourful banners of the local Brotherhood of Charity.

Menneval. – Pop 1 329. The village lies in one of the most attractive folds in the valley. Its small country church with renovated façade is delightful. The local Brotherhood of Charity is the oldest in the region, dating from 1060.

Bernay. – *Description p 44.*

Leave Bernay to the south on the D 33.

The road runs alongside the river.

Broglie. – *Description p 49.*

At Mélicourt take the D 819 to the right.

St-Denis-d'Augerons. – Pop 109. From the war memorial, near a beech wood, there is an attractive view of the Norman countryside highlighted by the two village churches of St-Denis-d'Augerons and St-Aquilin.

Return to Mélicourt then drive south on the D 33, D 252 and D 31 from la Ferté-Frênel.

St-Evroult-Notre-Dame-du-Bois. – *Description p 120.*

★ CLÈRES

Michelin map **52** fold 14 or **231** fold 23

One of Normandy's greatest attractions is the zoo which has occupied part of the park around the château, originally 14C but considerably rebuilt in the 19C, since 1920. The former castle occupied the site of the present château and its surroundings. Built in the 11C, only a few ruins remain. The neo-Gothic château consists of two main sandstone buildings decorated with motifs in brick and flint.
The wooden covered market with slate roof stands proudly on the market square.

★**Zoo.** – In an exceptional natural setting birds and mammals inhabit the rivers, lawns, groves, and trees.
From the garden populated by flamingos, ducks and exotic geese, go through into the park proper where antelopes, kangaroos, gibbons, different types of deer, cranes and peacocks roam in partial liberty. The lake is inhabited by more than 300 couples of palmipeds of 120 different species. Higher up indoor and outdoor aviaries are reserved for pheasants, doves, budgerigars and parrots... (around 2 500 birds of 450 different species). In the former main room of the château, a gallery houses rare exotic birds.

Car and Military Museum (Musée de l'automobile et militaire). – Besides the lovely old cars of various makes, such as the Panhard-Levassor (1894), the Georges Richard (1901), the Grégoire (1913) with its curious "monocle" windscreen fixed on the shaft of the steering wheel and a steam fire engine (1876), the museum displays bicycles from before 1900, motorcycles and, upstairs, military vehicles from the last war. Lorries, jeeps, armoured cars, tracked vehicles and aeroplanes are present and a diorama retraces the history of the Battle of Normandy.

EXCURSION

Bocasse Park (Parc du Bocasse). – *2km - 1 1/4 miles west on the D 6.*
Essentially an amusement park for children with many games and roundabouts, the park has a number of picnic areas.

★ CONCHES-EN-OUCHE

Michelin map **55** fold 16 or **231** fold 34 – Facilities

The town of Conches, bordering on the woodlands which mark the northern limits of the Ouche Region, is remarkably situated on a spur encircled by the Rouloir River.

HISTORICAL NOTES

Returning from a campaign against the Spanish Moors beside Don Sanche of Aragon (1034), Roger de Tosny, made a pilgrimage to Conques, in Aquitaine, and brought back relics from the site of the cult of Saint Foy. We may think that he gave the new town the name of the famous sanctuary. Roger dedicated to the young martyr a church replaced at the end of the 15C by the building we see today.

SIGHTS

★**Ste-Foy Church** (Église). – The south tower is crowned by a tall spire of wood and lead, a copy of the one blown down in a storm in 1842. The fine carved panels of the façade doors are early 16C. Notice the many gargoyles.
Inside there are some beautiful statues; in the south aisle and near the great organ that of St Rock (17C); at the entrance to St-Michael's chapel, the statue of St Suzanne (13C); in the north aisle a polychrome *Pietà* (16C); at the entrance to the Lady Chapel, a statue of St Peter wearing a tiara (16C); in the east end, Christ resurrected in stone (16C).

★**Stained Glass Windows.** – The Renaissance windows, dating from the first half of the 16C, have retained their unity in spite of restoration. Those in the north aisle depict the life of the Virgin. The second window (1510), showing the Virgin between St Adrian, on the left, and St Romanus, on the right, is, like its pair which evokes the life of John the Baptist, of an earlier date than those that follow, and probably adorned the original church.
The seven 10.50m - 34ft windows in the chancel are divided into two by a trilobed transom, the upper part being given to the illustration of the Life of Christ, the lower to that of St Foy and portraits of the donors. The whole series, inspired by German master engravers such as Dürer and Aldegrever, is said to be by Romain Buron, a pupil of Engrand the Prince of Beauvais.
The windows in the south aisle were made in either the Ile-de-France or at Fontainebleau. The Mystical Wine Press, fifth window, is the best known.
The houses facing the church are 15 and 16C.

The Town Hall Garden (Jardin de l'Hôtel de Ville). – Go through the town hall's Gothic doorway – entrance to the former castle – to the garden in which stands the ruined keep surrounded by 12C towers.
From the terrace with its wild boar in stone, there is a fine view of the Rouloir Valley and the elegant Flamboyant apse of St-Foy Church. Below there is another terrace with a Flamboyant balustrade and offering a similar view.

EXCURSIONS

Rouloir Valley. – *Round tour of 10km - 6 miles along narrow roads. Leave Conches by the Évreux road, the D 830.*
After 3km - 2 miles, turn left at a crossroads into a road which goes steeply downhill. After La Croisille turn into the first tarred road on the left (D 167) and 1km - 2/3 mile further on, at a crossroads, bear left into a downhill road which reaches the bottom of the Rouloir Valley in the pleasant setting of St-Elier Church. Return along the river for a superb view of Conches.

Breteuil. – *14km - 9 miles south on the D 840. Description p 48.*

CRÈVECŒUR-EN-AUGE   Pop 515

Michelin map 🆔 fold 17 or 🆔 fold 31 – Local map p 39

Crèvecœur is a welcoming town situated in the Auge Valley. 500m - 1/3 mile north and to the right of the N 13 is Crèvecœur Manor.

★ CRÈVECŒUR MANOR *time: 3/4 hour.*

Encircled by trees and moats, the half-timbered buildings of the manor were fortified in the 11C, altered in the 15C and restored in 1972. The result is particularly picturesque.
The gatehouse (15-16C) has a chequered brick and stone ground floor. The first floor is half-timbered. On either side the turrets with their "pepper pot" overhanging roofs are from the château of Beuvilliers near Lisieux. The farm (15C), barn (16C) and main building (15C) house the **Schlumberger Museum** on petroleum research, named after the

two Alsatian engineers who in 1927 invented the technique of electric logging which is used throughout the world today: drilling equipment, working models, mobile laboratories etc. Note the unusual square dovecot with its overhanging tiled roof. At the top two small windows enable the pigeons to fly away. The interior woodwork is pierced with 1 500 pigeonholes.
The 12C chapel has a fine panelled vault in the form of an upturned hull and contains an exhibit of Norman architecture – drawings, models and an audio-visual presentation.

Dovecot at Crèvecœur-en-Auge

EXCURSION

★**Manors of the Auge Region.** – *Round tour of 30km - 19 miles. Leave Crèvecœur to the south on the D 16 and then take the D 101ᴬ on the left.*

Mont de la Vigne Manor. – A shady drive leads uphill to the manor, built on the site of a former 14C fortress. It consists of a central yard around which stand the main building, chapel and outbuildings in a pleasant and restful setting. Visit the outside and discover the remains of the fortress.

At Monteille take the D 101ᴬ to the right and then the D 269 at Lecaude.

Grandchamp Château. – *(not open to the public)* The building is surrounded by a moat and consists of a 17C main building in brick and stone and a 15-16C half-timbered gateway, flanked by two four-storey turrets surmounted by slate domes with skylight windows. The main building has a raised projection terminating with a pediment. An attic makes up the top floor.

The D 269 leads to St-Julien-le-Faucon. Once here take the D 47.

Coupesarte Manor. – This charming residence surrounded by water on three sides is the main house of a farm building. The construction goes back to the end of the 15C or beginning of the 16C. From the field on the left beyond the small lock there is a good view of the half-timbered façade with its two corner turrets reminiscent of watchtowers.
The half-timbered outbuildings contribute to the originality of the whole.

Return to St-Julien-le-Faucon. Take the D 511 on the left. At Le Godet turn right. The D 154 and D 16 lead back to Crèvecœur-en-Auge.

★★★ DEAUVILLE

Pop 4 769

Michelin map **54** fold 17 or **231** fold 19 – Local maps p 39 and 128 – Facilities

Deauville is world famous: its dazzling luxury, its sea water swimming pool and thalasso-aesthetics centre (AZ), its variety of entertainment – racing, regattas, car rallies, galas, tournaments – make it a favourite international resort.

THE RESORT

High season in Deauville opens in July and closes on the fourth Sunday in August with the Deauville Grand Prix. Racing takes place alternatively on the La Touques (flat) and Clairefontaine courses (flat and steeplechase) and it is at Deauville that the international yearling sales are held (in August). Out of season the resort accommodates numerous seminars and conventions.

The coming and going of everyone on the **Planches** (AY) – a wooden plank promenade which runs the length of the beach – is the special characteristic of Deauville beach life. As a background, on the far side of the beach with its coloured tents, the *planches* are lined by elegant buildings such as the Pompeian Baths and the Soleil Bar where celebrities enjoy being seen.

The yacht basin on the Touques River the Yacht Club and such boulevards as the Eugène-Cornuché give the resort an air which has earned it the title *Plage Fleurie*.

Port Deauville (AY). – Contained to the east by the breakwater stretching from the beach to the mouth of the Touques and to the west by the jetty at the port side entrance to the channel, the port consists of three docks accessible through a double lock offering the advantages of deep water mooring and increased capacity – over 4 000 yards of floating quays enable more than 800 moorings. In the middle of the water, the buildings include the typical "marinas" with their slate roofs, the harbour master's office and the Deauville Yacht Club *(Quai des Marchands, near the lock)* and places reserved for shopping centres and the hotel industry.

⏱ AIR TRIPS

Flights over the coast and main resort, either by plane or by helicopter, may be organised from Deauville-St-Gatien.

AROUND DEAUVILLE-TROUVILLE

Trouville is described on p 132. Distances are measured starting from the bridge over the Touques (Pont des Belges) which connects the two resorts.

The endless horizons over the sea combine beautifully with the picturesque greenery of the hinterland. Between Honfleur and Cabourg the coast has become one of the busiest in France during the holiday season, but has nevertheless retained its charm.

★**Mount Canisy (Le Mont Canisy).** – Round tour of 15km - 9 miles – about 3/4 hour. Leave Deauville by ③, the D 513.
Bénerville Church stands overlooking a crossroads.

Turn left up the hill before the church and about 200 yards further left again by the town hall. At the top bear right into a road leading to Mount Canisy. Leave the car by a gate.

A path leads to the blockhouses where the **view** extends from Cape Hève to the Orne Estuary.

Return to the car and go right.

After the modern Canisy town there are views over the Touques Valley as the road descends to the St-Arnoult crossroads.

Turn left on the D 278 to Deauville.

★★**The Normandy Corniche: from Deauville-Trouville to Honfleur.** – 21km - 13 miles – about 1 hour. Leave Deauville-Trouville on ①, the D 513.
This very pleasant trip passes through magnificent scenery and affords views over the Seine Estuary between gaps in the hedges and orchards. Handsome properties are scattered along the road. Just before Villerville there is a fine view of the oil refineries on the estuary. To the left Le Havre can be recognised by its thermal power station and the belfry of St-Joseph's church.

★**Villerville.** – Pop 733. Facilities. This lively seaside resort, with its nearby meadows and woods, has kept its rural character. Notice the Romanesque belfry on the local church. Rocks stretch beyond the beach, notably the Ratier Bank which is visible at low tide. From the terrace overlooking the beach there is a view of Le Havre and Cape Hève. The road is thereafter narrow with hidden bends.

Criquebœuf. – Pop 172. The 12C **church,** with its ivy-covered walls, is a familiar feature on travel posters.

At Pennedepie, take the D 62 and then 2.5km - 1 1/2 miles further on, the D 279 to the right.

Barneville. – Pop 125. The church, hidden away in the greenery, stands against the magnificent park of the 18C **château.**

Turn round and after 4km - 3 miles – turn left by a château to reach Honfleur by the Côte de Grace.

★★**Côte de Grace.** – Description p 89.

★★**Honfleur.** – Description p 87.

DEAUVILLE

Morny (Pl. de) ...... **BZ** 28
République (Av. de la) **ABZ**

Fracasse (R. A.) ..... **AZ**
Gambetta (R.) .... **BY** 9
Le Hoc (R. D.) ...... **BZ** 24

Blanc (R. E.) .... **AZ** 4
Colas (R. E.) .... **AZ** 5
Fossorier (R. R.) ..... **AZ** 8

Gaulle (Av. Gén. de) . **AZ** 10
Gontaut-Biron (R.) . **AYZ** 13
Hoche (R.) .... **AZ** 20
Laplace (R.) .... **AZ** 23
Le Marois (R.) ...... **AZ** 25
Marine (Q. de la) .... **BY** 26

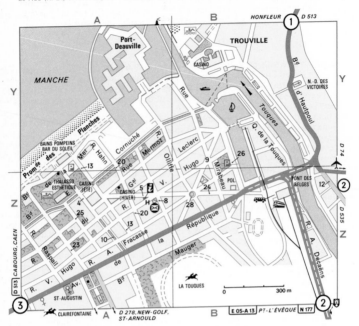

★★ The Fleurie Coast: from Trouville-Deauville to Cabourg. – *19km - 12 miles – Leave Deauville by ③, the D 513.*

Bénerville-sur-Mer. – Pop 527. The hillsides are dotted with villas overlooking a long sandy beach.

Blonville-sur-Mer. – Pop 889. Its long sandy beach stretches to the slopes of Mount Canisy. There is an amusement park near the sea. Notre-Dame Chapel houses some modern frescoes, the work of the artist Jean-Denis Maillart. The paintings have been created directly on the fresh plaster and depict scenes particularly from the Old and New Testaments.

★★ **Villers-sur-Mer.** – Pop 1 853. Facilities. This elegant seaside resort with its casino and very good sports facilities is known for its large beach and its wooded and hilly countryside. The beach extends 5km - 3 miles from Blonville to the Vaches Noires Cliff *(p 90).* Straight below Villers it is bordered by a promenade almost 2km - 1 1/4 miles in length.

The **Museum of Paleontology** (musée paléontologique) has exhibits of fossils and stuffed birds from the area together with a stone armchair and seashells of Ferdinand Postel, artist and photographer who lived in Villers from 1880 to 1917. He collected fossils and created many montages printed subsequently in the form of postcards. Access to the museum is by the information centre (syndicat d'initiative).

Just before Houlgate, in a downhill hairpin bend, a viewing table on the right of the road offers an extensive **panorama** from the mouth of the River Dives to that of the River Orne.

★★ **Houlgate.** – *Description p 90.*

The road runs along the coast and, before Dives-sur-Mer, passes in front of a monument commemorating the departure of Duke William for the conquest of England.

★ **Dives-sur-Mer.** – *Description p 63.*

★★ **Cabourg.** – *Description p 50.*

★★ DEUX AMANTS HILL (CÔTE DES DEUX AMANTS)

Michelin map **55** fold 7 or **231** fold 23 – Local map p 127

From the top of this spur overlooking the confluence of the Seine and Andelle Rivers there is an admirable view over the Seine Valley.

The legend. – Marie de France, the country's earliest female writer, told the touching story of Caliste and Raoul as early as the 12C. The king of Pitres did not want to give his daughter's hand in marriage and decreed that Caliste's future husband would have to be strong enough to run non-stop to the top of the nearby hill with Caliste in his arms. Raoul, the son of a count, made an attempt but collapsed and died from exhaustion at the top. Caliste fell dead beside him. The two young people were buried on the spot and the hill took on the name *Deux Amants* (two lovers).

★★ **View.** – Leave Amfreville-sous-les Monts by the D 20 which climbs rapidly to the top of the hill. From a bend in the road there is a **magnificent view** over the Seine Valley *(car park 50m beyond the TCF viewing table).*

Panorama des Deux Amants. – The most notable features of the landscape are Amfreville Locks and Dam and the bend in the Seine.

Michelin map **52** fold 4 or **231** fold 11 – Local map p 55 – Facilities

Dieppe, the beach closest to Paris, is the oldest French seaside resort; the harbour is modern but many old corners and alleys remain, making it one of the most unusual towns in Normandy. The town's past is evoked in its churches, castle and museum. The Maréchal Foch Boulevard runs the length of the shingle beach which gets ever more crowded as you approach the west end where the castle stands out high on the cliff top. On the town side are gardens and sports areas and a second parallel avenue, the Boulevard de Verdun. Near the casino can be seen the west harbour gateway, a part of the 14C town defences and now known as Les Tourelles. Below the castle and west cliff a monument in Square du Canada commemorates the Dieppe explorers of Canada in the 16, 17 and 18C and reminds us of the 350 years of common history uniting the two countries. A plaque recalls the 1942 Commando Raid.

HISTORICAL NOTES

Jean Ango and the Privateers' War (16C). – In the 16C the Portuguese treated as pirates any ships venturing off the coast of Africa but François I decided that reprisals should be undertaken and issued letters of marque. The master mariners of Dieppe, who were already renowned for their voyages of exploration, retaliated with the shipbuilder and maritime counsellor to King François, Jean Ango, constructing for the purpose, a fleet of privateers "such as would make a king tremble". Among the mariners were the brothers Parmentier who in 1529 when crossing the Equator had thought up the ducking ceremony, still practised, when crossing the line; another outstanding figure was **Verrazano,** the Florentine who, in April 1524, discovered the site of New York to which he gave the name Land of Angoulême.

Ango's fleet captured more than 300 Portugese ships in only a few years and the King of Portugal, fearful for his merchant fleet, was compelled to intrigue for the withdrawal, at a price, of the letters of marque. Finally, in 1530, Jean Ango gave up the war and built himself a splendid palace of wood in Dieppe and, at Varengeville *(p 134)*, a less sumptuous but equally stylish country residence. In 1535 the King appointed him Governor of Dieppe and in 1551 he died and was buried in the chapel he had had built in St James' Church.

The Canadian Commando Raid of 1942. – On 19 August 1942, Operation Jubilee, the first Allied reconnaissance in force on the coast of Europe, was launched with Dieppe as the primary objective.

Seven thousand men, mostly Canadians, were landed at eight points between Berneval and Ste-Marguerite but the only German strongpoint to be taken was the battery near the Ailly Lighthouse *(p 134)*. The Churchill tanks floundered hopelessly on the beach under intense fire and were finally sacrificed to protect the re-embarkation. Five thousand men were killed or taken prisoner; the Allies learned from this raid that German defences were concentrated round the ports and, as naval losses were small, that amphibious operations on a larger scale might be successful; the Germans, for their part, felt convinced that future Allied attacks would be directed particularly at the ports.

THE PORT

Dieppe port is interesting for its variety.

Passenger Port (Port de voyageurs) (BY). – This is the most unusual part of Dieppe harbour with tall, dark stone buildings surrounding the basin where the Newhaven-Dieppe ships moor. The coming and going beneath the arcades and around the fish market add to the old shipping harbour atmosphere.

In 1986 Dieppe was the 6th French passenger port owing to the Dieppe-Newhaven car-ferry services.

Fishing Port (Port de pêche) (BZ). – The fishing fleet brings in primarily the higher grade fish – turbot, brill, bass and sole. The early morning bustle of the fish market is full of local colour. The fishermen, who live mostly in the old Le Pollet quarter on the right bank of the river, landed 16 000 tons of fish in 1986 and a further 1 150 tons of scallops, thereby making Dieppe France's 5th fishing port.

Commercial Port (Port de commerce) (BZ). – The fruit trade has an important place in the port's activities. In 1986 Dieppe was the 3rd fruit importing port in France mainly due to citrus fruits from the Camaroons and bananas essentially from Morocco. With a trade of 2 168 000 tons in 1986, Dieppe is France's 12th port.

SIGHTS

The busiest part of Dieppe and the most interesting, apart from the streets around the exchange and the fish market, and the Grande Rue, a pedestrian street, is the Puits-Salé Square where six roads meet and the Café des Tribunaux pediment stands.

* **St-Jacques Church (Église) (BY).** – Begin by going round the outside which has been considerably rebuilt over the centuries.

The 14C central doorway is surmounted by a fine rose window; the restored façade tower is 15C, the east end and radiating chapels are 16C; the south transept, on the other hand, has been left untouched and is a good example of early Gothic.

Interior. – The well proportioned nave, which is 13C, was ornamented in the 14C with a triforium and given tall windows a century later.

The first chapel in the south aisle, the Chapel of the Holy Sepulchre, has a fine stone screen and is 15C.

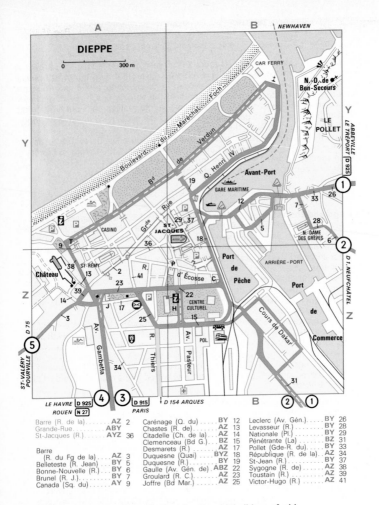

The other chapels were all given by the shipbuilders of old.

The transept, the oldest part of the church, supports the dome which was rebuilt in the 18C while above the chancel are star vaulting and a 16C pierced triforium. A fine 17C wooden statue of St Jacques stands above the high altar.

The Sacred Heart Chapel on the right facing the high altar has original Flamboyant vaulting; the centre chapel is known for its consoles on which are carved major events in the Life of the Virgin. Left, above the sacristy door, is a frieze (from Jean Ango's Palace destroyed by British naval bombardment in 1694); the upper frieze shows a file of Brazilian Indians and recalls the voyages of Dieppe explorers.

Castle (   ). – 15C. Dieppe Castle, faced with alternate blocks of flint and sandstone, was built round a massive circular tower which formed part of the earlier, 14C, town fortifications. 17C curtain walls link the castle to the square St-Rémy tower.

Formerly belonging to the Governors of the town, it now houses the municipal museum.

Museum (Musée). – On the ground floor are exhibited models of 18 and 19C boats, and 16 and 17C maps and navigational instruments, whereas the basement houses local archaeological collections. On the first floor there is a display of Pre-Columbian Peruvian pottery and several rooms are devoted to 19C Dutch and French painting.

The museum also possesses a unique collection of **Dieppe ivories★**. The meticulous craftsmanship is in every way equal to that associated with artistic achievements of the Far East whether it be certain model ships and navigational instruments mentioned above or,

Dieppe ivory

on the first floor, objects of a religious nature (crucifix, rosary beads, statuettes) or everyday items (toilet requisites, sewing instruments, fans, snuff boxes, clocks, sculptures and miscellaneous models).

A small workshop has been reconstituted to show the tools of the local ivory carvers, craftsmen who came to Dieppe to carve on the spot ivory being imported from Africa and the Orient. In the 17C there were 350 ivory carvers in the town.

One of the rooms is dedicated to the musician Camille Saint-Saëns: drawings, portraits, academic clothes, objects received after his concerts, holiday souvenirs (Egyptian statuettes, sunshades...).

The museum also has a collection of prints by Georges Braque.

Boulevard de la Mer (AY). – *Access by car direction "Château-musée Panorama" by* ⑤, *or on foot by the Chemin de la Citadelle.*
At the east end there is a magnificent view★ of the town and beach.

Notre-Dame de Bon Secours Chapel (Chapelle) (BY). – *Leave Dieppe on* ①, *the D 925. Half way up take the Route du Puys on the left as far as the cliff. Turn left along the cliff edge.*
Stand at the foot of the Calvary or beyond the signal pole, where there is an extensive **view★** of the town and port.

EXCURSIONS

★**Varengeville-sur-Mer.** – *8km - 5 miles: Leave Dieppe by* ⑤, *the D 75. Description p 134.*

Miromesnil Château. – *12km - 7 1/2 miles – about 1 hour. Leave Dieppe by* ④, *the D 925.*
A road lined with magnificent beech trees leads to Offranville.

Offranville. – Pop 3 134. The village has a 16C church and beside it a thousand year old yew tree more than 7m - 23ft in circumference.

Turn left on the road to St-Aubin-sur-Scie and follow the signs.

At the boundary of Miromesnil Château stands a statue of Guy de Maupassant who was born in the château in 1850.

Miromesnil Château. – *Description p 99.*

Join us in our never ending task of keeping up to date.

Send us your comments and suggestions, please.

Michelin Tyre Public Limited Company
Tourism Department
Davy House – Lyon Road – HARROW – Middlesex HA 1 2DQ.

★ DIVES-SUR-MER   Pop 5 732

Michelin map 54 folds 16, 17 or 231 fold 19 – Local map p 39

Dives faces Cabourg from across the river of the same name. At the mouth a small fishing harbour and marina have been built where there was in the Middle Ages a large port, now silted up.

If Cabourg is known as a holiday resort, Dives is more synonymous with history, for it was from here that William and his men set out to conquer England *(p 17)*.

The covered market at Dives-sur-Mer

SIGHTS *plan p 50.*

★ **The Covered Market** (Halles) (B). – 15 and 16C. The magnificent oak frame is in very good condition and goes perfectly with the tiled roof. Wrought iron signs characterise the different merchants.
On the other side of Place de la République one can see the 16C Bois-Hibou manor.

Notre Dame de Dives Church (Église) (B). – This massive building, once a centre of pilgrimage until the Religious Wars, is 14 and 15C except for the transept crossing, a remnant of an older sanctuary built in the 11C. Inside the elegance of the 15C nave is in sharp contrast with the massive pillars and plain arches of the Romanesque transept crossing. The transepts themselves, the chancel and the Lady Chapel were built in the Radiating Gothic style of the 14C. Notice on the back of the west wall a list carved in 1862 of William's companions in arms during his expedition to England.

William the Conqueror Village (Village Guillaume le Conquérant) (B E). – This pleasant enclave of art and craft shops is located within the precincts of the old inn of the same name, dating from the 16C. Guests included Mme de Sévigné and Alexandre Dumas. The shops with their individual signs stand around the yard of the former inn.

For a peaceful night
*the **Michelin Red Guide France** revises annually its choice*
of pleasant, quiet and well situated hotels.

★ DREUX
Pop 33 760

Michelin map 60 fold 7 or 231 folds 47, 48 – Local map p 72

Dreux stands on the boundary separating Normandy from the Ile-de-France and is a regional trade centre living from its diversified industrial activities.
The name Dreux is connected with **Jean Rotrou** (1609-1650), poet and lieutenant of the bailiwick of his home town. He died a victim of his devotion when returning to Dreux after it had been ravaged by the plague. On the square bearing his name a statue perpetuates his memory (AY).
Around the belfry the pedestrian precinct invites the visitor to take a stroll round and see the Main Street (Grande Rue) bustling with activity, above all on market day. On the corner of the Rue Illiers note the two picturesque timber-framed houses joined together by beams.

HISTORICAL NOTES

A Fronteer Town. – Dreux assumed its importance when the Normans settled beyond the River Avre and its fortress protected the fronteer of France against a very bellicose neighbour.
The castle, built on a hill occupied by St-Louis Chapel, underwent many sieges. In 1593 the town was partly burnt down by Henri IV for having taken sides with the League and refused to surrender for three years. On the king's orders the fortress was dismantled.

A Royal Necropolis. – In 1556 the Parliament of Paris decided that the county of Dreux would thereafter be the sole possession of the royal family of France, who had often pledged it to important families of the realm. In 1775 Louis XVI yielded Dreux to his cousin the Duke de Penthièvre, son of the Count of Toulouse. Eight years later, on the king's insistance, the duke had to give up his magnificent residence at Rambouillet. He then had the family tombs, until then grouped together in the parish church of Rambouillet, since destroyed, transferred to the collegiate church adjoining the castle at Dreux.
The duke's daughter had as her dowry the county of Dreux when she married Louis-Philippe of Orléans, also known as Philippe-Equality. Dreux, a simple family tomb before the Revolution, therefore gained the honour of keeping the remains of the Orléans Family.

SIGHTS

★ **Belfry** (Beffroi) (AY B). – The most ornate façade closes the former main street (rue Maurice-Viollette). Construction took 25 years (1512-1537). The ground and first floors are decorated in Flamboyant style whereas the second floor shows the skill of Clément Métézeau (1479-1555), a young architect from Dreux at the time of the Renaissance. Notice the windows flanked by pilasters with friezes above and the skylight turrets.

🕙 **Inside.** – *Entrance Rue des Changes.* The first floor room with ribbed vaulting was once a bailiff's court. It has a fine monumental hearth bearing salamanders, which were emblems of François I. Several old paintings depict the town of Dreux, together with an original collection dating from around 1893 by a local hairdresser, composed entirely of hair. The second floor room, formerly for storing flour, is characterised by its ribbed vaulting and a monumental fireplace. The oculus in the middle enabled the bell to be passed through into the belfry. Notice the carved oak door.
The attic houses the great bell under an immense chestnut framed roof. The bell dates from 4 August 1809, bears the arms of the town and used to be rung by four deaf men.

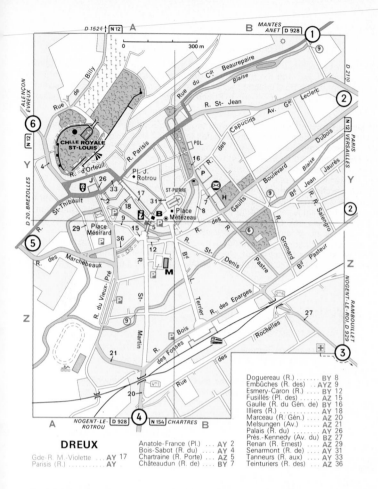

St-Louis Royal Chapel (Chapelle) (AY). – Before the Revolution the collegiate church of St-Stephen stood nearby where the remains of the Toulouse Penthièvre families were gathered. In 1816 the dowager duchess of Orleans, widow of Philippe-Equality, at the cost of major earthworks, had a neo-Classical chapel built in the form of a Greek cross and lit only by a dome.

The practical difficulties were due to the need to centre the church on the site of the grave where the remains of the princes had been thrown during the Revolution. Louis-Philippe as king enlarged the chapel and altered its out-ward appearance by adding "Gothic" pinnacles.

On the whole the building does credit to the 19C by the quality of the architecture and the contributions made by talented artists.

The high chapel benefits from better lighting after the installation of lateral windows under Louis-Philippe. Notice the stained glass devoted to the patrons of France and the royal family. The series on the left includes St-Philippe, St-Amélie, St-Ferdinand. The apse windows concern the life of St Louis.

Go down into the necropolis proper where the tombs of the princes of Orleans are to be found. The recumbent figures constitute a museum of 19C statuary art. Among the famous people buried here are: King Louis-Philippe and Queen Marie-Amélie, the Dukes of Orleans, Aumale and Nemours, the Prince of Joinville and the Duke and Duchess of Alençon. The incredibly minute engravings on the marble are truly remarkable.

On the lower level, five **stained glass windows★** made in the Sèvres factories, as was the other glasswork, are in reality one and the same piece. Impressive effects can be obtained in either natural or artificial light.

The crypt under the rotunda of the high chapel has twelve burial places prepared for the family of the Count of Paris. One of them has been occupied since 1983 by the Prince of Orleans who died for his country during the Algerian War. In a nearby crypt lies Prince Thibault of Orleans who died in 1983.

The park is quiet and contains several remains of former fortifications. A fine **view** can be had of the town.

Marcel-Dessal Art and History Museum (Musée d'Art et d'Histoire) (AZ M). – Set in a former chapel the museum's ground floor contains remains from the collegiate church of St-Stephen which occupied the site of the chapel before the Revolution. Notice the four historiated Romanesque capitals and stained glass fragments. The paintings exhibited include works by Monet, Vlaminck, Montézin and Valtat, accompanied by a bust of Jean Rotrou. A number of Merovingian funerary objects and furniture are presented in the archaeology room.

On the first floor a collection of documents, posters, drawings, engravings and plans evoke Dreux and the surrounding region from the Middle Ages up to the present time.

DUCLAIR

Michelin map 54 fold 10 or 231 fold 22 – Local map p 129 – Facilities

Duclair has developed on the outer side of a bend on the Lower Seine where the Austreberthe flows into the main river. The Liberation Quay, shaded by lime trees, makes a good spot from which to watch cargo boats, seemingly so out of place in this country setting, moving upstream to Rouen or to follow the comings and goings of the ferry.

St Denis Church (Église). – The church, though restored during the last century, has retained its 12C belfry which was crowned in the 16C with a spire.

As you enter note the vaulting of the base of the belfry, and the half column of pink marble surmounted by a capital with acanthus leaves: the half column (there are six others in the church) is from a Gallo-Roman temple.

Leaning against the pillars of the bay beneath the bell tower, bounded by circular relieving arches, are two stone panels (late 14C) with many small figures. In the north side aisle is a 14C stone statue of an Apostle, from Jumièges Abbey. In the lower nave the wooden statues representing the Holy Trinity, the Virgin of the Assumption and St John are also 14C. On the wall of the belfry, the calvary, in wood, showing Christ on the cross, the Virgin and St John is 15C.

There are many stained glass windows, most of which are 16C including the beheading of St Denis in Renaissance decor. The window at the rear of the church and the window depicting Pentecost (1968) are the work of Max Ingrand who also helped in the general restoration work.

★★ EAWY Forest

Michelin map 52 folds 14, 15 or 231 folds 11, 23

Eawy Forest – a name of Germain origin meaning wet pastureland and pronounced Ee-a-vi – covers a jagged crest 6 600 ha - 16 300 acres bordered by the Varenne and Béthune Valleys.

Eawy Forest, with that of Lyons, is the most beautiful beech woodland in Normandy. A straight divide, the Allée des Limousins, cuts through it, crossing deeply shaded valleys.

FROM DIEPPE TO NEUFCHATEL-EN-BRAY

67km - 41 miles – about 2 hours

★★**Dieppe.** – *Description p 61.*

> *Leave Dieppe by ④, the D 915.*

The road crosses the plateau between the Varenne and the Scie rivers.

> *Turn left on the D 107.*

After Le Bois-Robert the downhill road offers pretty views of the wooded crest separating the Varenne from one of its tributaries.

> *Turn right on the D 149.*

The D 149 and D 154 go up the quiet Varenne Valley speckled with brick manor houses and where, on the left, the beeches of the Eawy Forest grow ever more densely.

> *At Rosay bear left on the D 97.*

The D 97 is aptly named the "Road of the Long Valleys".

> *At the Epinette crossroads turn right on the D 12.*

The D 12 winds through the woods then leads directly to St-Saëns offering attractive views of this small town.

St-Saëns. – Pop 2 342. The town is located on the edge of the Varenne Forest. Its church is imitation Romanesque.

> *On leaving St-Saëns, turn left on the D 929.*

The road goes up the side of a valley and on the other slope can be seen the last trees of Eawy Forest.

> *Immediately after the les Hayons crossroads, turn right on the D 136.*

The road descends in a great curve to the Bray Region *(qv)* which can be seen from the car.

> *The N 28 leads to Neufchâtel-en-Bray.*

Neufchâtel-en-Bray. – *Description p 101.*

★ ECOUIS

Michelin map 55 southeast of fold 7 or 231 fold 24 – Local map p 33

The village of Ecouis in the Normandy Vexin Region centres on the twin towers of its old collegiate church. This was built between 1310 and 1313 by Enguerrand de Marigny, Superintendent of Finances to Philip the Fair. Victim of the feudal leagues in reaction to the king's financial policies, his life ended tragically upon the gibbet in 1315. His politics have been outlived by his policy of local artistic patronage as may be seen from the remarkable works of art in the church, the result of his encouragement towards local sculptors.

Notre-Dame Collegiate Church (Collégiale). – *time: 1/2 hour.*

The sober building – the roof timbers were replaced by the present brick and stone vaulting at the end of the 18C – has an immense chancel terminating in a three sided apse. The chancel is flanked by two chapels with pointed arch barrel vaulting and contains some beautiful furniture and remarkable **statues**★ dating from the 14 to the 17C.

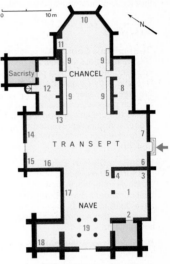

1) Chapel of the Immaculate Conception (16C) with attractive lierne and tierceron vaulting.
2) Christ on the cross (early 15C).
3) St-Nicaise.
4) St-Ann and the Virgin (14C).
5) Notre Dame d'Écouis (14C).
6) Statue of St Margaret (14C).
7) Statue of Jean de Marigny, brother of Enguerrand, who died Archbishop of Rouen in 1351.
8) St John Chapel – the wooden vault enables us to imagine the former vault of the large nave. Statue of Alips de Mons, wife of Enguerrand de Marigny. Stained glass depicting the Crucifixion with St John and St Mark at the foot of the cross.
9) 14C choir stalls. 16C doors and woodwork.
10) Door of former rood-screen.
11) Christ and his shroud.
12) North side chapel: St Martin, St Francis, St Laurent (14C), St Cecilia.
13) "Madonna of the King" (14C).
14) St Agnes.
15) St Veronica.
16) Ecce Homo in wood.
17) Annunciation (15C). The statue of the Virgin is supported by a charming group of small angels reading prophecies relating to the mystery of the Incarnation. The hands and face of the Virgin, together with the face of Angel Gabriel, are in marble encrusted in stone.
18) St John the Baptist (14C).
19) Organ case (17C).

⊙ In a **room** on the first floor beautiful works of art are displayed including a cope chest and the chalice of Jean de Marigny (14C).

Avoid visiting a church during a service.

ELBEUF
Pop 17 362

Michelin map **54** fold 20 or **231** southeast of fold 22 – Local maps pp 42, 127 and 129

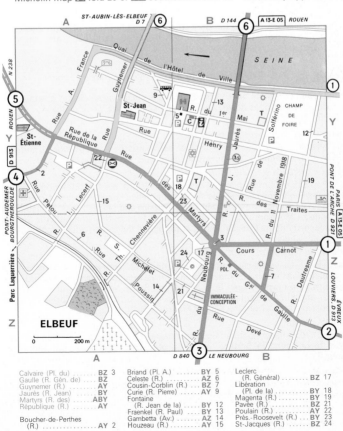

Situated on one of the Seine's meanders, Elbeuf together with its neighbouring towns St-Pierre, Caudebec, St-Aubin and Cléon, forms an agglomeration of 60 000 inhabitants. Formerly one of France's major textile centres, the drapery industry developing from the 15C, reaching its peak at the end of the 16C and benefitting from mechanisation after 1870, Elbeuf has seen the arrival of the chemical, electrical, mechanical, metallurgy and automobile industries. Today there is a Renault plant in Cléon specialising in engine and gearbox manufacture.

SIGHTS

⊙**St-Stephen's Church** (Église St-Étienne) (AY). – This Flamboyant church has retained its 16C stained glass windows. Note the Crucifixion on the top window to the right in the apse and other windows retracing scenes from the life of the Virgin in the north aisle. Near the Lady Chapel in the north aisle there is a fine stained glass representation of the Tree of Jesse.

St Roch is depicted in the stained glass of a chapel in the south aisle. One of the panels shows the drapers in working clothes.

Woodcarving is represented by a Louis XV style rood beam, a 13C recumbent figure of Christ (lower north aisle) and on either side of the chancel statues of St Stephen and St John.

⊙**St John's Church** (Église St-Jean) (AY). – A Gothic church but with Classical ornament and furnishings. Notice the 16C stained glass windows on the 1st, 3rd, 4th and 5th windows in the north aisle and the 1st in the south aisle. They are the oldest (1500) and best conserved. Two of the windows in the south aisle date from the same period but have been restored.

There are also a number of modern windows. The new and the old form an attractive combination.

⊙**Natural History Museum** (Musée d'Histoire naturelle) (BY H). – Nine rooms display large collections of zoological (stuffed animals, skeletons and shells), mineralogical and archaeological (remarkable Gallo-Roman burial places) exhibits. One room is devoted to local history: iconography, paintings and sculptures treating the Elbeuf agglomeration.

Laquerrière Park (AZ). – *Approach by Rue Isidore-Lecerf and the footpath Sente des Echelettes.*

This wooded park dominating the town belonged to the Duke of Elbeuf until the Revolution. It bore the name of its owner in 1901 and now belongs to the town. Four footpaths lead through this reserve of greenery and fresh air.

The EPTE Valley

Michelin map 55 folds 8 and 18 or 237 folds, 3, 4

The Epte River, which rises in the Bray countryside to the north of Forges-les-Eaux, crosses the Vexin plateaux and enters the Seine on its north bank, has played an important part in the history of Normandy (p 17).

FROM GISORS TO VERNON 41km - 25 miles – about 2 hours.

The road follows the right bank of the Epte and is often very shaded in contrast with the bareness of the slopes hewn out of the chalk bed of the Vexin plateaux.

★ **Gisors.** – *Description p 78.*

Leave Gisors to the west on the D 10.

Neaufles-St-Martin. – Pop 806. The village is dominated by a keep upon a perfectly preserved artificial mound. The only remaining walls are those facing France.

At the crossroads with the D 181, turn left.

⊙**Dangu.** – Pop 515. The main features of the Gothic **church** are the 18C woodwork and painted panelling in the chancel, the 16C Montmorency Chapel in which a monotone window above the altar shows St Denis, St Lawrence and, on his knees, William, fifth son of Anne of Montmorency, High Constable of France. Near the pulpit is an 18C Beauvais tapestry of the Crucifixion and at the end of the church a fine wood carving of the Annunciation.

The D 146 runs down into the valley.

Château-sur-Epte. – Leave the car in front of the fortified 13C entrance to the farm and ask permission to visit the ruins. Standing on an artificial mound surrounded by a moat are the remains of a massive keep built by William Rufus, second son of William the Conqueror and King of England from 1087 to 1100, to protect the Norman frontier against possible attack from the King of France.

Aveny. – 15C bridge.

From the D 170 a shaded footpath leads to a **covered alley,** a megalithic monument such as those to be found in Brittany, made up of upright stones covered with slabs *(1/2 hour Rtn).*

Return to the D 146. At Bray-et-Lu turn right.

Baudemont Castle (Château). – Only the ruins of the 11C castle remain. From the mound on which they stand there is a pretty view over the valley.

★ **Giverny.** – *Description p 79.*

★ **Vernon.** – *Description p 138.*

Michelin map 🔢 folds 7, 8 or 🔢 fold 8 – Local map p 54 – Facilities

Étretat, now an elegant resort, has always had a great reputation because of the originality of its setting. The grandeur of the high cliffs and crashing waves is unforgettable whatever the season. It is hardly surprising to learn that the town has inspired many writers, artists and film directors.
Étretat was formerly at the end of a Roman road stretching from Lillebonne.

The Setting. – The shingle beach, skirted by a sea wall promenade, lies between the well known cliffs; to the east the Amont (Upstream) Cliff with its small chapel and to the west the Aval (Downstream) Cliff with its monumental arch cut through the chalk, known as the Porte d'Aval, the Downstream Gateway.
Offshore stands a solitary needle rock, L'Aiguille, 70m - 200ft high. On the beach are three traditional thatched fishermen's huts which have been restored. They were used for storing fishing equipment.

SIGHTS

★★★ **Aval Cliff** (Falaise d'Aval) (A). – *1 hour on foot Rtn.*

Climb the steps at the west end of the promenade to arrive at the path which scales the cliff face. Walk along the edge of the cliff as far as the Porte d'Aval crest. The view is magnificent. To the left we see the massive Manneporte arch, the Aiguille opposite and the Amont Cliff on the far side of the bay. The variations in colour according to the time and natural lighting are truly enchanting.
Walk on round to the Manneporte where there is a view towards Cape Antifer. Continue on to the promontory overlooking the second arch. From this point the view extends south to the petroleum port of Le Havre-Antifer.

★★ **Amont Cliff** (Falaise d'Amont) (B). – *1 hour on foot Rtn.*

Take the stairway (180 steps, handrail) at the end of the promenade. Cut out off the chalk cliffs, the steps, followed by a footpath, lead to the top of the cliff. From the seamen's chapel dedicated to **Notre-Dame-de-la-Garde** there is a magnificent **view** of Étretat and its surroundings. The long shingle beach lies below as far as Aval Cliff and the Aiguille.

Behind the chapel an immense spire points towards the sky. The monument was erected as a memorial to Nungesser and Coli, the two French aviators who made the first and unsuccessful attempt to fly the Atlantic on 8 May 1927. It was here that their aircraft was seen for the very last time.

Climbing the steps behind the spire, we encounter the base of the former monument which had the form of the aeroplane. Notice its name in large white letters, its nose, the markings of the French flag on the tips of its wings, and finally its tail.

Access by car. – *Take the D 11 "Fécamp par la côte". Just before the sign indicating the limits of the built-up area, turn sharp left on a steep and narrow uphill road. Leave the car at the end near the monument.*

The cliffs at Étretat

ⓥ **Nungesser and Coli Museum** (Musée). – Standing opposite the monument it contains mementoes of the two aviators, "the first to dare...".

Covered Market (Halles) (B). – This reconstitution of an old wooden covered market gives the Place du Maréchal Foch its distinctive character.
Nearby the **Boulevard Président René Coty** leads to the sea and is lined with elegant timber-framed houses.

Notre Dame Church (Église) (B). – Once a dependency of Fécamp Abbey, it has a Romanesque gateway with a 19C tympanum. Around the church is a cornice with carved modillions.
Inside, the first six bays (11C) are characteristic of Romanesque style with geometrical decoration and gadrooned capitals. The rest of the building is 12C. Go forward to the transept crossing to admire the 13C lantern turret.

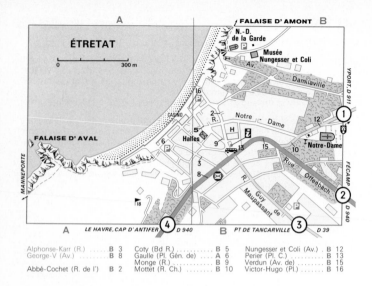

Alphonse-Karr (R.) ..... B 3	Coty (Bd R.) .... B 5	Nungesser et Coli (Av.) . B 12
George-V (Av.) .... B 8	Gaulle (Pl. Gén. de) .... A 6	Perier (Pl. C.) .... B 13
	Monge (R.) .... B 9	Verdun (Av. de) .... B 15
Abbé-Cochet (R. de l') B 2	Mottet (R. Ch.) .... B 10	Victor-Hugo (Pl.) ...... B 16

EXCURSION

Le Havre-Antifer Port and Terminal. – *15km - 9 miles to the south. Leave Étretat by ④, the D 940, and take the D 111 to the right, direction "La Poterie cap d'Antifer".*

⊙ **Cape Antifer Lighthouse** (Phare). – From the top of the lighthouse which stands on a cliff 102m - 334ft above sea level, there is an extensive view of the coast south to Cape Hève with Le Havre-Antifer terminal in the foreground.

Turn round and at La Poterie take the D 111 on the right.

Bruneval. – A German radar installation not far from the beach was the objective of an Allied raid on the night of 27-28 February 1942 when three detachments of British parachutists landed and, after destroying the enemy position, re-embarked almost without loss. The monument, up from the beach, on the left, commemorates the part played by the French Resistance and the British Paratroops.

Between Bruneval and St-Jouin, the winding road passes through picturesque countryside and vegetation of different colours.

The long downhill road leads to the oil terminal.

Le Havre-Antifer Terminal. – The Le Havre-Antifer port was created in 1976 to receive oil tankers exceeding the capacity of Le Havre's facilities *(p 86)*. Located near the St-Jouin beach it has a 43 ha - 106 acre total area of which 8 ha - 20 acres are for tugs, the other 35 ha - 86 acres for port installations, including 4 150 000 m³ reservoirs. Protection to the north is ensured by a 3 500m - 11 487ft sea wall. Two piers, linked by pipelines to the storage tanks, can cope with the arrival and unloading of 555 000 ton oil tankers. A pipeline 26.5km - 16 miles long carries the oil to Le Havre, assuring a continuous supply to the refineries in the Seine Valley.

To the right on the road back to St-Jouin there is a belvedere (restaurant) with a fine **view** over the beach and the port installations.

★ EU

Michelin map 52 fold 5 or 231 fold 12

Pop 8712

Eu, a small town between the sea and the forest from which it gets its name, lies peacefully grouped round its beautiful collegiate church built in the times when this was a "land of princes" – from Rollo in the 11C to the last of the powerful dukes of Orléans in the 19C.

★NOTRE-DAME AND ST-LAURENT *time: 1/2 hour*

The collegiate church, dedicated to Our Lady and St Lawrence O'Toole, Primate of Ireland who died in Eu in the 12C, was erected in the 12 and 13C in the Gothic style. In the 15C the apse was remodelled and in the 19C, Viollet-le-Duc undertook a general restoration of the building.

The exterior is marked by the number of pinnacled and turreted buttresses supporting the aisles and east end.

The **interior** is striking in size and harmonious proportions. The second ambulatory chapel on the right, the Chapel of the Holy Sepulchre, has, beneath a Flamboyant canopy, a 15C Entombment; opposite is a magnificent head of Christ in Sorrow, also 15C. The statue of Our Lady of Eu, attributed to one of the Anguier Brothers *(see College Chapel p 71)*, is in the apsidal chapel, while the north transept chapel contains a lovely statue of the Virgin (16C). A shrine at the back of the chancel contains the remains of St Lawrence.

⊙ **Crypt.** – Located just beneath the chancel, the crypt was restored in 1828 by the Duke of Orléans and future King Louis-Philippe (who reigned from 1830 to 1848 when he abdicated and fled to England where he died – at Claremont in Surrey – in 1850) where he grouped the effigies of the Counts of Eu, House of Artois (14 and 16C), their graves having been desecrated at the time of the Revolution. The 12-13C recumbent statue against the north wall is of St Lawrence.

EU

Château. – Nothing remains of the original castle where William the Conqueror married Mathilda of Flanders in 1050. It was destroyed in 1475 on the orders of Louis XI. The present château, a huge brick and stone building begun by Henri of Guise in 1578, has been restored several times since. It passed to the Orléans family and became one of the favourite residences of Louis-Philippe, who received Queen Victoria there twice. Viollet-le-Duc was asked to do the redecorating between 1872 and 1879 for the Count of Paris, grandson of the King.

The château, which now belongs to the town of Eu, is occupied by the Town Hall and the communal archives, and houses the Louis-Philippe Museum.

Bignon (R. P.) 3

Abbaye (R. de l') 2
Carnot (Pl.) 4
Collège (R. du) 5
Hélène (Bd) 7
Lecomte (R. O.) 8
Morin (R. Ch.) 9
Normandie (R. de) 10

Louis-Philippe Museum (Musée). – On the ground floor are two rooms, one of which, the *Salon Bragance,* was decorated by Viollet-le-Duc with painted wall hangings. The room is so called after two marriages between the Houses of Bragance and Orléans. On the first floor a suite of rooms contains furniture and portraits of previous owners. Note *La Grande Mademoiselle's* (Anne Marie Louise d'Orléans, Duchess of Montpensier, 1627-93) bedroom decorated with restored green and gold woodwork, the former **dining room** of Louis-Philippe enhanced by a 17C caisson ceiling, a handsome floor of inlaid work and an early 18C Flemish wall hanging, and the huge **Galerie des Guise** containing the library of the former Jesuit college with more than 10 000 volumes. The adjacent guardroom contains a collection of stuffed birds, the Kings' Room (Salon des Rois) busts of Queen Victoria and Prince Albert given to Louis-Philippe when he visited Windsor in 1844. Finally there are the former private apartments (Breste Valley museum, and a reconstitution of a glass workshop). Go down the staircase to visit the chapel decorated with Sèvres stained glass windows.

The Park. – Consisting primarily of beech trees, one of which is 400 years old and is known as the *Guisard,* the park also has rhododendrons, azaleas and conifers planted by the Count of Paris.

College Chapel (K). – Today, the college, founded by Henri de Guise in 1582, bears the name of the 17C Anguier Brothers, one time students of the Jesuit college and gifted sculptors.

The college chapel was built in 1620 by Catherine de Clèves, Henri's widow, to whom she brought the County of Eu as a dowry earlier in 1570. The Louis XIII façade is harmonious.

In the chancel are the two magnificent 17C marble **mausoleums★** of the Duke of Guise, assassinated at Blois on the orders of Henri III, King of France in 1588, and of his Duchess.

They are the work of four sculptors, Tremblay, Gissay, Nicolas and Guillain and were requested in 1627.

EXCURSION

Eu Forest (Forêt d'Eu). – *Round tour of 57km - 35 miles – about 3 hours.*
The Eu Forest consists of three isolated massifs. Only the Triage d'Eu and the Upper Eu Forest are described here; beautiful beech glades spread out along the plateau between the Bresle and the Yères Rivers.

Leave Eu to the southwest on the D 49. At Incheville turn right on the D 58.

To the right of the entrance to the forest is St Martin's Priory Chapel with its pretty gateway.

At the Hêtre-des-Princes crossroads turn left on the D 126 towards Millebosc. Then drive to Guerville and take the D 14 as far as the Montauban crossroads.

The edge of the Upper Eu Forest has now been reached. The dead straight road is lined by very tall trees.

Take the winding forest road. At St Catherine's Post, turn right to St Catherine's forest lodge.

St Catherine's Viewpoint. – *3/4 hour on foot Rtn. Leave the car near the gate. Go past the lodge on the left to the edge of the wood.* Walk beneath the trees and discover the peaceful countryside of the Yères Valley.

Return to St Catherine's Post and go right along the road by which you came.

La Bonne Entente. – *20m-65ft off the road to the right.* This Agreement *(Entente)* has arisen from an oak and a beech growing so close together that, as the trunks have enlarged, they appear to spring jointly from a single bole.

At the St-Rémy Post, turn sharp right into the D 149 which leads out of the forest and affords a view of the Yères Valley. Follow the D 16 along the river bank to St-Martin.

St-Martin-le-Gaillard. – Pop 270. The 13C **church**, altered in the 16C, has a slender slate belfry. Inside, the capitals are carved with humorous figures and the font is 16C. Notice the 18C Virgin and Child.

Drive along the left bank through Criel-sur-Mer, then return to Eu on the D 925.

The EURE Valley

Michelin maps **55** fold 17 and 60 fold 7 or **231** folds 35, 36, 47, 48

The Eure Valley runs through some most attractive countryside between Dreux and Louviers. The green river banks below bare hill slopes hold many delightful surprises.

① FROM DREUX TO PACY-SUR-EURE
42km - 26 miles – about 2 hours

★ **Dreux.** – *Description p 64.*

Leave Dreux by ①, the D 928, then turn left onto the D 16[1].

The aqueduct on the right across the valley takes water from the Avre River to Paris. The woodlands on the far bank form part of the Dreux Forest. Notice the church in the small village of Montreuil. Just before Ezy-sur-Eure, once specialised in the manufacture of combs made of horn, the old hump-back bridge of St-Jean links the left bank to Saussay. The bare slopes, hollowed out here and there into caves, become steeper.

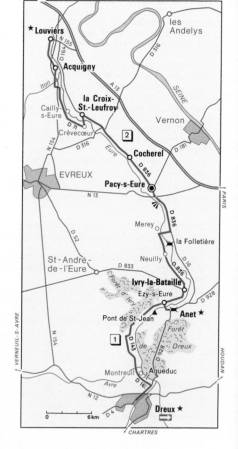

★ **Anet Château.** – *Description p 35.*

Between Neuilly and the Merey mills one can see through the trees **Folletière Château,** an impressive late 16C brick edifice standing in a park. From Chambines to Pacy-sur-Eure the D 836 overlooks the river as it winds through the greenery.

Take the D 58 to the right and cross the river.

Pacy-sur-Eure. – Pop 3 773. Pacy-sur-Eure became known, together with Cocherel (see below), through Aristide Briand who was greatly attached to the area. His monument stands at the entrance to the town. The **Church of St Aubin** is a fine 13C Gothic building, remodelled in the 16C, and has a nave remarkable for its symmetry and unity of style. The modern ornaments include four glass powder paste low reliefs round the altar and amber coloured stained glass windows by Décorchemont depicting the Ascension. There are also beautiful 16C stone statues – the Virgin and Child attributed to Germain Pilon, St Anne and a *Pietà* – and an early 17C statue of St Michael slaying the dragon.

② FROM PACY-SUR-EURE TO LOUVIERS
34km - 21 miles – about 1 hour

Pacy-sur-Eure. – *See above.*

Leave Pacy-sur-Eure to the north on the D 836.

Cocherel. – The exploits of a man at arms and an apostle of peace have between them brought fame to Cocherel.

A pyramid beside the Jouy-sur-Eure road, the D 57 west from Cocherel, commemorates the victory of Bertrand Du Guesclin in this spot over the Anglo-Navarre forces in 1364.

From 1908 until his death in 1932, **Aristide Briand,** statesman and "apostle of peace" spent all his leisure time in three houses which he owned successively in Cocherel. He lies buried in the local cemetery beneath a massive dark granite stone. A statue, *Meditation,* on the far bank of the Eure, is also in his memory.

Return to and continue along the D 836.

⊙ **La Croix St-Leufroy.** – Pop 732. The **church** has a carved Renaissance font and an interesting collection of pictures from the former Abbey of Croix-St-Ouen.

The drive, which is attractive between Cocherel and Chambray-sur-Eure, becomes even more so along the left bank betwwen Crèvecœur and Cailly-sur-Eure where the river is lined by fine estates.

Acquigny. – Pop 1 059. There is a good view of the late 16C castle from the bridge over the Eure.

The park and outbuildings complete the scene.

★ **Louviers.** – *Description p 95.*

★★ ÉVREUX   Pop 48 653

Michelin map **55** folds 16, 17 or **231** fold 35

Évreux, the religious and administrative capital of the Eure, standing on the Iton River which here divides into several arms, is the great agricultural market for the surrounding regions. Industry centres primarily on the manufacturing of electrical equipment and automobile accessories.

Flower gardens have been planted on the banks of the Iton, offering pedestrians a pleasant, serene place to stroll in the heart of the city, at the foot of some ancient Gallo-Roman ruins.

A French City throughout the Wars of History. – Évreux's story, like that of many towns in France, is a lengthy chronicle of fire and destruction:

5C – The Vandals sacked Old Évreux, a prosperous market town on the plateau going back to the time of the Gauls.

9C – The Vikings destroyed the fortified town established by the Romans on the present site beside the Iton.

1119 – Henry I, King of England, set fire to the town when fighting the Count of Évreux who was supported by Louis VII.

1193 – King Philippe-Auguste, betrayed here by King John of England, fired the city in reprisal.

1356 – Jean the Good, King of France, laid siege to Évreux in his struggle against the House of Navarre, and set fire to the town.

1379 – Charles V besieged the town which suffered cruelly.

June 1940 – Following German air raids the centre of the city burned for nearly a week.

June 1944 – Allied air raids razed the quarter round the station.

After each disaster the people of Évreux have rebuilt their town from the ruins and worked to restore its prosperity.

Évreux Today. – The opportunity was taken when the city centre was rebuilt after 1945, to provide attractive settings for the last of the town ramparts, the old bishopric, the cathedral and the 15C belfry, all of which remained undamaged.

MAIN SIGHTS

★ **Notre-Dame Cathedral** (BZ). – The great arches of the nave are the only part remaining of the original church, which was rebuilt between 1119 and 1193, and once more set on fire. The chancel was built in 1260; the chapels added in the 14C.

Following the fire of 1356 the church was not repaired for two centuries when the lantern tower and the Lady Chapel were added.

At the beginning of the 16C the master builder Jean Cossart devised the magnificent north transept façade and doorway. The reconstruction was completed by remodelling the south tower in the Henri II style and the termination, in the 17C only, of the north tower.

It was the upper parts of the cathedral which suffered in the 1940 conflagration: the "silver belfry", a lead spire above the transept lantern tower melted, and the west façade towers lost their crowns.

Exterior. – *Walk along the north side.* The aisle windows were redesigned in the 16C in the Flamboyant style. The north door is a perfect entity in which all the richness of the Flamboyant, then at its height, can be seen.

Interior. – To view the **stained glass★** and the **carved wood screens★** of the ambulatory chapels stand in the transept, between the pillars supporting the graceful lantern tower. The lower part of the lantern tower is ornamented with Flamboyant decoration. The nave – completely restored – has the original massive Romanesque arches and, above, an elegant triforium of Gothic bays. The monotone glass dates from 1400.

The light chancel is closed by a superb 18C wrought iron grille and is very beautiful. The apse windows have been declared the most beautiful, the most limpid, of the 14C.

Fine wood screens dating from the Renaissance mark the ambulatory entrance in which the first chapel on the right, the Treasury Chapel, is entirely enclosed in a 15C wrought iron grille bristling with spikes and hooks. The screen to the fourth chapel is a masterpiece of imagination and execution, particularly the lower figures; the chapel glass is early 14C.

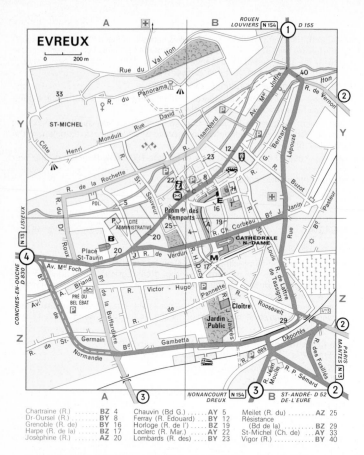

EVREUX

The central or Lady Chapel, given by Louis XI, has 15C windows of considerable documentary interest. The upper parts, including *fleurs-de-lis,* depict the peers of France at the King's coronation; the central window has a Tree of Jesse in which the Virgin is surrounded by a crowd of people. Two windows further on is Louis XI himself. On the altar is the venerated statue of Our Lady which is said to be late 15C.

The chapels off the ambulatory are also enclosed by screens: the second of Gothic design, has Renaissance motifs in its lower part.

The third, fourth and sixth chapel screens are the oldest and purely Gothic – note the fantastic animals at the base of the sixth screen.

Former Bishopric (Ancien évêché) (BZ M). – Built in the 15C by the architect Pierre Smoteau on the orders of Bishop Raoul du Fou, its façade looks out onto the cathedral and has a fine Flamboyant air with dormer windows, ornamented window pediments and a staircase tower. The municipal museum is inside.

★★ **Museum (Musée).** – On the ground floor the first two rooms are devoted to the history and geography of the Eure region and of the town itself (engravings, paintings). Costumes, banners and *torchères* of the Brothers of Charity illustrate popular traditions.

The former chapter house (room 3) has a monumental fireplace and contains medieval and Renaissance collections, such as 16C stalls and wooden polychrome statues. Notice the series of 17C Aubusson tapestries on the theme of the Prodigal Son. Room 4 contains medieval exhibits: tomb inscriptions in engraved stone, capitals... The 15C hearth bears the arms of Bishop Pottier de Novion.

In the basement the **archaeological room★** uses the former Gallo-Roman rampart enhanced by an appropriate lighting arrangement. The collections include domestic and religious objects, statuettes, jewels, etc. from the Paleolithic (300 000-9 000 BC) age to the Gallo-Roman era (1-4C AD). Among the finest exhibits are bronzes of Jupiter Stator and Apollo and a late 3C glass goblet.

The first floor contains 17C and 18C paintings as well as various decorative items: furniture, crockery, including apothecary jars in Nevers and Rouen china from Évreux hospital. A contemporary art exhibition takes up the second floor, whereas the third floor, with its diagonal vaulting at the top of the stairway, has a temporary exhibition room with panelled ceiling.

St-Taurin Church (Église) (AZ B). – This former abbey church established in 660 and dedicated to the first Bishop of Évreux dates back to the 14 and 15C. A beautiful Romanesque blind arcade runs along the foot of the north aisle to the Renaissance font. The well proportioned 14C chancel is lit by superb 15C windows. Three windows in the apse trace the life of St Taurinus.

★★ **St Taurinus's Shrine.** – Displayed in the north transept, this masterpiece of 13C French craftsmanship was given by St Louis to the abbey to contain St Taurinus's relics and was probably made in the abbey workshops. The silver gilt reliquary enriched with enamel (the best are low down) is in the form of a miniature chapel and even shows St Taurinus with his crosier.

Walk on the Ramparts (Promenade des remparts) (BYZ). – The walk runs beside the Iton River. It takes the name of Robert de Flocques, who liberated the town in 1441, as far as the Rue de Grenoble Bridge. Thereafter it is named after Charles II (King of Navarre and Count of Évreux, 1332-1387), until it reaches the Clock Tower.

Clock Tower (Tour de l'Horloge) (BY E). – An elegant 15C tower, built on the site of one of the two towers which flanked the town's main gateway. It is crowned by a spire decorated with lead covered wooden pinnacles.

Public Gardens (Jardin Public) (BZ). – Laid out on a slope, they have fine shady trees and a rose garden, and have been enlarged by the restoration of the cloister belonging to the former Capuchin convent (17C).

Former Capuchin Cloister (Cloître des Capucins). – Consisting of four galleries with timber roofs and monolithic columns, its walls are engraved with morals. The whole is embellished by a flower garden with a well in the middle.

★★ FÉCAMP
Pop 21 696

Michelin map **54** fold 8 or **231** fold 8 – Local map p 54 – Facilities

Fécamp is known today as a fishing port – it is France's most important port for cod, landed from the boats which sail regularly to the Newfoundland Banks. The town is also famous as the home of Benedictine liqueur – a link with its monastic past.
Guy de Maupassant lived in the town, which figures in several of his works.

The Heavenly Gate. – From the 7C there was always a monastery in Fécamp to shelter the relic of the Precious Blood which, according to tradition, was "entrusted to the sea and the Grace of God" by Isaac, nephew of Joseph of Arimathea.
Richard II, whose father, not content with having rebuilt a magnificent church to the Holy Trinity, had made him promise to found a Benedictine abbey, was much struck by the reformed Cluny style which he saw in several monasteries in Burgundy. These Cluniac reforms had been instigated by the Abbot of St-Bénigne at Dijon, **Guglielmo da Volpiano**, who was persuaded by Richard in 1003 to move with his monastic following to Fécamp.
The new abbey assumed considerable importance and its influence was felt throughout the Duchy. Until the advent of Mont-St-Michel, Fécamp was the leading pilgrimage centre in Normandy with the dukes traditionally coming there at Easter; from the 11C, troubadours and minstrels, particularly favoured by the abbots, helped to spread the renown of the Precious Blood and the Holy Trinity Church. The Bishop of Dol was to write of this centre which attracted religious and popular devotion and added prestige to the dukes of Normandy that "The monastery can be compared to a heavenly Jerusalem: it is called the Heavenly Gate, the Palace of Our Lord. Gold, silver and silken ornaments shine everywhere."

The Port. – Fécamp, a major deep sea cod fishing port until 1973, had only four deep sea trawlers in operation in 1986, two with deep freeze facilities, but has developed into a busy pleasure boat harbour.
The port handles commercial traffic as well, including wood from the North and heavy materials from Morocco and western Europe. The Freycinet Basin is the liveliest: the Marne Quay is used for landing fresh or deep frozen fish, the Verdun Quay for unloading gravel and sand for the glass industry, salt and wood, pre-cut or in logs. The Bérigny Basin's Sadi-Carnot Quay is reserved for cargo-boats carrying wood and miscellaneous goods.
Associated industries are to be found all around: cod drying plants, herring curing works, shipyards.
The boat basin already has moorings for 550 boats on floating pontoons.

The port of Fécamp

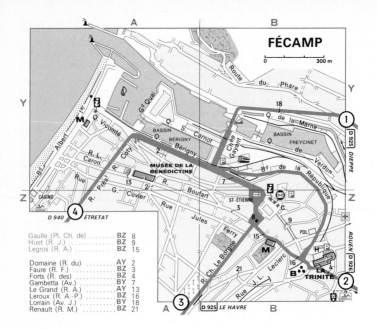

SIGHTS

★★ La Trinité Church (Église) (BZ). – Richard I's church, struck by lightning, was rebuilt in the 12 and 13C and several times between the 15 and 18C. The town hall abutting on the north wall is in what were formerly monastic buildings of the latter period.

Pilgrims flock on the Tuesday and Thursday following Trinity Sunday to venerate the Precious Blood relic within this ancient abbey.

Exterior. – In length 127m - 416ft the cathedral is one of the greatest in France. The Classical façade does not go well with the rest of the building, and the walls of the nave are severe. Walk along the south wall to a porch restored in the 19C and where an inner door has a tympanum, a good example of Norman Gothic decoration *(details p 23)*. The square lantern tower rising 65m - 210ft over the transept evokes, though on a grander scale, the typical Norman belfry.

Interior. – The majestically proportioned nave of ten bays with but little adornment ends at the transept where the lantern tower rises in a sweep to 40m - 125ft.

The south transept contains a beautiful late 15C **Dormition of the Virgin★** (1). Two groups of figures, taken from the former rood screen, frame the altar. On the right of the altar is the Angel's Footprint. In 943, when the reconstructed church was being consecrated before William Longsword, an angel pilgrim appeared before the bishops deliberating on the church's patronage and commanded them to dedicate the sanctuary to the Holy and Indivisible Trinity. Before disappearing in a blaze of light, the angel left his footprint on the stone for all to see for ever.

The chancel's dimensions make it magnificent. The stalls (2), baldachin and high altar (3) are all good 18C works by the Rouen artist, De France. A Renaissance altar (4), commissioned by Abbot Antoine Bohier from Girolamo Viscardo, stands behind the high altar. The altarpiece is adorned with five low reliefs – the abbey's two benefactors, Richard I and Richard II, are depicted at either end. In the centre of the sanctuary is an ancient shrine (5) adorned with low reliefs dating from the 12C.

The chapels off the chancel aisles and radiating chapels were given wonderful **carved screens★** in the 16C through the munificence of Abbot Antoine Bohier. In the fourth chapel, on the right, is the **tomb★** (6) of Abbot Thomas of St-Benoît who died in 1307; the tomb is decorated with scenes from the abbey's history on its base. The radiating chapel (7) contains abbots' tombs.

The **Lady Chapel★**, rebuilt in the 15C on a crypt of the same dimensions, forms a separate group in the Flamboyant style. The wood medallions are 18C; the windows are 13, 14 and 16C. Facing the chapel is the white marble **tabernacle★** of the Precious Blood (8) by Viscardo.

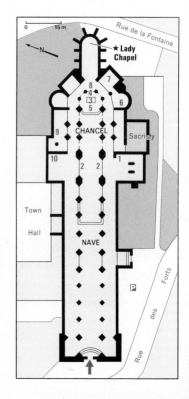

The following two radiating chapels are the only remains of the earlier Romanesque church destroyed by lightning. From the first a door leads to the crypt below the Lady Chapel which served as a charter library. The door itself is surmounted by a Flamboyant decoration in which the donor's initials, R.C., can be seen intertwined with thistles – his name was Robert Chardon, the French for thistle.

The 17C tomb (9) in the chapel of the Sacred Heart belongs to Guglielmo da Volpiano, first Abbot of Fécamp, who returned to the abbey he had founded to die in 1031. The north transept contains fragments of the former rood screen (10) and a 17C timepiece showing the tides and phases of the moon.

★ **Benedictine Museum (Musée)** (AY). – In 1510, a monk named Vincelli thought of distilling the aromatic plants growing on the cliffs: the famous liqueur *Benedictine* was born. The buildings, combining Gothic and Renaissance styles, date from the end of the 19C. To the museum's original collection of different fragments coming from the celebrated Abbey of Fécamp (remains of the rood screen, statues, charters of the monastery, books from the monks' library) have now been added collections of enamels, ivories and wrought iron. Documents and objects related to the production of Benedictine from the end of the 19C to the present are also displayed.

The *salle des plantes* exhibits the 27 plants and spices which go into the making of the liqueur. The visit ends with the laboratory where the transmutation process of alcohol and plants takes place, and then the cellars where the spirits age in oak casks. On the way out the corridor contains remains of the rood screen from Fécamp Abbey.

Museum of Local Art (Centre des Arts) (BZ M). – The ground floor of this elegant 18C mansion contains a collection of ceramics (faïence) from Rouen, Nevers and Delft, ornate chests and marriage cupboards, and an original collection of antique and contemporary babies' bottles donated by Doctor Dufour, founder of the *Goutte de Lait* ("drop of milk") organisation against childhood mortality. The first floor houses 19C landscape paintings and ivories, and the second historical weapons and archaeological exhibits. On the third floor there is a reconstruction of the inside of a room typical of the Caux region. The gardens around the mansion have been laid out in the English style and are home to a ceramic monument to those lost at sea.

Terre Neuvas and Deep Sea Fishing Museum (AY M). – The adventures of the Fécamp codfishermen who sailed for months at a time to the Banks of Newfoundland are now depicted rather appropriately in this museum directly on the sea-front. There are old model ships, navigational instruments, studies of Viking sailing techniques and herring fishing, shipbuilding workshops and authentic vessels, both old and modern.

Abbey Remains (BZ B). – *23 Rue des Forts.* From this former choir school there is a fine view of the chevet of the Trinity Church.

EXCURSION

Bailleul Château (Château de Bailleul). – *10km - 6 miles to the southeast on the D 73. Description p 40.*

FLEURY-LA-FORÊT Château

Michelin map 55 fold 8 or 231 fold 24 – 7 km - 4 miles northeast of Lyons-la-Forêt – Local map p 97

A beautiful drive lined with lime trees leads to this early 17C château built of red brick, flint and sandstone. The two low, symmetrical wings flanking the main building with Mansart style roofing were added in the 18C.

TOUR *time: about 3/4 hour*

The ground floor rooms include Diane's bedroom with a fine canopy bed and a huge kitchen amply decorated with copper, porcelain and pewter utensils and, on the hearth, a plaque bearing the arms of Charles de Caumont who rebuilt the château in 1647 as a result of a fire. On the first floor a series of rooms such as the *boudoir blanc,* the *chambre rouge* and the Empire and Directory Chamber reveal interesting pieces of furniture – 17C Italian cabinets, wardrobe, dressing table which can be converted into a bureau and an armchair which also serves as a praying stool.

The 18C chapel has *fleur-de-lis* decoration on the ceiling.

★ FONTAINE-GUÉRARD Abbey

Michelin map 55 fold 7 or 231 fold 23 – Local map p 33

The ruins of the 12C abbey, standing isolated on the right bank of the Andelle, are both evocative and moving, so menacing is the threat of flooding by the river.

TOUR *time: about 1/2 hour*

As you walk up the path you will see, first, St Michael's Chapel, built in the 15C over vaulted cellars. An underground passage links these with the abbey storerooms. Straight ahead lie the ruins of the abbey church, consecrated in 1218. The flat east end with its many elegant windows remains as does a part of the apsidal vaulting.

To the right is the chapter house, a fine example of Norman architecture of the first half of the 13C, with three aisles divided by a double row of small columns with crocheted capitals. Further on is a second vaulted chamber, possibly the workroom which resembles the knights' room in Mont-St-Michel Abbey. Go up a staircase to the sleeping quarters on the storey above. Each cell is lit by a narrow bay.

FORGES-LES-EAUX

Pop 3756

Michelin map 🔢 fold 16 or 🔢 fold 24 – Local maps pp 33 and 47 – Facilities

Forges-les-Eaux, a town where metal was worked until the 15C, is today a spa resort and an extremely pleasant place in which to relax, set in the green depression of the Bray Region *(qv)* where this opens out to its fullest extent. Several well-maintained parks make the town even more attractive.

As you approach the entrance to the spa park along the Avenue des Sources, immediately beyond the railway bridge on the left, there is a 17C façade which once formed part of the Carmelite Convent of Gisors. Overlooking the park is another beautiful façade, that of a hunting pavilion formerly erected near Versailles, which belonged to Louis XV.

Several half-timbered structures (17-18C) stand in the centre of town, especially in Rue de la République.

The Spa Park. – The spa – the waters are only used for drinking (at a *buvette* at the park entrance) – offers, in elegant modern surroundings, all the distractions proper to a watering place. The ferruginous waters of Forges are clear, refreshing and stimulating. As you walk through the park, on your left is the "grotto" where Louis XIII, his Queen and Richelieu took the waters. You come after a short while to the pool formed by the Andelle.

GAILLON

Pop 5856

Michelin map 🔢 fold 17 or 🔢 northeast of fold 35 – Local map p 127

The property of the archbishops of Rouen since the time of Philippe-Auguste, Gaillon was made famous at the end of the 15C by **Georges d'Amboise,** first of France's great Cardinal-Ministers. After an expedition to Italy, led by Louis XII, the prelate rebuilt the Castle of Gaillon in the new Italian style (1497-1510), thus launching the Renaissance movement in Normandy.

Note in the main street near the church, an attractive 16C wooden house.

Château. – The approaches branch off on the right, at the top of a rise in the N 15 to Rouen. This vast building, property of the Fine Arts School, is well situated. The dispersal of the château's riches began with the Revolution. The entrance lodge, flanked by two towers, has, however, preserved its graceful Renaissance decoration.

★ GISORS

Pop 8859

Michelin map 🔢 folds 8, 9 or 🔢 fold 4 – See town plan in current Michelin Red Guide France

Gisors, a one time frontier town in the possession of the dukes of Normandy, is the capital of the Normandy Vexin *(qv)*. Although badly battered in 1940, the town has retained considerable historical character.

The town owes its origins to the castle, several times coveted for its strategic location. The fortress formed part of a line of defence running from Forges-les-Eaux to Vernon and including the castles of Neaufles-St-Martin and Château-sur-Epte *(qv)*.

★★ **Castle (Château fort).** – The castle was built as early as 1097 by William II, King of England and son of William the Conqueror. It was fortified in the 12C by Henry II. In 1193 it was taken by Philippe-Auguste of France. During the Hundred Years War it changed hands several times before returning to the French crown in 1449.

This magnificent group of 11 and 12C Norman military architecture dominates the town and commands a view of it, including the Church of St Gervase and St Protase, built, as can clearly be seen, throughout many different architectural periods.

The 11C **keep,** on its 20m - 65ft artificial mound in the centre of the fortified perimeter and surrounded now by a public garden where once there was a moat, is flanked by a watch tower. This, and a solid surrounding wall, were added by Philippe-Auguste at the end of the 12C.

A staircase leads to the top from where there is a fine **view** over the surrounding woodland.

★ **St-Gervase and St-Protase Church (Église St-Gervais et St-Protais).** – The oldest parts of the church go back to the 12C but construction continued to the end of the 16C as is evident both outside and inside. The Gothic chancel was completed in 1249; the side chapels which form the ambulatory were added in 1498 and 1507 and are immediately noticeable outside by their pointed gables well separated from the main east end which they nevertheless surround. The transept doors are 16C and Gothic as is the very tall nave. Finally the monumental west front is Renaissance: the doorway is delicately carved and flanked by two towers, that on the north being built in 1536 in François I style and crowned by a cupola, that on the south in Henri II style and left unfinished in 1591.

In spite of the mixture of architectural styles the church as a whole appears perfectly harmonious, particularly inside. Enter through the south transept and you will see how the uncluttered light walls add to the architectural lines and richness of the carved decoration. The large monochrome window in the north chapel is 16C.

Walkers, campers, smokers
please take care

Fire is the scourge of forests everywhere

Michelin map 55 middle of fold 18 or 231 fold 36 – 2km - 1 1/4 miles southeast of Vernon

Claude Monet lived in the village from 1883 until his death in 1926. It was here, inspired by the lily pond he created, that he painted the huge canvases of the *Nymphéas* series which can be seen in the Orangerie Museum in Paris.

Giverny. *The Garden* by Claude Monet

★**The House of Claude Monet.** – The house and gardens formerly owned by Monet are today a museum where reproductions of this most famous works are displayed.

The *Nymphéas* studio (visitor centre and exhibits) is the former main studio.

The house, pink and green, long and low, contains reproductions of the painter's works and the collection of Japanese prints (18-19C) he gathered. The dining room with its yellow painted wooden furniture, the bedroom, the "blue" reading room, and the kitchen with its attractive wall tiles are especially memorable.

The adjacent flower garden, replanted according to the original designs of Monet, is a spectacular array of colour; and on the other side of the road (tunnel) is the water garden. Japanese in inspiration, the water garden has a lily pond, gracefully curved bridges, and is bordered by bamboo trees, rhododendrons and a majestic weeping willow.

Musée Américain Giverny. – Founded by Daniel and Judith J Terra within a few hundred yards of the house of Claude Monet, this museum commemorates the fruitful interrelationship of French with American art.

The collection of about one hundred works of art by forty American artists has come largely from the Terra Museum of American Art in Chicago. It is housed here in three adjoining galleries; the first two galleries containing the core collection and the third presenting collections on different themes. The exhibition opens with two pictures of major historical interest: *Gallery of the Louvre* by Samuel F B Morse, which reflects the great attraction held by the Louvre for American artists, and *The Wedding March* by Theodore Robinson, which has been described as a graphic representation of the "marriage of French Impressionism with American Art".

The first two galleries present views of Giverny by the first wave of American artists to visit the area in the 1880s, and by the second wave of 1895-1920 (artists include John Leslie Breck, Theodore Butler and Frederick Frieseke). Many of the paintings were executed out-of-doors and show the spontaneity of plein-air painting methods.

The third gallery houses works of art from the period 1840-1920; American artists' impressions of other parts of France, in particular of Brittany and Paris (artists include Mary Cassatt, Winslow Homer and John Singer Sargent).

*The **Michelin Maps**, **Red Guides** and **Green Guides** are complementary publications. Use them together.*

Michelin map 55 fold 8 or 237 folds 3, 4 – Local map p 47 – Town plan in the current Michelin Red Guide France

Gournay and Ferrières are the busiest towns in the Bray Region *(qv)*; the local dairy industry supplies the major part of the fresh cheese consumed in France. In 1850 a local farmer's wife, helped by a Swiss cowherd, had the idea of mixing fresh cream with curds before these had been broken. The *Petit Suisse* met with instant success.

St-Hildevert Church (Église). – The church, which is largely 12C, has withstood several wars but the late 12C doors have suffered from overmuch restoration.

Inside, the massive columns are surmounted by capitals interestingly carved with animal and plant motifs. The oldest and most worn, at the end of the south aisle, are among the earliest examples of attempts at human portrayal and date from the Romanesque period.

In the side aisles the polychromed wooden statues of the Virgin and St-Hildevert are 15C.

HARCOURT Pop 934

Michelin map 🗺 fold 19 or 🗺 fold 34 – 7km - 4 1/2 miles southeast of Brionne – Local map p 42.

Harcourt stands on the crossroads of a road network connecting the village to the banks of the Risle and the Charentonne, as well as to the Forest of Beaumont. It is located on the Brionne-Le Neubourg road, the latter giving its name to the vast cultivated plain.

★ **Castle (Château).** – Harcourt Castle, cradle of the celebrated family of the same name, ⊙together with its 247 acre park, has belonged to the French Agricultural Academy since 1828.

The castle was built at the end of the 12C by Robert II of Harcourt, companion to Richard Lionheart. Modernised and fortified by Jean VI of Harcourt in the 14C, it was eventually transformed into a residence in the 17C by Françoise de Brancas, herself Countess of Harcourt.

From the entrance drive with its two enormous cedars we discover the castle's imposing dimensions. To the left a path is marked out and enables the visitor to follow the 20m - 66 feet wide moat surrounding the fortified enclosure flanked by towers. On the inside the assembly area is separated from the keep by another ditch. The medieval entrance and bridge have been restored.

Notice the 70m - 230 feet deep well (14C) in the left corner of the terrace created in the 17C.

Arboretum. – Adjacent to the main courtyard, the 15 acre arboretum contains more than 200 species of conifers and deciduous trees from Europe, America, Asia,. North Africa etc.

Forest. – In more than 230 acres of forest there are superb rare trees from all parts of the world (larches from Poland, beeches from Chili, fir trees from the Caucasus, sequoias, thuyas...) as well as exotic species of decorative interest and beneficial to the forest.

⊙**Church (Église).** – Built in the 13C, it has conserved a remarkably elegant apse. An old timber-framed covered market stands nearby.

★★ Le HAVRE Pop 197 730

Michelin map 🗺 fold 7 or 🗺 fold 19 – Local maps pp 54 and 128

Le Havre, a great seaport and the final milestone along the beautiful Seine Valley, spreads its modern installations to the edge of the furthest Caux promontory. In 1945 Le Havre bore the least enviable title of Europe's worst damaged port; today it is France's second largest port and ranks third in Europe.

Two lines of car ferries also operate to England and the Republic of Ireland. Le Havre-Octeville airport handles regular traffic both within France and abroad (London, Brussels, Rotterdam).

Le Havre town, including the residential area of Ste-Adresse and the old port of Harfleur, is a remarkable example of large scale reconstruction and successful town planning.

1986 saw the opening of a new university and the considerable increase in higher education facilities already in place.

HISTORICAL NOTES

The port, created on the decision of a king in the 16C, has been repeatedly enlarged and modernised by the industry and tenacity of the local Havrais.

A Judicious Choice. – In 1517, to replace Harfleur which was silted up, **François I** ordered the construction of a harbour – *havre* – and fortification on the Côte de Grâce. The marshy site chosen did not look promising except that the floodwaters at high tide remained there for two hours or more and this, in fact, proved decisive in Le Havre's development.

In 1518 the first flagship entered the Bassin du Roi, forerunner of the modern port; the King bestowed his name, provisionally, on the town and his arms: a salamander on a red field – which it retains.

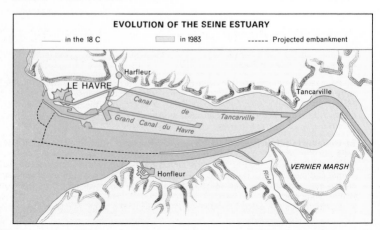

EVOLUTION OF THE SEINE ESTUARY

───── in the 18 C   ▨ in 1983   ------ Projected embankment

Gateway to the Ocean. – Le Havre's present importance as a trading and transatlantic port began during the American War of Independence when it supplied the "rebels". All produce such as cotton, coffee, sugar, tobacco and exotic woods from the one time colony were distributed from Le Havre to all parts of Europe, bringing considerable prosperity to the town. The exchange was founded in 1784. Le Havre is a close parallel to Liverpool in many senses, particularly cotton, both being traditional ports of entry with a textile industry founded close by, and each having a cotton exchange closely in touch with the other.

In the 19C relations with New York grew even closer: in 1850 the vessel *Franklin,* using sails and paddles, crossed the ocean in a fortnight; in 1864 came the first steamship, the *Washington.*

The came the turn of the *Normandie, Ile-de-France, Liberté* (former German liner) and *France,* names ringing with nostalgia for the local people, reminding them of a bygone era, the days of the great transatlantic liners when they left the port to the sound of the three blows, escorted by the tug boats known as the *Abeilles (p 82).*

The Place du Havre became a synonym for the powerful international commercial and banking organisation which had developed in the town.

Le Havre during the War. – Le Havre suffered 146 raids, more than 4 000 killed, 9 935 dwellings totally destroyed and 9 710 partially destroyed. The town's siege began on 2 September 1944 – the Battle of Normandy was over and Paris liberated, but Le Havre was still occupied.

Allied air raids went on ceaselessly for eight days from 5 September; the Germans were determined to blow up any port installations still in existence. On 13 September 1944 Le Havre was liberated. It took two years, even with the aid of the Allies, to clear the destruction and reconstruction was, therefore, able to begin only in 1946.

★THE MODERN TOWN *time: 2 hours*

The old town which had been planned on a chessboard principle by the Italian architect Belarmato in 1541 was virtually wiped out in 1944. A new town was, therefore, planned by **Auguste Perret** (1874-1954), the pioneer of reinforced concrete construction (he also designed the *Théâtre des Champs-Élysées*). A remarkable architectural unity has been achieved; a balance between the volumes and spaces. The centre offers wide perspectives made possible by the vast living units whose horizontal lines are broken by tall tower blocks. The notable town hall and Church of St Joseph, both by Perret, pierce the sky.

The impressive perspective which the Avenue Foch offers towards the Porte Océane symbolises the important part the sea has always played in and on the town.

Commercial Dock (Bassin du Commerce) (FGZ). – The dock has been made the focal point of the new quarter accessible by the Pont de la Bourse (foot bridge). Overlooking the north side of the dock is the Chamber of Commerce which houses the Stock Exchange; at the end stands the International Centre of Commerce.

At the west end opposite the war memorial the urban landscape has had a face lift with the new **Espace Oscar Niemeyer** complex, Place Gambetta. The concrete curves contrast with the rectangular buildings nearby. The work of Brazilian architect Oscar Niemeyer, the ultra-modern centre's vocation is cultural. Cinemas, theatres and exhibition halls are to be found within. The square in front is lined with shops and forms part of a pedestrian precinct with Rue Racine.

François I, founder of the town, stands near the bridge separating the Bassin du Commerce from the Bassin du Roi.

★ **Place de l'Hôtel-de-Ville** (FY 47). – The square, as designed by Auguste Perret, is one of the largest in Europe. Three storey buildings with flat roofs line the sides, the horizontal lines being broken by six ten storey tower blocks. The **town hall (H)**, also by Perret, is a plain building with good lines and is dominated by 72m - 236 feet high concrete tower. In the centre of the square there is a lovely public garden where in the middle a monument to the Resistance has been erected.

The **Rue de Paris (FZ)**, Le Havre's finest street in the 18C, leading off the square opposite the town hall is lined by arcades of luxury shops.

The Avenue Foch opens up to the west.

★ **Avenue Foch** (EFY). – This long shaded avenue entices the stroller to walk on a sunny day all the way down to the end where the Porte Océane (EY) and the sea welcome you.

Said to be the most beautiful street in Le Havre with its shady lawns, its buildings displaying a high degree of architectural unity.

★ **St-Joseph Church (Église)** (EZ). – Auguste Perret designed this bare construction, built in reinforced concrete between 1951 and 1957. Topped by an octagonal bell tower, the church stands out on the city skyline (109m - 325ft) like a beacon. The **inside★★**, strikingly monumental, is designed on a square plan, four groups of four square towers support the base of the bell tower which forms a lantern tower (84m - 275ft). The stained glass windows along the walls of the church and on the sides of the bell tower sparkle throughout the day.

★ **André Malraux Fine Arts Museum** (Musée des Beaux-Arts André Malraux) (EZ M[1]). – The building, built entirely of glass and metal, looks at the sea through a monumental concrete sculpture known locally as the Eye. The roof, designed to provide the best possible light to the galleries inside, is highly original. It consists of six sheets of glass covered by a horizontal slatted aluminium sun blind through which natural light passes, together with electric light which is subsequently filtered through clear or opaque ceiling lights. The galleries are linked on different levels by gangways similar to those on the outside of the building and reminiscent of those on board ship.

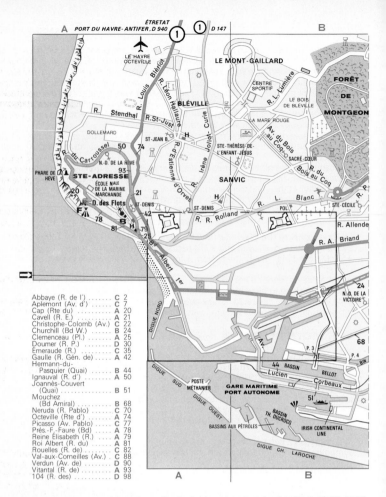

Displayed on the ground floor is a **collection**★ of works of art by **Raoul Dufy** (1877-1953). Dufy, who was born in Le Havre, belonged to the Fauve movement. His subject matter is drawn from life: concerts, regattas, racecourses, esplanades, Normandy beaches, village festivities, streets, etc. The figures are dabbed on the canvas, a background of flat washes of colour, in simplified form and bright colour. His paintings with their touch of humour seem like a pictorial essay of the 1900s.

Also on the ground floor is **Impressionism** represented by Boudin and Jongkind, Monet (a student of Boudin), Pissarro (who worked at Le Havre), Sisley and Renoir; and **Fauvism,** characterised by an expressive power of colour; belonging to this movement are Marquet, Friesz and Van Dongen.

Among the acquisitions of a more recent date are works by Léger and Jacques Villon. The first floor displays an important **collection**★ of the works of **Eugène Boudin,** consisting of paintings, drawings and watercolours bequeathed to the museum by various donors among which was the artist's brother, Louis Boudin. Born in Honfleur, Boudin was one of the first French landscape painters to paint in the open air; admired by Baudelaire, he was a precursor of Impressionism. His animated seashore scenes (of beaches in Trouville and Deauville) where the atmosphere of earth, sky and sea melt into a colourful image are exquisite. His collection is presented showing the artist's development: from the early period when he painted like the Dutch Masters *(The Pardon of Ste-Anne-de-la-Palud)* to his later paintings. He excelled in the portrayal of the Normandy countryside and beach scenes in Deauville and Trouville.

His contemporaries Corot (who influenced Boudin), Manet and Millet are also exhibited as well as other French (Vouet, Fragonard, Courbet, Fantin-Latour), Dutch, Flemish and Italian painters from the 16 to the 19C.

Signal Station (Sémaphore) (EZ). – All available means of communication between land and sea are concentrated in the station whose tower rises to a height of 52.4m - 172 feet. The tugs known as **Abeilles,** literally "bees", and pilot ships moor alongside. From the very end of the pier the **view** takes in the outer harbour and entrance, protected by the long southern breakwater. In the foreground stand the liquid methane reservoirs and the berths of the methane tankers. From this vantage point the manœuvres of all the vessels can be seen.

North Breakwater and Beach (Digue Nord et plage) (EYZ). – The north breakwater shelters the pleasure boat harbour. At the end of this very long breakwater there is a beautiful view; in front the outer harbour (avant port) and behind Ste-Adresse and the city with the Church of St Joseph overlooking the pleasure boat harbour. The beach which extends from the north breakwater to Cape Hève, some 2km - 1 mile, offers views of the Seine Estuary.

During the summer season small wooden beach huts painted white can be seen scattered along the shore. Ste-Adresse is a favourite spot for windsurfers.

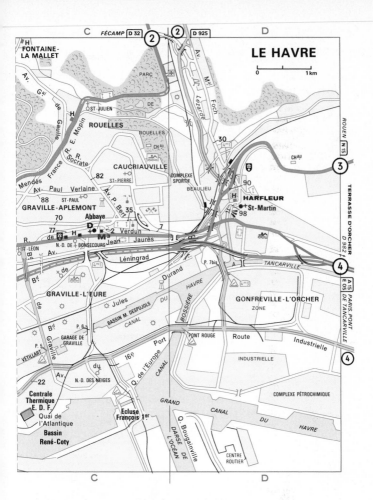

ADDITIONAL SIGHTS

ⓥ **Natural History Museum (Musée d'Histoire Naturelle)** (FZ M⁴). – Installed in the former 18C Law Courts, the museum contains a collection on ornithology. Notice the model of the Tilleul Cliff, north of Le Havre together with the different species of birds which nest there. Other collections include bee-keeping and mineralogy.

Notre Dame Cathedral (Cathédrale Notre-Dame) (FZ). – Built between 1575 and 1630, the building is a harmony of Gothic and Renaissance styles and bristles with buttresses decorated with gargoyles in the shape of salamanders. The north door, with its attractive Ionic columns, is called the "door of the Avé Maria" because of the inscription above the Flamboyant rose window. Three pairs of ringed Ionic columns surmounted by urns stand on the west side. Inside are two side naves and a central nave and chapel. The organ dates from 1637 and was offered by Richelieu.

ⓥ **Old Havre Museum (Musée de l'Ancien Havre)** (GZ M²). – In the heart of the old St-François Quarter, this museum is in a restored 17C house. It is characteristic of Norman town housing of the time, built in a combination of stone and flint.
The museum relates the town's history from 1517 to the present day, each room devoted to a particular period. The Augustin-Normand shipyards have a special place in the 19C. One room evokes street music under the 3rd Republic.

Montgeon Forest (Forêt de Montgeon) (BC). – *Access by the tunnel Jenner* (HY) *which comes out at the Cours de la République (go towards the upper town).*
This large area (280 ha - 691 acres) of woods (oak, beech, birch) has been carefully laid out and contains a boating lake, games areas, camping site and sports fields.

Graville Abbey (Abbaye de Graville) (C). – *Access by Rue Aristide-Briand, then Rue de Verdun (follow directions Rouen-Paris), then left to Rue de l'Abbaye (sign-posted). Enter by the cemetery.*
A sanctuary was erected in the 6C on this spot to shelter the relics of St Honorine. These, however, were later removed to Conflans near Pontoise to preserve them from the "fury of the Normans". On the left of the entrance, stands a **Black Madonna**, so called because of the colour of the metal it is composed of, placed here after the Franco-German War of 1870. **St Honorine Church** (D), the former abbey church dating from the 11 to 13C, has beautifully embellished capitals.
Walk down through the terraced gardens (left of the church) bordered by conventual buildings (13C but rearranged in the 17C), offering pleasant views of the industrial zone and the Seine Estuary, to Rue du Prieuré where a little further stairs take you to the museum located in the conventual buildings.

ⓥ **Graville Priory Museum** (Musée du Prieuré de Graville) (C M³). – Tombstones, capitals, stone statues (12-15C), low reliefs, polychrome wood statues, folk art and a collection of models of 13-17C Norman houses can be seen.

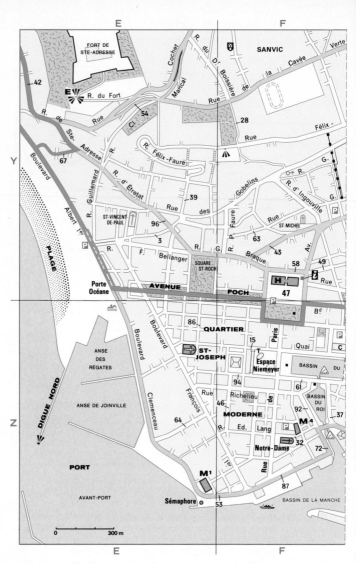

LE HAVRE

SIGHTS BEYOND THE TOWN CENTRE

★★ **Ste-Adresse** (A). – Pop 8 212. *Time: 1 hour.* In the 14C Ste-Adresse, then known as St-Denis Chef de Caux, was a busy maritime centre when its port was laid waste by a tidal wave. Today, this pleasant town extends from Le Havre to Cape Hève. The resort and the old town, orientated to the south, with its mansions surrounded by gardens form a succession of terraces up the steep slopes of Cape Hève. Views of Le Havre and the Seine Estuary.

Following the German invasion of Belgium during the First World War, the Belgian government operated out of Ste-Adresse where it benefitted from the privileges of extraterritoriality.

★★ **Panorama from the Ste-Adresse Fort** (EY E). – *Access: start from Place de l'Hôtel de Ville, left on Rue Georges-Braque, Rue d'Étretat then, on the right, Rue Crochet and left on Rue du Fort.*

Stairs climb to the terrace from which there is a magnificent **view** of the city, port, Seine Estuary and the Côte de Grâce. On a clear day you can see as far as the Calvados Coast on either side of the mouth of the Orne.

On the far side of the Ignauval Valley, to the right, is the *Pain de Sucre* (Sugar Loaf) a memorial erected as a mariners' landmark.

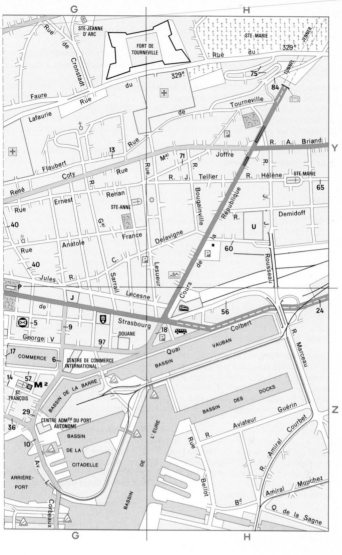

★ **Round Tour of Ste-Adresse** (A). – Follow Boulevard Albert Iᵉʳ alongside the beach to Place Clemenceau and its statue of Albert I, king of the Belgians from 1909 to 1934.

Follow the signs for Pain de Sucre and N-D des Flots.

After a few bends in the road we arrive at the **Pain de Sucre** (B), erected by the widow of General Lefèbvre-Desnouettes who disappeared during a shipwreck off the Icelandic ⊙ coast in 1822. A little higher up on the right the **Notre-Dame des Flots Chapel** contains sailors' votive offerings.

Take the Cape road to the left, Route du Cap.

The road passes in front of the Merchant Navy College (École Nationale de la Marine Marchande), one of the most modern in Europe.

Cape Hève (Cap de la Hève) (A). – *In front of the lighthouse (1/4 hour on foot Rtn).* This rocky site overlooks the mouth of the Seine and the entrance into the harbour. View of Second World War casemates.
The Boulevard du Président Félix-Faure to the right and facing the ocean offers extensive **views**★ *(viewing table – telescope)* of the beach, city, port and Seine Estuary.

Return to the Place Clemenceau.

Harfleur (D). – *Access by the Rue Aristide-Briand and the Rue de Verdun following the direction of Rouen.*

Harfleur (pop 9 703), once a port in its own right at the mouth of the Lézarde Valley, has retained a certain character, in spite of now being at the centre of Le Havre's industrial zone.

The bell tower (83m - 272ft) of **St Martin Church** has been famous in the Caux Region since the 15C. Inside, there are beautiful keystones; the pillars on the north side have foliated capitals, those in all other parts of the church rise in a single sweep. The first chapel on the south aisle contains an 18C altarpiece and a 14C tombstone of a local lord and lady. The organ case which dates from the 17C is ornamented with delicately carved sculptures.

Go from the church along the Rue des 104 and Rue Gambetta, on the right, and continue to the **bridge over the Lézarde** from which you will get a good view of the church belfry.

★★ THE PORT

The Traffic. – Located on the right bank of the Seine Estuary, Le Havre with a total traffic of 50 million tonnes is the second largest port after Marseilles. The imports (39.5 million tonnes) consist chiefly of crude oil, coal, chemical products, fruit and vegetables, coffee, cotton, rubber, natural phosphates and hydrocarbons etc. Petro-chemical products account for half of the exports (17 million tonnes).

Le Havre is a complex of three maritime terminals (one for cruising ships and two for Le Havre-Southampton, Le Havre-Portsmouth, Le Havre-Cork and Le Havre-Rosslare lines) which enabled 900 000 passengers to be transported in 1985 across the Channel to England and further afield to Ireland.

The opening of the Tancarville suspension bridge (1959) connecting the commercial and industrial firms of the Le Havre Region with the areas on the south bank of the Seine has also brought additional traffic to the city.

The Future of the Port. – The alluvial land along the north bank of the Seine, which extends to Tancarville *(see plan p 80)* affords excellent opportunities for extending the port, so enabling it to receive even larger ships.

The **tidal basin** (Bassin René-Coty) (C), 2.5km - 1.5 miles long and 15m - 49 feet deep, has been designed to take cargo ships and tankers up to 250 000 tonnes as well as 150 000 tonne ore carriers feeding the Le Havre Thermal Power Stations and those in the Paris region.

Le Havre being the first French port for container traffic, three specialised wharfs have been built (CD): the Quai de l'Europe, Quai de l'Atlantique, and the Quai Bougainville. At the end of the tidal basin is the **François I Lock** (Écluse maritime François Ier) (C), the largest in the world of its type (length: 400m - 1 312 feet, width 67m - 220 feet, depth 24m - 79 feet), which was first operated in 1971. It connects the tidal basin to the **Canal Bossière** (CD), itself linked to the Tancarville canal, and to the **Grand Canal du Havre** (CD) which serves the industrial area.

Thanks to these installations 250 000 tonne vessels can unload in the industrial area irrespective of the tides.

However, given the Port's limited capacity of ships up to 260 000 tonnes, the **Le Havre-Antifer Terminal** *(p 70)*, 22km - 14 miles north of Le Havre between St-Jouin and Bruneval, was constructed in 1972. This deep water port (25m - 82 feet) can accommodate 555 000 tonne supertankers.

The Industrial Complex. – The area is developing over 8 000 ha - 19 678 acres, 21km - 13 miles in length, and includes an oil refinery, chemical and petro-chemical complexes, fertilizer plant, a car manufacturing plant (Renault Sandouville) a cement factory, and a vast processing and storage centre for bulky products and foodstuffs etc. The EDF power station covering 32 ha - 79 acres alongside the tidal basin supplies energy for the vast industrial area.

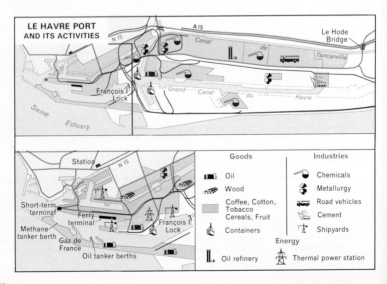

LE HAVRE PORT AND ITS ACTIVITIES

Goods		Industries	
Oil		Chemicals	
Wood		Metallurgy	
Coffee, Cotton, Tobacco Cereals, Fruit		Road vehicles	
Containers		Cement	
		Shipyards	
Energy			
Oil refinery		Thermal power station	

The Basins. – The port, made up of 1 100 ha - 2 718 acres of basins and 28km - 17 1/2 miles of docks consists of three distinct areas.
- The modern **tidal docks** (Théophile-Ducrocq, René Coty), linked to the sea, used by ships limited to 260 000 tonnes but principally intended for tankers, ore ships, container carriers and cargo ships with rapid turn-round.
- The seven **wet docks** (the most important is the Bassin Bellot) limited to cargo ships.
- The **closed docks** where the water level is kept constant: the Bassin Vétillart (linked with the wet docks), the Graville Dock, the Bassin M. Despujols and the wharves of the *Compagnie Française de Raffinage,* the Ocean Dock, the Canal Bossière as well as the Grand Canal du Havre. The last two receive container carriers.
In addition, the **Canal de Tancarville,** beyond the CFR, receives river traffic.

⊙**Thermal Power Station (Centrale Thermique)** (C). – With a capacity of 2 050 000kW it is one of the biggest in Europe powered by oil and coal. It has two spectacular 240m - 788 feet high chimneys.

Tour of the Port. – Information on the port and boats can be obtained from the receptionist of the Port Autonome, Centre Administratif, Terre-plein de la Barre (GZ). Cassette-guides are available for unaccompanied visits.
⊙ Harbour-boats take visitors around the port facilities. They leave from the Quai de la Marine.

⊙ BOAT TRIPS

Seine Cruises. – Upstream to Villequier or Rouen.

Across the Estuary. – Le Havre-Honfleur or Deauville.

EXCURSIONS

★★ **Étretat.** – *28km - 17 1/2 miles. Leave Le Havre ①, the D 940. Description p 69.*

★★ **Fécamp.** – *12km - 7 1/2 miles from Étretat on the D 940. Description p 75.*

⊙ **Orcher Castle (Château d'Orcher).** – *10km - 6 miles. Leave Le Havre by ③, the N 15, then take the Gonfreville-l'Orcher road to the right.* The castle stands on a cliff overlooking the Seine. In the 11C it was part of a defence line protecting the estuary. So as not to fall into English hands it was dismantled in the 14C.
It was purchased in the 18C by a Rouen dealer who had three sides demolished and the fourth redone in Louis XV style.
The visit takes in the library, the dining room (fine collection of plates from the East India Company) and the salons containing an attractive collection of rocaille woodwork. Note the octagonal buttressed **dovecot** in stone and blue flint.
An enjoyable walk can be taken along the shaded terrace near the castle.

★★ HONFLEUR   Pop 8 376

Michelin map 54 fold 8 or 231 fold 20 – Local maps pp 39 and 128 – Facilities

Honfleur on the Seine Estuary, at the foot of the Côte de Grâce hill, is a delightful town. Its old dock, its church and old streets combine in singular harmony. Fresh fish and shellfish are regularly unloaded from the local fleet in the outer harbour.
The town, an important strongpoint until the 15C, acquired true glory through the part played by its mariners in the 17C Norman voyages of discovery.

HISTORICAL NOTES

Canada, a Norman Colony. – Ever since the early 16C navigators had been anchoring briefly along the coast of a land named Gallia Nova by Verrazano, the discoverer of the site of New York *(p 61);* in 1534, however, **Jacques Cartier** stepped ashore and claimed the territory in the name of France. He named it Canada, the Huron word for village. François I, however, was disillusioned as the explorer brought back no spices, no gold, no diamonds. Canada was left unexplored until the 17C when the experienced navigator, **Samuel de Champlain,** received orders to colonise this vast territory. He set sail from Honfleur, and in 1608 founded Quebec.
As a result of Louis XIV's interest, on Colbert's advice, Canada was rapidly developed into virtually a Norman and Percheron colony populated by more than 4 000 peasants who emigrated across the Atlantic. Fishing, hunting, fur trading and agriculture flourished.
The Iroquois Indians, however, bitterly opposed the French colonists and by 1665 these had to appeal to France for aid against mounting attacks. A thousand soldiers arrived; simultaneously a decree was published compelling each to marry within a fortnight one of the "King's daughters", chosen with the approval of the Queen, dispatched from France to help increase the sparse population.
From Canada, **Cavalier de la Salle** journeyed south to explore and colonise Louisiana in 1682 and establish the communication route along the Ohio Valley which was to lead to war with the British and finally the loss by the French of Canada in 1760.

Honfleur, the Artists' Paradise. – The character and the atmosphere of Honfleur have inspired painters, writers and musicians.
At a time when the coast of Normandy was in fashion with the Romantics, Musset came to stay on St-Gatien and Honfleur began to fill with painters and not only those who were Norman born such as Boudin, Hamelin and Lebourg but also Paul Huet, Daubigny, Corot and others from Paris and foreigners such as Bonington and Jongkind.

The old dock at Honfleur

It was in the small St-Siméon Inn, at Mère Toutain's that the Impressionists *(p 25)* first met. Artists have continued ever since to visit Honfleur.
Baudelaire, who stayed in the town with his mother in her old age, declared "Honfleur has always been the dearest of my dreams" and while there wrote his *Invitation au Voyage.*
Other Honfleur citizens include the composer Erik Satie (1866-1925), the poet and novelist Henri de Régnier (1864-1936), Lucie Delarue-Mardrus, the economist Frédéric Le Play and the historian Albert Sorel.

★★THE OLD TOWN *time: 2 1/2 hours*

Walking along the streets and alleys of the old town, stopping to admire an old house or a painter at work, sipping a bowl of cider on a café terrace on a fine sunny day are unforgettable experiences.

★★ **The Old Dock (Vieux Bassin)** (AZ). – The quaysides of the Old Dock are picturesque, enhanced by the pleasure boats alongside. The contrast is striking betwwen the **St-Étienne Quay** with its splendid two-storey stone dwellings, and **Ste-Catherine Quay** where the tall – rising up to 7 storeys high – slender houses are faced with slate and timber. The Governor's House (La Lieutenance), next to the swivel bridge completes the scene. From the St-Étienne Quay look across to the façades on Ste-Catherine Quay reflected in the water.

The Governor's House (Lieutenance) (AY). – Only a relic now remains of the 16C house in which the King's lieutenant, Governor of Honfleur, once lived. The Caen Gate, once part of the town ramparts, has been inset between two wicket gates in the façade overlooking the square while that on the harbour bears a plaque commemorating the sailing of Samuel Champlain for Canada. From the corner of the passenger quay you get a good view of the house, the Old Dock and, on the other side, the outer harbour.

The Enclosure (Enclos) (BZ). – To the east of the Old Dock, this was formerly the heart of the old fortified town.

⊙ **Maritime Museum** (Musée de la Marine) (AZ **M¹**). – Installed in the now disused church of St Étienne the museum traces the history of the port of Honfleur and contains a large number of scale models and topographical information on the town. Maritime activities are not forgotten: fishing, shipbuilding etc. Note the series of 18C documents relative to the slave trade and an accounts book.

Rue de la Prison (BZ 27). – A line of old timber-framed houses.

⊙ **Folk Art Museum** (Musée d'Art Populaire) (AZ **M²**). – Normandy interiors have been reconstructed in this museum located in the former prison. Note particularly the timbered manor house (Pré d'Auge pottery and carved chests), the bourgeois dining room, the weaver's and printer's workshop, the bedroom and a shop on the ground floor.
A large variety of objects are displayed: pewter, weapons, furniture, paintings, measuring instruments and an original collection of theatrical costumes from the theatre created by Louis XIV at Beaumont-en-Auge.

⊙ **Salt Stores** (Greniers à sel) (BZ 35). – *Rue de la Ville.* These tile-covered stone buildings were constructed in the 17C on the instructions of Colbert in order to store the salt needed for cod fishing. The fine oak beams are visible only during temporary exhibitions.

Place Arthur-Boudin (BZ 4). – Old slate-shingled houses stand around the square. At no 6, a Louis XIII house with stone and flint chequered decoration. The Saturday morning flower market brings colour and life to the area.

Ste-Catherine Quarter. – Once a suburb, the quarter was linked to the Enclosure in the 19C when the ditches separating them were filled in. Place Ste-Catherine with its Saturday morning market is the heart of the district.

- ★ **Ste-Catherine's Belfry** (Clocher) (**AY B**). – The belfry, a building covered in chestnut weather boarding, stands apart from the church on a large foundation which contained the bellringer's dwelling. Inside there are fine wooden beams and displays of religious art (wood polychrome monk, 16C, a glass statue of Christ from the liner Ile-de-France), ornaments and *torchères* used by the Brothers of Charity and medallions.

- ★ **Ste-Catherine Church** (Église) (**AY**). – This church is a rare example in western Europe of a building constructed, apart from the foundations, entirely of wood. After the Hundred Years War all masons and architects were employed on the inevitable postwar reconstruction, but the Honfleur "axe masters" from the local shipyards determined to thank God immediately for the departure of the English and built a church by their own skill. The interior has twin naves and side aisles, the timber roof over each nave being supported by wooden pillars. The carved panels ornamenting the gallery are 16C, the organ 18C. There are also many wooden statues.

  Old Streets (**AY**). – Stone and timber houses line the old streets. Examples include: **Place Hamelin**, birthplace of Alphonse Allais, a humorous writer, at no 6, **Rue Haute**, formerly a pathway outside the fortifications where many shipbuilders lived (Erik Satie was born in no 88), **Rue de l'Homme-de-Bois**, overlooking Rue Haute on the garden side, **Rue des Lingots**, narrow and winding with its original paving, and **Rue des Puits** where the Dutch painter Jongkind stayed at no 23.

- ○ **Eugène Boudin Museum** (Musée) (**AY M³**). – The museum is primarily devoted to the Honfleur school of painting and works by painters of the Seine Estuary. Two galleries on the second floor contain oils and pastels by Eugène Boudin and his friends, Isabey, Huet, Courbet, Monet, Jongkind and others. On the third floor a gallery is given over to Dufy, Marquet and Villon and their contemporaries (Oudot, Effel, etc.).
  Finally, on the first floor, a gallery displays Norman furniture, costumes, headdresses, paintings most of which depict life in the 18 and 19C.
  Notice in the stairway the painting by André Hambourg which once decorated the Normandy apartment of the great liner *France*.

★★COTE DE GRACE (AY)

The peaceful beauty of this famous hillside appreciated by all Honfleur enthusiasts is also appealing to passing tourists.

- ★★ **The Calvary** (Calvaire). – There is a good **panorama** from the Cross of the Seine Estuary, the Le Havre roadstead and, to the extreme right, of Tancarville Bridge. *Telescope.*

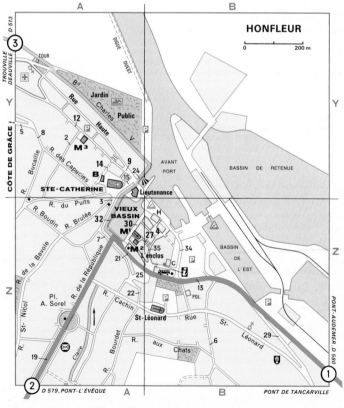

Cachin (R.)	**AZ**		Charrière St-Léonard (R.)	**BZ** 6	Passagers (Q. des)	**AY** 24	
Dauphin (R. du)	**AZ** 7		Delarue-Mardrus (R.)	**AY** 8	Porte-de-Rouen		
Hamelin (Pl.)	**AY** 9		Homme-de-Bois (R. de l')	**AY** 12	(Pl. de la)	**AZ** 25	
République (R. de la)	**AZ**		Le-Paulmier (Q.)	**BZ** 13	Prison (R. de la)	**BZ** 27	
			Lingots (R. des)	**AY** 14	Revel (R. J.)	**BZ** 29	
Albert-1er (R. du Roi)	**AY** 2		Logettes (R. des)	**AY** 15	St-Étienne (Q.)	**AZ** 30	
Berthelot (Pl. P.)	**AZ** 3		Manuel (Cours A.)	**AZ** 19	Ste-Catherine (Q.)	**AZ** 32	
Boudin (Pl. A.)	**BZ** 4		Montpensier (R.)	**AZ** 21	Tour (Q. de la)	**BZ** 34	
Charrière-de-Grâce	**AY** 5		Notre-Dame (R.)	**AZ** 22	Ville (R. de la)	**BZ** 35	

⊙ **Notre-Dame-de-Grâce Chapel (Chapelle).** – In the centre of the esplanade beneath tall trees, stands the small Chapel of Our Lady of Grace and within it the statue after which it is named. This graceful 17C building which has replaced a sanctuary, said to have been founded by Richard II, 4th Duke of Normandy, is visited by pilgrims throughout the year *(p 143)*. It was here that navigators and explorers came to pray before leaving on journeys of discovery or colonisation to the North American continent and the north transept chapel is dedicated to all Canadians of Norman origin. There are numerous small, ex-voto vessels.

Mont-Joli Viewpoint. – The view complements the one from the Calvary: in the foreground are the town, the port and the coast; to the east is the semicircle of hills. The Tancarville Bridge can be seen in the distance.

OTHER SIGHTS

Public Gardens (Jardin public) (AY). – This is a pleasant park with borders of flowers, set out along land reclaimed from the sea. The walk on the new western dike along the channel is pleasant at high tide.

St-Léonard Church (Église) (BZ). – The church's façade associates, in bizarre amalgam, an ornate Flamboyant doorway and a 17C belfry tower.
Inside are two immense shells which have been converted into fonts. The narthex has restored quadripartite vaulting. The entrance to the chancel has statues of Our Lady of Victory and St Leonard with two prisoners kneeling; note in the chancel the wooden statues of St Peter, St Paul and the four Evangelists. The narthex has an 18C copper lectern from Villedieu-les-Poêles.

★★ HOULGATE   Pop 1 784

Michelin map 54 fold 17 or 231 fold 19 – Facilities

Houlgate is the perfect type of Normandy resort where the coast and the surrounding countryside are equally lovely. The shady avenues, the houses and gardens all add to the attraction of the green Drochon Valley in which the resort is set.
The magnificent fine sand beach is bordered by a breakwater promenade which extends to the foot of the Vaches Noires Cliff. Bathers congregate on the beach section of the promenade; anglers and those in search of shellfish at the end beneath the jagged cliffs.

EXCURSION

★ **Vaches Noires Cliff (Falaise des Vaches Noires).** – Between Villers-sur-Mer and Houlgate, the Auberville Plateau ends in a crumbling and much hollowed-out cliff, known for the strangeness of its appearance and for the many fossils found there. To see this strange place at its best, follow the beach at low tide starting from Houlgate or Villers *(about 2 hours Rtn on foot)*. The panorama stretches from Trouville to Luc-sur-Mer and over most of the Seine Bay.
The cliff has steep sides of dark clay and marl, cut by ravines. Erosion by the sea attacks the foot of the cliffs and the trickle of fresh water from the Auge Plateau brings about a hollowing of the rock and the formation of a mud flow. Further on, standing back a little, the Auberville Plateau ends in a small chalk cliff, from which large pieces have broken away, split up near the beach and become covered with seaweed – these are the so called "Vaches Noires" (Black Cows).

IVRY-LA-BATAILLE   Pop 2 065

Michelin map 55 fold 17 or 231 fold 36 – Facilities

The battle in the town's name is the one in which Henri IV defeated the Leaguers of Mayenne on the 14 March 1590.
The area has retained a few picturesque half-timbered houses. At No 5 Rue de Garennes there is a typical dwelling where Henri IV is said to have put up in 1590, and closing Rue de l'Abbaye the 11C gate with its three carved archings which belonged to the former abbey of Ivry, destroyed at the time of the Revolution.

St-Martin Church (Église). – Founded late 15C – early 16C by Diane of Poitiers, the building is attributed partly to a famous architect of the time, Philibert Delorme. The church is remarkable for its Gothic pinnacled tower decorated with gargoyles and dragons and above all for its south entrance (the door is walled up) surmounted by an elegant pediment and boasting fluted pilasters with Corinthian capitals. Inside the nave and aisles are covered by fine panelled barrel vaulting.

EXCURSION

Ivry Obelisk (Obélisque). – *7km - 4 1/2 miles to the northwest on the D 833 and D 163.*
La Couture-Boussey. – Pop 1 534. The village has been famous since the 16C as a major centre for the making of reed instruments. On the village square the craft and industrial ⊙ **museum of wind instruments** proposes a large variety of instruments made over the centuries.
Turn right on the D 163.
Obelisk. – Commemorating the Battle of Ivry, the obelisk was constructed on the plateau by Napoleon in 1804. A tree-lined drive indicates its position.

Jumièges, in a splendid setting on the Lower Seine, is one of the greatest ruins in France.

To experience the deep emotions that can be awakened by a visit to the ruins let your imagination free, now, to re-create in the open the tribunes, the timbered roof of the nave, the transept crossing, the semicircle of the choir, and the galleries of the cloister.

The Jumièges Almshouse. – In the 10C Duke William Longsword rebuilt Jumièges on the ruins of the former abbey founded in the 7C by St Philibert and destroyed by the Vikings *(details p 125)*. The new Benedictine abbey soon became popularly known through its benefactions as the Jumièges Almshouse. But charity did not preclude learning and Jumièges also became widely recognised as a centre of scholarship and wisdom.

The large abbey church was consecrated in 1067 in the presence of William the Conqueror.

The last monks dispersed at the Revolution and in 1793 the abbey was bought at a public auction by a timber merchant from Canteleu who undertook to make use of Jumièges as a stone quarry and to that end blew up the lantern in the church. A new proprietor in 1852 set about saving the ruins which now belong to the nation.

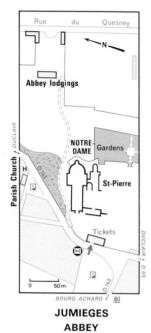

JUMIEGES
ABBEY

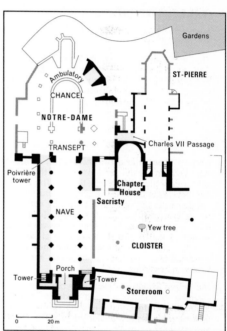

★★★ **THE ABBEY** time: 1/2 hour

⊙ **Notre-Dame Church (Église).** – The twin towers of the façade are square at the base, octagonal above, and rise 43m - 141ft on either side of the main door. Inside, the entire nave, which rises to a height of 27m - 89ft together with part of the transept and chancel, remains.

Backing on the façade, a wide gallery overlooks the nave; one of the features which makes the latter outstanding is the arrangement of massive square pillars quartered by columns alternating with slender piles of single columns. On either side are galleries covered with groined vaulting.

The transept was largely destroyed in the 19C and only the west wall of the lantern remains, supported with great effect still by a high and sweeping arch.

The original chancel, round which traces of an ambulatory have been discovered, was enlarged in the 13 and 14C but today all that remains are two vaulted chapels.

Charles VII Passage. – The arched passageway leads to the smaller St Peter's church. Its name dates back to the King's visit to Jumièges.

St Peter's Church (Église St Pierre). – The porch and first bays of the nave are Norman Carolingian (round windows and twinned arcades), the remaining ruins 13 and 14C. The porch, pierced by an arch, is flanked by two small doors behind which are steps to the towers and galleries. The first two bays are a rare example of 10C Norman architecture; the rounded hollows above the semicircular arches were once covered in frescoes. Above, a gallery opens on the nave through small twin bays with rounded arches.

Chapter house. – *To the left of St Peter's church.*
In accordance with monastic tradition, the chapter house, which dates from the early 12C, opened on the cloister. The square bay and apse were covered by pointed arches which are among the oldest known examples of this type of vaulting.

Sacristy. – It had barrel vaulting and was strengthened by buttresses.

Cloister. – An ancient yew tree marks the centre of the cloister. Its four galleries formerly had twenty-six bays. The south side was occupied by the refectory.

Storeroom. – The west wall of the very large storeroom, which is late 12C, is decorated outside with bays encircled by arcades or surmounted by trilobed tympana.

Gardens. – A 17C stairway winds up to a large terrace and gardens.

Abbey Lodgings. – Beyond the lawn stands a majestic rectangular 17C building with a Mansart-style roof and pedimented projection on the façade.

ADDITIONAL SIGHT

⊘**Parish Church** (Église). – The nave is 11 and 12C. In the 16C a vast chancel and ambulatory were added with the idea of the new church's replacing the abbey. A few works of art – altarpieces, 15 and 16C stained glass, etc. – were brought from the abbey to the church at this time.

LILLEBONNE
Pop 9675

Michelin map **54** fold 9 or **231** fold 21 – Local map p 128 – See town plan in the current Michelin Red Guide France

The small industrial town of Lillebonne was once a capital city. After the conquest of Gaul by Julius Caesar, the military camp of Juliobona, named in honour of the Proconsul, became a major port on Bolbec Bay. It is now silted up.
Lillebonne flourished towards the end of the 19C with the arrival of textile factories in the region. From Bolbec to Lillebonne the valley came to be called the "Golden Valley".

SIGHTS

Roman Theatre and Amphitheatre. – From the main square (place de l'Hôtel-de-Ville) you can see the general layout of this 1C amphitheatre transformed into a theatre with a capacity of 10 000 in the 2C. The arena's major axis measured 48 metres – 157 feet – as in Lutetia. The central arena was surrounded by a **podium** made up of two parallel walls and lined with a ditch for collecting water. The audience sat on the tiers of the **cavea** divided into the first or lower maenianum and the second or higher maenianum. Access was through the **vomitorium.** To the east and west the two large entrances and principal cloakrooms show just how big the construction was. Six metres – nearly twenty feet – wide they were covered over by a vault. Near each entrance, large rectangular buildings known as **parascaenia** were probably used for storing accessories.

⊘**Municipal Museum** (Musée). – *Jardin Jean-Rostand.*
Devoted to popular art and traditions it exhibits craftsmen's tools, objets d'art, furniture and documents relating to the history of Lillebonne and Normandy. The basement houses archaeological finds from local excavations (cremation urns, pottery and ironwork from 1-3C). From the garden there is a view of the medieval castle and enclosure.

⊘**Castle** (Château). – *Access by 46 Rue Césarine.*
There remains of this fortress (rebuilt in the 12 and 13C) where William the Conqueror assembled his barons before invading England, one wall of an octagonal tower and, on the left, a bold round tower built on three floors.

⊘**Notre-Dame Church** (Église). – This 16C building has a double entrance with central pillar. The sweeping spire rises 55 metres – 181 feet – above a square tower. Inside there is a stained glass window devoted to the story of John the Baptist. The stalls were originally from Valasse Abbey.

EXCURSION

Valasse Abbey (Abbaye de Valasse). – *6km - 4 miles northwest on the D 173. Description p 133.*

Times and charges for admission to sights described in the guide are listed at the end of the guide.

The sights are listed alphabetically in this section either under the place – town, village or area – in which they are situated or under their proper name.

Every sight for which there are times and charges is indicated by the symbol ⊘ in the margin in the main part of the guide.

Michelin map 54 fold 18 or 231 fold 32 – Local map p 39 – Facilities

Lisieux has become the most important commercial and industrial town in the prosperous Auge Region *(qv)*.

The town's renown centres today on the "Lisieux of St Teresa".

During the summer season, discover the different parts of the town on a tourist train leaving from the basilica or Les Buissonnets *(see below)*.

ST TERESA OF LISIEUX

An Early Calling. – Born on 2 January 1873, to a well to do and very religious family in Alençon, Thérèse Martin was an eager and sensitive child, who soon showed intelligence and will-power. On the death of her mother, M. Martin brought the family to Lisieux where they lived at Les Buissonnets. Thérèse grew up in an atmosphere of kindness and piety and at nine years felt the call of the Church. Notwithstanding her father's permission given on Whit Sunday 1887 that she might join her sister at the Carmelite Convent, the authorities felt she was too young, and it was only in April 1888, after a pilgrimage to Rome and a request to the Holy Father, that she entered the Order finally at the age of fifteen and a quarter years.

"Little Teresa". – "A soul of such quality should not be treated as a child; dispensations were not intended for her", said the Prioress of the new postulant who undertook the severe life of a Carmelite.

Leading a solitary life in the cloisters where she had come "to save souls and, above all, to pray for the priests", Sister Teresa of the Child Jesus, with humility and courage, mounted the difficult path to perfection. Her gaiety and simplicity cloaked a consuming energy. She wrote the story of her life, *History of a Soul,* finishing the last pages only a few days before entering the Carmelite hospital in which, after a slow and agonising illness, she died in 1897. She was beatified in 1923 and canonised on 17 May 1925. On her beatification her remains were transferred to the Carmelite chapel.

THE PILGRIMAGE *see p 143*

⊙ **Les Buissonnets** (BY B). – This is where Thérèse Martin lived from the age of 4 1/2 to 15. The house can be visited and includes the dining room, Thérèse's bedroom, where she was miraculously cured at the age of 10, her father's bedroom and a mementos room – Communion dress, toys and games.

In the garden a group of statues represents Thérèse asking her father permission to enter the Carmelite Convent.

Carmelite Chapel (BZ). – The Saint's shrine, a recumbent figure in marble and precious wood, is in the chapel on the right and contains her relics.

⊙ **Reliquary Chamber (Salle des Reliques).** – A series of display windows with recorded commentary shows relics relating to the Saint's convent life (bowl, footwear, white gown and veil).

St Teresa Basilica (Basilique Ste-Thérèse) (BZ). – This impressive basilica was consecrated on 11 July 1954 and is one of the biggest 20C churches. Its total surface area measures 4 500m² – over 150 000 square feet and its dome is 93m high – 305 feet. The **dome** is open to visitors.

The construction of the bell tower was interrupted in 1975. 45m - 147 feet high, surmounted by a terrace it contains the great bell and the 45 smaller carillon bells. Notice on the tympanum of the door the carvings by Robert Coin depicting Jesus teaching the Apostles and the Virgin of Mount Carmel. The single and immense nave is brightly coloured and decorated with marble, stained glass and mosaics by Pierre Gaudin, a pupil of Maurice Denis. On either side of the central doorway stand statues of the Virgin and St Joseph, protectors of the Carmelite order. In the south transept stands a reliquary offered by Pope Pius XI containing the bones of the Saint's right arm. The **crypt** *(entrance outside, beneath the galleries)* is decorated with mosaics (scenes in the life of St Theresa). Behind the apse are the tombs of the Saint's parents.

⊙ **Display "St Teresa's Life as a Carmelite".** – *Beneath the north cloister.*

The history and life of the Carmelites are traced with the reconstruction of a cell and the papal enclosure behind which the sisters lived and which could be crossed only with the permission of the Pope.

⊙ **Diorama St Teresa's Life** (BZ). – Wax figures evoke the main moments in the life of Thérèse Martin.

★ ST-PIERRE CATHEDRAL (BY) *time: 1/4 hour*

The cathedral was begun in 1170 and only completed in the middle of the 13C.

Exterior. – The façade, raised above the ground on stone steps, is pierced by three doors and flanked by towers. The one on the left, though incomplete, is beautiful with bays and quartering columns.

Walk round the church by the right to the south transept's Paradise Door. The massive buttresses linked by an arch surmounted by a gallery were added in the 15C.

Interior. – The transept is extremely simple with the lantern rising in a single sweep at the crossing. The nave has great unity with blind bays topped by relieving arches and robust round pillars surmounted by circular capitals supporting the wide arches. Walk round the 13C chancel, to the huge central chapel which was remodelled in the pure Flamboyant style on the orders of Pierre Cauchon, Bishop of Lisieux, after the trial of Joan of Arc *(details p 109)*. His tomb lies to the left of the altar. It was in this very chapel that Thérèse Martin attended mass. Note the series of 15C carved low reliefs.

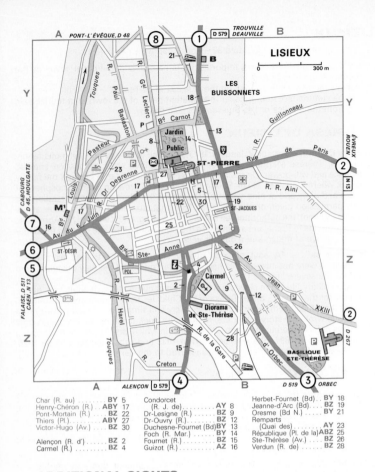

ADDITIONAL SIGHTS

Law Courts (Palais de Justice) (BY J). – *(not open to the public)* The courts are in the old Louis XIII style Bishop's Palace. The **Gold Room** (Salle Dorée) is the Bishop's dressing room decorated with gilded panelling and a beautiful coffered ceiling with painting by Le Sueur representing the arms and emblems of the Bishop. The walls and chairs are covered with Cordovan leather.

Beyond stretch the **public gardens,** formerly belonging to the Bishop.

Old Houses. – No 34 Rue du Dr-Lesigne, Rue Henry-Chéron and Rue du Dr-Degrenne where a timber-framed house stands next to a building with chestnut shingled roof.

⊙ **Old Lisieux Museum (Musée du Vieux Lisieux)** (AZ M¹). – A lovely timber-framed house contains this museum which displays an important iconographic collection from Old Lisieux, and the Auge Region. Space is devoted to arts and regional folk traditions. Notice on the 1st floor an interesting collection of Rouen porcelain, pewters and a Flemish jewelry chest (17C) in wood and ebony veneer. The 2nd floor houses a reconstruction of a dressmaker's workshop alongside sacred art statues, ornaments of the Brothers of Charity and Pré-d'Auge pottery.

EXCURSION

Upper Valley of the Touques. – *Round tour of 75km - 47 miles – about 3 hours – Local map p 39. Leave Lisieux by ④ the D 579, and take the D 64 on the left.*

⊙ **Fervaques.** – Pop 514. The **château** is a vast, well-proportioned 16 and 17C brick and stone construction, washed by the waters of the Touques. For 22 years the town was the retreat of Delphine de Custine, the companion of Chateaubriand who also stayed there himself.

Turn right at Notre-Dame-de-Courson into the D 4. After 3km - 2 miles – bear left.

Bellou. – Pop 107. Bellou Manor, a timbered 16C house, stands in the centre of the village.

The D 110 leads into the forest of Moutiers-Hubert. Chiffretot Manor stands on the right just before the village.

At Moutiers-Hubert take the D 64 to the right towards Gacé. At the crossroads with the D 16 turn left and then right. Cross the river at Canapville on the D 33, then continue straight ahead under the railway bridge just after the station. Cut across the D 79 and follow the D 242 for 1km - 1/2 mile. At the first fork bear right for Vimoutiers.

Vimoutiers. – *Description p 139.*

Take the D 979 and then the D 579 to the north and after 2km - 1 mile turn right on the steeply rising D 268.

⊘ **Lisores.** – Pop 248. 500m - about 550 yards to the northwest in a pretty hillside setting stands the little **Fernand Léger Museum** installed in the former barn, now modernised, of the Bougonnière farm where the painter (1881-1955) liked to rest. On display are scale models of stained glass, paintings, mosaics, bronze statues, carpets and Aubusson tapestries representative of the artist's personal style. There is also a model of the ceramic-mosaic decorating the façade of the museum at Biot *(see Michelin Green Guide French Riviera).*

Return to the D 579 by the D 110 and St-Ouen-le-Houx.

Livarot. – Pop 2 759. Home of the cheese bearing the same name, Livarot possesses
⊘ some lovely old houses and a **conservatory** (conservatoire des traditions fromagères), which explains the different stages in cheese making.

★ **St-Germain-de-Livet.** – *Description p 120.*

Return to Lisieux by the D 268 and the D 579.

Gourmets ...

The country's gastronomic specialities and fine wines are described on page 29.

*Each year the **Michelin Red Guide France** proposes a revised selection of establishments renowned for their cuisine.*

LONGNY-AU-PERCHE
Pop 1 650

Michelin map **60** fold 5 or **231** fold 45 – Local map p 104 – Facilities

Longny has a pleasant setting in the green Jambée Valley; it is also quite near the forest of the same name.

Notre-Dame-de-Pitié Chapel (Chapelle). – *Access by Rue Gaston-Gibory to the right of the town hall.*
There is a good view of the town from this delightful 16C chapel where a large stairway leads up to the apse.
The square belfry set obliquely to the façade and a buttress crowned by an open pinnacle add considerably to the building's design. The main door is surmounted by delicate Renaissance decoration flanked by finely carved pilasters which, however, lack statues as these were destroyed during the Revolution.
Above the lintel is a statue of Our Lady of Mercy, higher is the head of the Eternal Father, and still higher a medallion illustrating Abraham's sacrifice.
The beautiful carved doors are by a local 19-20C artist: the Visitation and Annunciation are shown on the west door panels; in medallions on the north and south doors are the Virgin in Sorrow and a representation of the face of Christ from the imprint on Veronica's veil.
The nave has pointed arching with liernes, tiercerons and hanging keystones; two side chapels at the beginning of the chancel form a false transept. The miraculous statue of Our Lady of Mercy (annual pilgrimage), stands upon the high altar.

⊘ **St-Martin Church (Église).** – The façade of this late 15C – early 16C church is flanked by a square belfry supported by ornamented buttresses and a staircase tower.
The belfry's great blind window frames three statues. Above, in a niche, St Martin on horseback can be seen, dividing his cloak.

EXCURSION

★ **Tour in the Normandy Perche.** – *128km - 80 miles – about 4 hours.*
This drive described on p 104 as departing from Bellême, can be made equally well from Longny.

★ LOUVIERS
Pop 19 413

Michelin map **55** folds 16, 17 or **231** fold 35 – Local map p 127

Located in the middle of the Seine, Eure and Iton Valleys, Louviers is an interesting town to pass through with its modern trading area and an old town north of Notre-Dame church with its pretty half-timbered houses, such as in Rue Tatin, Rue du Quai, Rue Pierre Mendès-France. Those who like fishing have three rivers to choose from. The woollen textile industry, particularly the making of sheets traditionally associated with the town since the 13C, has progressively disappeared. However, in the industrial estate to the north new plants manufacture batteries, television aerials, records and plastic foam.

SIGHTS

⊘ **Museum of Theatre and Opera Scenery and Film Sets (Musée des décors de théâtre, d'opéra et de cinéma) (AY M).** – The museum houses a collection of works by the stage and film set designer Georges Wakhévitch (1907-1984) who lived between Louviers and Les Andelys. The ground floor exhibits tableaux of theatre and opera costumes and sets and has a temporary exhibition room. A winding staircase leads to the attractively arranged top floor where the designer's film sets are portrayed including those for producers Jean Cocteau, Jean Renoir and Peter Brook (*King Lear* 1970).
A slide projection with appropriate musical soundtrack is regularly proposed on the first floor.

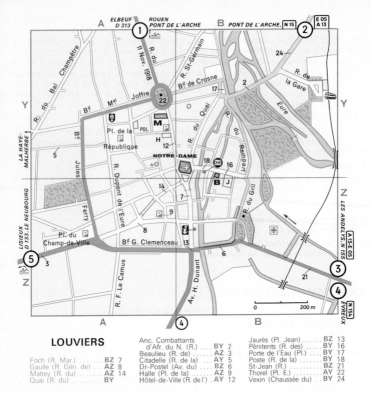

LOUVIERS

★**Notre-Dame Church (Église) (BY).** – This plain 13C church was renovated at the end of the 15C in the Flamboyant style which brought its local renown.

Exterior. – The **south wall**★ is the most astonishing part of the church for it is there that the brilliance of the Flamboyant style appears in a profusion of pointed gables, openwork balustrades, pinnacles, festoons and gargoyles. The buttresses support interesting statues.

The **porch**★ (on the south side) has been described as more closely resembling silver work than masonry. The door panels are Renaissance. Notice the hanging keystones in the Gothic arcades.

A beautiful Virgin stands at the 14C west door.

Interior. – The 13C nave, flanked by double aisles on either side has a considerable elegance and contains numerous **works of art**★:

1) Entombment (late 15C).
2) Marie-Salomé and her sons (16C).
3) Throne.
4) Above the altar, 3 statues. Christ, the Virgin and St John (15C). On each side are carved panels depicting the Virgin Mary and the Centurion at the Calvary (14C).
5) Altar decorated with carved panels depicting the life of the Virgin (16C).
6) and 7) Early 17C tableaux by local artist Jean Nicolle: The *Nativity* and *Adoration of the Magi.*
8) Mausoleum by Robert d'Acquigny (late 15C).
9) Restored Renaissance stained glass.

Former Penitents' Convent (Ancien couvent des Pénitents) (BY B). – All that remains of this Franciscan convent, built in 1646, on a branch of the Eure, is the inhabited main building together with three small arcaded galleries belonging to the cloister. The western gallery is in a semi-ruined state but lined with a square with lawn and trees.

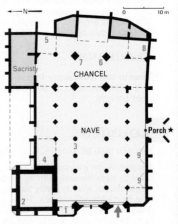

Maison du Fou du Roy (BZ). – This lovely half-timbered house located in the main street is also the Tourist Office. It is said to have belonged to Guillaume Marchand, apothecary and Henri IV's jester on the death of Chicot, killed during the siege of Pont-de-l'Arche.

EXCURSION

Vironvay. – Pop 169. *5km - 3 miles by ③, N 155 and the road on the left which crosses the A 13 and N 15.*
The church stands alone overlooking the Seine Valley. As you approach there are views over the river spanned by the bridge at St-Pierre-du-Vauvray, and further east the ruins of Gaillard Castle dominating Les Andelys.

Michelin map 55 fold 8 or 231 fold 24 – Local maps p 33 and below – Facilities

The village of Lyons, lying in the heart of the forest of the same name on the slope of the left bank of the Lieure, is a beautiful, tranquil place to stay. It is a picturesque traditional Norman village with a fine group of half-timbered houses. One of them, located in the steep downhill street leading off from the square, was occupied by the musician Maurice Ravel and it was here that he composed his piece *le Tombeau de Couperin*.

Covered Market (Halles). – The market is covered by a fine 18C timber roof. Nearby is a house with unusual window supports in wrought iron, the birthplace of the poet Isaac de Benserade (1613-1691).

⊙ **St Denis Church (Église).** – The church dates from the 12C but was extensively remodelled in the 15C. On the outside, note the stonework and the timber belfry. Inside, the great wooden statues are very appropriate in this woodmen's village. Notice in the chancel a statue of St Christopher carrying the child Jesus.

EXCURSION

★★ **Lyons Forest.** – *Description below.*

★★ LYONS Forest

Michelin map 55 folds 7, 8 or 231 fold 24

Lyons Forest, favourite hunting ground of the dukes of Normandy, has been considerably reduced over the centuries but it still extends for more than 10 700 ha - 40 sq miles principally in the Eure Department. Its particular glory is that it is a beech forest. Tree trunks often rise to a height of over 20 metres - 66 feet.

TOWNS AND SIGHTS

⊙ **Beauficel-en-Lyons.** – Pop 136. The **church,** preceded by a 17C porch, contains beautiful statues, particularly a 14C Virgin in polychrome stone inlaid with glass.

★ **La Bunodière Beech** (Hêtre de la Bunodière). – Indicated by a signpost on the right as you leave the N 31 to enter the forest, this magnificent tree which is 40 metres - 131 feet tall stands near the **Câtelier Reserve** where oak, ash and maple trees thrive.
Its circumference measures 3.3 metres - 11 feet.

⊙ **St-Jean Chapel.** – A path at the back of the 17C chapel leads to a tree known as St John's Oak (Chêne St-Jean), which has a circumference of 5m - 16ft at a height of 1.30m - 4ft above the ground.

Croix-Vaubois Crossroads (Carrefour de la Croix-Vaubois). – The plain memorial is to the foresters who died in the Resistance.

La Feuillie. – Pop 1 038. The slender church **spire★** is a bold piece of carpentry.

Fleury-la-Forêt Château. – *Description p 77.*

Fouillebroc Spring (Sources du Fouillebroc). – A pleasant forest setting.

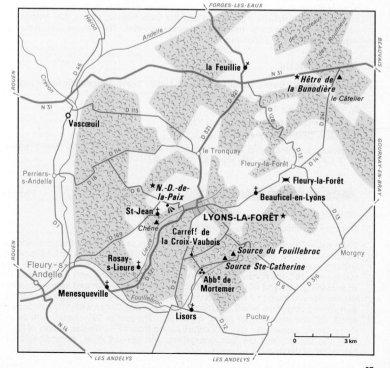

Lisors. – Pop 264. The **church** contains a crowned Virgin dating back to the 14C and which was found buried in 1936.

★ **Lyons-la-Forêt.** – *Description p 97.*

Menesqueville. – Pop 387. The small 12C country **church,** which has been skilfully restored, contains some very old statues. The Canticle of Canticles is the theme of the stained glass windows by Decorchemont.

Mortemer Abbey. *Description p 101.*

★ **Notre-Dame-de-la-Paix Viewpoint.** – Good **view** of Lyons in its setting from the approach to the statue.

Rosay-sur-Lieure. – Pop 443. The small **church** surrounded by a well-kept burial ground is in a pleasant setting.

Ste-Catherine Spring (Source). – A signpost points the way beside a wall to the oratory where young girls come to pray for a husband. Leave the car in a lay-by and cross over the stream on a wooden footbridge.

Vascœuil. – *Description p 134.*

MAMERS   Pop 6747

Michelin map **60** fold 14 or **231** fold 44 – See town plan in current Michelin Red Guide France.

Mamers lies in a hollow in the Dives Valley, the capital of the Saosnois, a small transitional area between the Perche hills and the flat countryside of Le Mans. Two stretches of water have been created for fishing and water-cycling.
It is a prosperous small town as can be seen from its well-kept spacious squares and old covered market; large fairs are held there regularly. The manufacture of household and camping equipment and trimming materials has replaced the traditional net making.

Notre-Dame Church (Église). – The church, which was founded in the 12C as part of a Benedictine priory, was almost entirely rebuilt in the 16C.
The nave has an unusual triforium within wide mullioned bays. At the back of the façade, on the left, there is a 16C terracotta study of the Dormition of the Virgin.
On the façade to the right of the small door is a plaque indicating the water level during the floods of 1904.

MARTAINVILLE   Pop 559

Michelin map **55** fold 7 or **231** fold 23 – 16km - 10 miles east of Rouen

The village is situated between the Crevon and Andelle Valleys which meet at the edge of Lyons Forest.

Château. – This elegant residence of brick and stone was erected at the end of the 15C. On the outside, the great brick chimneys have remarkable Gothic decoration. Note also, near the outbuildings, the massive 16C pigeon house and 18C half-timbered cart shed.
The inside, which houses the **Regional Museum of Arts and Traditions of Normandy,** has for the most part kept its original plan. The rooms, often embellished with beautiful chimneys, display 15-19C furniture from Rouen and the Caux Region, chests, 17C buffets, 18C cupboards, earthenware, pottery, glassware, pewter, Norman copper pans and regional ceramics and costumes.

EXCURSION

Round tour of 16km - 10 miles. – *About 1 hour. Leave Martainville to the east and take the D 13 to the left, towards the Crevon Valley.*

Ry. – *Description p 120.*
Follow the D 12 up the rural Crevon Valley.

Blainville. – *Description p 46.*
   Return to Martainville on the D 7 from southwest of Blainville and 2 1/2km - 1 1/2 miles – further take the D 85 on the left.

MESNIÈRES-EN-BRAY   Pop 827

Michelin map **52** fold 15 or **231** fold 12 – Local map p 48

The majestic château houses a private institution.

★ **Château.** – This Renaissance construction, which is said to be the most majestic civil monument in the Bray Region, was started late 15C and is flanked by powerful although purely ornamental machicolated towers. The grand staircase to the main courtyard is 18C, the right wing 19C. The main central building with its steep roof has an arcaded gallery and all the classical adornment of superimposed orders, ornamented dormer windows and Antique style busts. The tour includes the gallery adorned with carved stags (the wood is natural), the *Salle des Cartes* with 17C paintings on wood, and the main chapel dating from 1860. The earlier 16C chapel, with an axe shaped roof, is decorated with woodwork dating from 1670, life-size statues of Christ, John the Baptist, and the four evangelists, and stained glass, reconstituted with fragments of the original windows.

MIROMESNIL Château

Michelin map 52 fold 4 or 231 fold 11 – 6km - 4 miles south of Dieppe

The château was built after the Battle of Arques (1589) on the former fief of the Marquis of Miromesnil. The main building has a high slate roof and grand Louis XIII façade looking onto the main courtyard. Pilasters surmounted by carved stone urns punctuate the brickwork at regular intervals. One either side stand slender turrets and low wings.

⏱ **TOUR** *time: 3/4 hour*

Inside. – Guy de Maupassant was born here on August 5 1850. A showcase in the **vestibule** contains documents related to the event: birth certificate, records of his Christening and a letter written by his mother. Also to be seen are mementoes of Albert de Mun (1841-1914), politician and Catholic orator. The **Montebello salon** is devoted to Marshal Lannes, Duke of Montebello. The furniture is Empire style. A clock offered by Napoleon stands over the fireplace.
The **bedroom** of the Marquis of Miromesnil contains his book collection bearing his arms. The nearby **study** displays the only copy of the marquis' land register.

South Façade. – Flanked by two round pepperpot towers, the south side is totally different from the north. The construction is mainly of brick with stone around the windows and on the projecting corners.

Gardens. – The kitchen garden is lined with flowers (daffodils, roses, dahlias).

Park and Chapel. – Through a magnificent beech grove we arrive at the 16C chapel. The sobre sandstone and flint walls make a striking contrast with the richly decorated interior. Note the stained glass, the wood carving and painted stone statues.

MONTIVILLIERS   Pop 15 037

Michelin map 52 fold 11 or 231 fold 20 – Local map p 54

Founded on a monastery, from which it took its name, the town is now a suburb of Le Havre.

★ **St Saviour Church (Église St-Sauveur).** – Walk along the north side to see the 11C lantern
⏱ tower in the transept crossing. A Romanesque belfry complete with spire restored in the 19C dominates the façade. Inside are two naves, one Romanesque, the other 16C Gothic, added when the church passed to the parish. Notice the 17C solid oak pulpit in the nave and, at the back of the belfry, a charming Flamboyant gallery in three sections.

Brisegaret Cemetery (Cimetière). – *Access road from road to Fécamp, to the left in front of a marble mason's.*
Once a charnel house, all that remains is a 16C gallery with timber roof. Miscellaneous carvings are to be seen on the pillars – skeletons, coats of arms...

EXCURSION

⏱ **Filières Château.** – *14km - 9 miles – east on the D 31 and Gommerville.* The château can be seen at the end of the avenue leading to the main courtyard which is surrounded by a moat. All around is a park landscaped by Le Nôtre in the 17C.
The château, which is built of white Caen stone, is in two very distinct parts: the left wing from the late 16C, and the central building and right wing dating from the 18C. The plain classical façade of this later addition is ornamented with a pediment bearing the arms of the Mirvilles who built the castle and whose descendants still own it.
The collections include Oriental porcelain and wall hangings, mementoes of the kings of France (Sèvres biscuit medallions), furniture and Fragonard lithographs.
Return to the courtyard and turn right for the **cathedral★**, a magnificent avenue, set a little apart in the park, where the branches of seven rows of beech trees meet overhead.

★ MORTAGNE-AU-PERCHE   Pop 5 200

Michelin map 60 folds 4, 5 or 231 fold 45 – Local map p 104 – Facilities

The former capital of the Perche Region stands on a mound overlooking a green and valleyed landscape, the home of the Percheron horse.
The best view of Mortagne, its brown tiled roofs attractively grouped together, is as you approach from the north along the D 930. The local speciality is black pudding.

SIGHTS

Public Gardens (Jardin public). – These gardens are well laid out with pretty flower beds and are perfectly situated looking out over the undulating hills of the Perche countryside.

⏱ **Notre-Dame Church (Église).** – The church was erected from 1494 to 1535 and is an example of the Flamboyant and early Renaissance styles being combined in one building with a resulting loss of unity on the outside.
Magnificent 18C **woodwork★** surrounds the apsidal altar. This, the altarpiece, two panels from the altar surrounds rising to above the aisles, the choir stalls and pulpit, all come from the Valdieu Carthusian Monastery which was built, and of which a few traces remain, in the nearby Réno Forest. A stained glass window in the third chapel in the north aisle evokes the role of the Mortagnais in the colonisation of 17C Canada (*details p 87*).

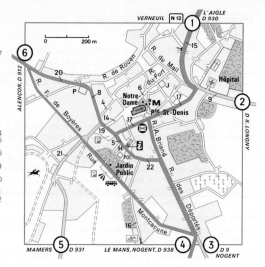

*The maps and plans
are orientated
with north at the top.*

Hospice (Hôpital). – There remain a delightful 16C cloister with panelled vaulting and an 18C chapel of the former Convent of St Clare.

St Denis Gate (Porte St-Denis). – The gate is the only sizeable piece of the fortifications still standing. The original 15C arch was crowned by a two storey building in the 16C. Inside, the **Perche Museum** exhibits archaeological remains and illustrates the history of the Perche Region.

House of the Perche Counts (Maison des comtes du Perche) (M). – This 17C building stands on the site of a former manor house.

Alain Museum (Musée). – The French philosopher Alain, whose real name was Émile Chartier, was born in Mortagne in 1868. His memory is evoked by photos, manuscripts, correspondance and personal belongings. His study is reconstituted on the second floor such as it was in his Vésinet house where he died in 1951. The armchair and walking stick recall the difficult years when he suffered with rheumatism.

EXCURSION

Perche and La Trappe Forests. – *Round tour of 51km - 32 miles – about 1 1/2 hours – Leave Mortagne by ① N 12; turn right after 11km - 7 miles into the D 290.*
Beech, oak and pine trees are to be found in these forest areas.

Autheuil. – Pop 117. The Romanesque church has a very purely styled apse. Inside, the arches of the nave and the capitals surmounting the pillars at the transept crossing are remarkable. Note, also, the 16C statue of St Leonard.

Turn round and continue along the D 290 to Tourouvre.

Tourouvre. – Pop 1 627. The **church** still has its 15C stalls and, more importantly, above the altar a 15C **canvas★**, *The Adoration of the Magi,* which has been incorporated in the 17C altarpiece.
Two stained glass windows relate the comings and goings of local families at the time when Quebec was founded.

Turn right after the church.

The road, at the top of a steep climb, enters the **Perche Forest.** After 2km - 1 mile you come to the clearly marked Étoile du Perche crossroads, a relic of the days when the forest was used for hunting.
Continue straight ahead. At the beginning of the Avre Valley you will notice a series of small lakes in one of which stands reflected the white Château des Étangs surrounded by dark pine trees.
After Bresolettes, the road runs into **La Trappe Forest.**

Turn right at the crossroads with the D 930.

The Chaumont pond is visible through the trees.

La Trappe Abbey (Abbaye). – The abbey, founded in 1140 by monks who came from the Abbey of Breuil-Benoît, stands alone in a forest with many pools. It was here that the strict reform of La Trappe, which was the origin of the present Order of the Cistercians, was brought about under the leadership of the Abbot de Rancé in the 17C. There is an audiovisual presentation on the life of the monks.

Return to the D 930 and back to Mortagne.

*The **Michelin Sectional Map Series (1:200 000)** covers the whole of France.*

When choosing your lunchtime or overnight stop use the above maps as all towns listed in the Red Guide are underlined in red.

When driving into or through a town use the map as it also indicates all places with a town plan in the Red Guide. Common reference numbers make the transfer from map to plan easier.

MORTEMER Abbey

Michelin map 55 fold 8 or 231 fold 24 – 4km – 2 1/2 miles south of Lyons-la-Forêt – Local map p 97

In the hollow of a valley and surrounded by forest stand the ruins of the 12 and 13C Cistercian abbey. Its church was 90m - 295 feet long and 42 metres - 138 feet wide. Of the former chapter house only the entrance remains with its two pointed arch bays and dormitory windows above. Under the conventual building reconstructed in the 17C a **museum** has been installed. It is concerned with monastic life and evokes the stories and legends connected with the abbey. In the cellars wax figures and effective sound and lighting effects create an atmosphere of magic and mystery. Notice a 14C stone Virgin at the end of one of the corridors. In the furnished **domestic quarters** on the 1st floor stands a 19C fireplace and a table with inlaid work lined with ebeny and ivory. Notice the 15C parchment antiphonary (a collection of liturgical verse), in colour and protected by a studded leather cover. On the outside the 15C **dovecot**, partially rebuilt in the 17C, was once a prison. A small train of wagons takes visitors around the buildings and pond where deer, poneys and birds roam free.

NEUFCHÂTEL-EN-BRAY   Pop 5 823

Michelin map 52 fold 15 or 231 fold 12 – Local map p 48 – See town plan in current Michelin Red Guide France

Neufchâtel, former capital of the Bray Region, is the home of the *bondon* which first brought fame to this part of Normandy as a cheese region.
The well known *Petit Suisse*, a sort of light creamy cheese, is also made here.

A Famous Cheese. – Neufchâtel cheese has its own *appellation d'origine*, i.e. the whole production process is carried out locally. Essentially a farm cheese, it can be presented in various shapes and sizes.

Notre Dame Church (Église). – The slate-covered belfry-porch houses three bells and has a 15C door. The early 16C nave contains Renaissance capitals. The aisles are lit by eight windows on which are depicted local saints. In the 13C chancel round columns hold up the pointed vaultings and a crowned Virgin in gilt wood stands by the entrance.

J.B. Mathon - A. Durand Museum (Musée). – The museum is devoted to Bray arts and traditions and to the art of iron-working (wrought iron). In the garden there is a 1746 cider mill and 1837 press, typical of the region.

EXCURSIONS

The Bray Region. – *Round tour of 49km - 31 miles – about 1 1/2 hours. Description p 47.*

Round tour of 63km - 39 miles. – *about 2 hours. Leave Neufchâtel northwards by the N 28, then the N 29.*

Aumale. – Pop 3 023. Aumale, which in the 17C belonged to the Duke of Maine, passed by marriage into the Orléans family. The title of Duke of Aumale was given to the fifth son of Louis-Philippe, donor of Chantilly. Today Aumale is an important dairy farming centre.

St-Pierre and St-Paul Church exhibits both Flamboyant and Renaissance styles. The portal on the south side, attributed to Jean Goujon, has been damaged. Inside, note the storiated keystones of the arches, particularly those of the chancel and the Lady Chapel. 16C stained glass window in St Joseph's Chapel.

Return towards Neufchâtel by the N 29, soon after turn right into the D 920.

Foucarmont. – Pop 954. This concrete **church** rebuilt in 1959-64 has a squat silhouette. However the stained glass windows and the precious stones encrusted in the walls lighten this somewhat casemated edifice. The interior consists of a vast nave, a baptistery and a chancel which is illuminated by a glass dome. The stained glass windows, with their irregular shape and size and their rich warm colours are very effective.

The N 28 leads back to Neufchâtel.

NOGENT-LE-ROTROU   Pop 13 209

Michelin map 60 fold 15 or 232 fold 12

On the banks of the Huisne River, dominated by its castle, Nogent-le-Rotrou is the capital of the Perche Region. Its agricultural products are poultry and cider, and Percheron horses are also raised. It is also an important slaughtering centre which serves the Chartres and Paris Region as well as Germany (6 000 tons).
The orchards and materials (especially muslin) of yesteryear have been succeeded by electrical components, radio technology, car heaters and pharmaceutical laboratories. The old town stretches along the N 23 at the foot of St-Jean Hill. Settled on plains along the Huisne is the new town.
The Gallo-Roman town became from 925 to 1226 a powerful fief of the Rotrou family, counts of Perche, who gave the town its name (Nogent from the Gallic word for "new market": *novio-magos*). Nogent was burned in 1449 at Charles VII's command to prevent the English from capturing it and using it as a base for operations. The town was rebuilt soon after which explains why many of the buildings are in the Flamboyant or Renaissance style.

NOGENT-LE-ROTROU

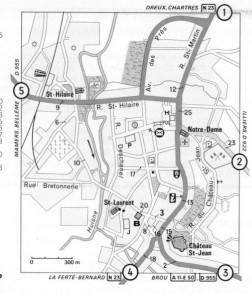

To find a hotel, restaurant, garage or car dealer look in the current **Michelin Guide France**

Famous Locals. – Rémi Belleau (1528-77) possessed one of the seven "stars", as a member of the Pléiade to which Pierre de Ronsard, Joachim du Bellay and Jean Antoine de Baïf also belonged. Belleau was a poet of nature writing pastoral odes, sonnets and amorous verse *(Les Bergeries);* in another of his works *Les Amours et Nouveaux Échanges des Pierres Précieuses* he wrote on exotic stones and their secret virtues. He gained the patronage of Charles IX and Henry III. He was also tutor and counsellor to the powerful Catholic Guise family.

In 1624 Henri II of Condé sold the castle and domain of Nogent to Sully, Henri IV's Minister of France whose family kept it until the Revolution. Sully (1560-1641) who also possessed Rosny, Sully, La Chapelle-d'Angillon, Henrichemont and Villebon collected the rents of these domains as well as those of the Church of St-Benoît-sur-Loire. He administered strictly the revenues of the domain and encouraged agriculture and stock raising.

SIGHTS

St-Jean Castle (Château). – *Access by Rue du Château St-Jean which offers glimpses of Nogent and the Huisne Valley.*

On the outside a path leads rounds the enceinte. The walls and massive towers of this impressive castle stand on a rocky spur. Further protection against attacks is assured by a wall and moat. The rounded enceinte forms two terraces separated by a wall.

The Rotrou family, counts of Perche, lived in the massive rectangular keep 35m - 115ft high (note its unusual buttresses) lightened in the 13C by double openings. In the 12-13C the enceinte was marked out by towers. The gatehouse is flanked by machicolated towers with arrow slits. The whiteness makes a striking contrast with the rest of the greyish stone. Above the entrance is a 15C terracotta medallion of the Italian school. From the courtyard is a beautiful view of the Huisne Valley and the town.

Perche Museum (Musée). – Housed in the castle the museum presents objects pertaining to the region: 15C armour, a reconstituted Perche interior, and art objects.

Notre-Dame Church (Église). – The 13-14C church, the former chapel of the Hôtel-Dieu, has been greatly restored. In the north aisle is a crib (16-17C) with painted terracotta figures. Note the sculptured keystones of the chancel vaults and the organ (1643).

Hôtel-Dieu. – *Sully's tomb can be seen. Enter at 3 Rue Gouverneur, after the church. Walk up a few steps and after the telephone booth turn left to cross the ground floor of the hospital wing. The tomb is in a small yard on the other side.*

Near the Church of Notre-Dame, a domed hexagonal oratory, with a Classical doorway whose façade carries Sully's coat of arms, houses Sully's **tomb**. Sully, a Protestant, did not want to be buried in the church. Thus he had this small mausoleum constructed. Barthélemy Baudin a sculptor from Chartres was commissioned in 1642. Sully is represented beside his wife Rachel de Cochefilet (whose statue, in comparison, is less expressive) in ceremonial dress. The slightly inclined head shows a great deal of expression reminding us of the great man he was.

Bailiff's House (Maison du Bailli) (B). – *47 Rue St-Laurent.*
This handsome 16C *hôtel* was built by Pierre Durand the Bailiff of St Denis Abbey and his wife Blanche Février. Note the finely carved dormer windows.

Rue Bourg-le-Comte (3). – Nos 2, 3, 4 are worthy of interest. No 2 is a 13C construction with tower, no 3 a Renaissance house with mullioned windows and No 4 is 16C. No 2 can best be seen from Rue des Poupardières.

St-Laurent Church (Église). – Located in the square this Flamboyant style church is linked to the house of the Father of St Denis Abbey by an arch. Inside, right of the chancel, is an Entombment (late 15C) – eight very expressive figures surround Christ.

St-Hilaire Church (Église). – 13-16C. On the shady banks of the Huisne this church with its 16C square tower possesses a rather original polygonal chancel (13C) copied from the Holy Sepulchre in Jerusalem. Above the bays are two attractive oculi.

NONANCOURT

Michelin map **60** folds 6, 7 or **231** north of fold 47

Like Verneuil and Tillières, Nonancourt was a Norman frontier fortress, on the Avre defence line facing France. Built in 1112 by Henri I, its rôle was to protect the Duchy of Normandy against the Capetians.

The Place Aristide Briand boasts several half-timbered houses typical of the region and a fine corbelled house stands on the corner of the main street.

St-Martin Church (Église). – A Flamboyant construction built in 1511, its belfry dates from 1204. The fine stained glass in the tall windows of the nave (16C) recount the Holy Week, the Passion and the Ascension of Christ. The Renaissance organ is particularly interesting. Notice the 15C statue of St-Anne in the north aisle above the font and a 14C Madonna and Child in the Lady Chapel.

St-Lubin Church (Église). – At St-Lubin-des-Joncherets.

Rebuilt in the 16C in Flamboyant style, the church has a Renaissance façade. The nave has panelled vaulting and is flanked by aisles with lierne and tierceron vaulting and Renaissance medallions. The font is 17C and decorated with the Nativity scene. Notice the fine marble statue by Coustou in the south aisle.

ORBEC

Michelin map **54** fold 18 or **231** fold 32 – Facilities

Orbec, a small and lively town, goes back over the centuries as can be seen from the commercial Rue Grande, where there are still some old houses whose half-timbered structure has been restored. It stands close to the source of the Orbiquet in one of the pleasantest valleys in the Auge.

Notre-Dame Church (Église). – The Church of Our Lady is flanked by a massive tower of which the base was built in the 15C and the upper part at the end of 16C.

The four 16C windows have been twice restored – in the 19C and since the Second World War. A small 17C carved wood statue of St Rock stands in the south aisle. In the chancel are a statue of the Virgin also of carved wood and also 17C, and a 14C tombstone engraved with the effigy of Dame Juliane Chardonnel.

Municipal Museum (Musée). – The museum is located in a beautiful 16C timber-framed house built for a rich merchant and bearing the name **Vieux Manoir**★. Carved figures decorate the walls which present a pleasant blend of tile fragments, flint and stone triangles. Displays include local history, popular arts and traditions, archaeology, ceramics (milk jugs, hot water bottles, pitchers), paintings by local artists, household objects...

EXCURSION

Spring of the Orbiquet (Source de l'Orbiquet). – 4.5km - 3 miles. Leave Orbec by the Vimoutiers road. Then take the D 130 and the D 130^A.

Go straight on without crossing over the Orbiquet and keep along the pleasant road of La Folletière-Abenon on the right bank of the river. Leave the car just before a bridge and take the path leading to the spring, in a picturesque setting.

The PERCHE

Michelin map **60** folds 4, 5, 6 and 14, 15, 16 or **231** fold 45 and **232** folds 11, 12

The Perche appears, if you have come from a flat area, as an undulating landscape of wooded hills, wide green valleys, and rolling pastures grazed by cattle. There are delightful villages that one discovers on leaving the hedge-bordered main roads.

The Perche has a somewhat complicated geological structure, lying as it does between the Paris Basin and the Armorican Massif. A predominance of non-porous soils and a damp climate produced perfect conditions for a dense vegetation of woods on the primary limestone, pastures and fertile arable crops on the secondary marls and clay. The Normandy Perche has, therefore, evolved with its rich grasslands as a stock breeding area and particularly as the cradle of the Percheron (p 14).

The Normandy Perche, to the north, may be distinguished from the Perche-Gouët or Lower Perche (Bas Perche), to the south (See Michelin Green Guide Châteaux of the Loire).

★ THE NORMANDY PERCHE

For those arriving from the Ile-de-France, after crossing the flat, monotonous Beauce, the Normandy Perche appears as a rugged, yet picturesque region of wooded hillsides, broad green valleys, rolling pastures, and charming villages discovered from roads which wind through the open countryside.

The Manor Houses. – While Auge manors (p 37) appear as welcoming country houses, those in the Normandy Perche emerge as small castles, standing a short distance from the road, built of stone and more or less fortified. Although most of these late 15 or early 16C lordly houses have long since been converted to farmhouses, they have retained such defensive features as towers, turrets and watch towers. But these towers, elegant turrets and the delicate carved ornaments decorating many façades have nothing to do with military architecture.

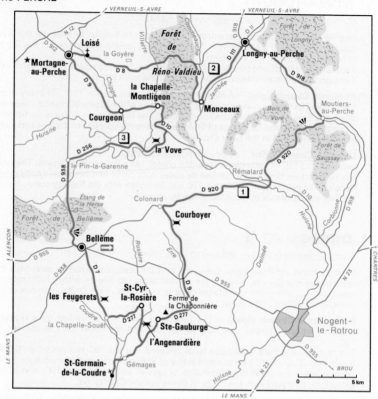

① FROM BELLÊME TO LONGNY-AU-PERCHE

68km - 43 miles – about 2 hours – Local map above

Bellême. – *Description p 43.*

Leave Bellême to the south on the D 7.

The drive begins through open landscape. The occasional outline of a tower can be seen on the horizon.

ⓥ **Feugerets Château.** – A harmonious group of buildings – two square pavilions with a fine balustrade and moat and an elegant 16C main living quarter – stand out against the green setting.

At la Chapelle-Souëf take the D 277 on the left.

St-Cyr-la-Rosière. – Pop 255. The church in this small village has a beautiful Romanesque doorway with a triple archivolt. Inside there is a remarkable 17C polychrome terracotta **Entombment★**, and a 17C painting of the martyrdom of St Sebastian.

Go south towards Theil.

St-Germain-de-la-Coudre. – Pop 714. The church has an 11C crypt containing a beautiful Madonna and Child in stone.

Angenardière Manor House (Manoir de l'Angenardière). – This manor house built in the 15 and 16C, although restored, retains a feudal air. Note the massive towers.

Continue south and turn right at the crossroads towards Gémages.
Turn back at Gémages and take the road to Ste-Gauburge.

ⓥ **Ste-Gauburge.** – The now deconsecrated church has been transformed into a **Museum of Popular Art and Traditions.** Local crafts of yesteryear are brought back to life (shoeing smith, saddler, cartwright, woodcutter, cooper etc.) A slideshow on the region is offered. Outside, a school typical of the turn of the century has been reconstituted together with a country dance. The church, pure Gothic, houses temporary exhibitions of local interest. Behind the church there remain the buildings of a former priory which depended in the 17C on the Royal Abbey of St Denis.

Continue along the D 277. Turn left at the crossroads with the D 9.

On the left as you leave the village to the east, is the **Chaponnière Farm**. A round tower links the living area and a late 16C square pavilion.

Courboyer Manor House. – This delightful manor house built of white stone at the end of the 15C, stands out on a hillside, and is one of the finest in the Perche. Four graceful watch towers on machicolations quarter the main wing. The massive round tower, which greets the visitor below the level of the road, is linked by a heavy ridgepole to the slender octagonal staircase turret which adds considerable elegance to the west front.

At Colonard turn right into the D 920.

The road beyond Rémalard, in a more hilly and green countryside, is very picturesque, crossing the delightful valley in which Moutiers stands and then, bordered with trimly cut hedges and white gates, continues to Longny-au-Perche.

Longny-au-Perche. – *Description p 95.*

② FROM LONGNY TO MORTAGNE-AU-PERCHE

25km - 16 miles – about 1/2 hour – Local map p 104.

Longny-au-Perche. – *Description p 95.*

Leave Longny on the D 111.

The road follows the green Jambée Valley.

Monceaux. – Pop 87. This village stands at the junction of two small valleys.

The D 291 follows the edge of the Réno-Valdieu Forest. After 6km - 4 miles enter the forest on the forest road westwards.

Réno-Valdieu Forest. – The forest has beautiful clumps of very old trees – oaks and beeches more than 260 years old and rising to more than 40m - 131ft. A farm in a restful setting has replaced the former Abbey of Valdieu which gave its name to the forest which in 1789 was joined with that of the comte de Réno.

The undulating D 8 crosses a remarkable landscape of hills, leaving la Coyère Castle on its right as it rises to Mortagne.

Loisé. – The 16C church is flanked by a monumental square tower.

★ **Mortagne-au-Perche.** – *Description p 99.*

③ FROM MORTAGNE-AU-PERCHE TO BELLÊME

35km - 22 miles – about 1 hour – Local map p 104.

★ **Mortagne-au-Perche.** – *Description p 99.*

Leave Mortagne-au-Perche by ③, the D 9.

⊘ **Courgeon.** – Pop 297. The late 11C Romanesque **church** was flanked in the 17C by two aisles and a four storey tower crowned by a stone shingle dome topped by a lantern. The unity of style will be appreciated by admirers of Classical ecclesiastical architecture.

La Chapelle-Montligeon. – Pop 858. This village is dominated by an immense Neo-Gothic basilica with modern stained glass windows. The basilica receives numerous pilgrims. The premises of the printing works (240 employees) around the central courtyard are a reminder of the original community.

There is a good view of the surrounding countryside from the basilica terrace.

Turn right at the crossroads with the D 213, then left on the D 10.

La Vove Manor

⊘ **La Vove Manor House** (Manoir de la Vove). – This large manor house with its military appearance defends the Huisne Valley and is one of the oldest in the Perche region. The roof of the 12C keep is supported by oak beams. The living quarters on three floors are served by a spiral staircase located in an octagonal tower flanked by a round turret. The long wing, built at rightangles, with its pilasters and high windows, was added in the 17C. The detached chapel to the left is reinforced with solid buttresses.

Beyond Le Pin-la-Garenne, the road (D 938) rises towards Bellême Forest *(qv)* where the trees are glorious and the La Herse Pool is extremely pleasant.

As you emerge from the forest there is a good view of Bellême from the road.

Victor Hugo's exile in Jersey and Guernsey
Discover Victor Hugo's favourite haunts
in the Channel Islands
*by using the **Michelin Green Guide Normandy Cotentin**.*

Michelin map 🟦54🟦 fold 19 or 🟦231🟦 fold 21 – Local map p 128

Pont-Audemer, formerly a tanners' town standing at the beginning of the embanked Lower Risle, has specialised in metallurgy, electronics and the paper industry. It still has character with its 17C corbelled half-timbered houses and there are picturesque views of the arms of the river.

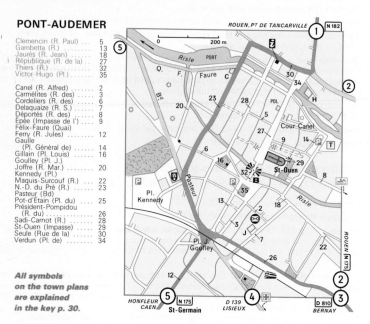

PONT-AUDEMER

Clemencin (R. Paul) ...	5
Gambetta (R.)	13
Jaurès (R. Jean)	18
République (R. de la) ..	27
Thiers (R.)	32
Victor-Hugo (Pl.)	35

Canel (R. Alfred)	2
Carmélites (R. des)	3
Cordeliers (R. des)	6
Delaquaize (R. S.)	7
Déportés (R. des)	8
Épée (Impasse de l') ...	9
Félix-Faure (Quai)	
Ferry (R. Jules)	12
Gaulle	
(Pl. Général de)	14
Gillain (Pl. Louis)	16
Goulley (Pl. J.)	
Joffre (R. Mar.)	20
Kennedy (Pl.)	
Maquis-Surcouf (R.) ...	22
N.-D. du Pré (R.)	23
Pasteur (Bd)	
Pot-d'Étain (Pl. du) ...	25
Président-Pompidou	
(R. du)	26
Sadi-Carnot (R.)	28
St-Ouen (Impasse)	29
Seule (Rue de la)	30
Verdun (Pl. de)	34

*All symbols
on the town plans
are explained
in the key p. 30.*

SIGHTS

St-Ouen Church (Église). – The church was begun in the 11C and enlarged in the 16C but its west face was never completed. The nave, which has a coffered vault, was given a Flamboyant veneer at the end of the 15C. The decoration of the triforium is unusually rich. The lancet arches are ribbed in Flamboyant style.

The aisles have hanging keystones and are lit through magnificent Renaissance **stained glass windows★**, the most interesting of which illustrate: the Legend of St Ouen (second chapel south aisle), the Redemption (first chapel north aisle walking towards the façade), the legend of St Nicholas (second chapel). Notice the 16C font in the first chapel north aisle.

The modern glass in the chancel and above the organ, including the striking reds and greens in a Crucifixion, is all by Max Ingrand.

Old Houses. – Half-timbered houses consist of an oak beam framework completed by a "wall" of daub, a mixture of earth and straw.

Rue de la République (27), **Impasse St-Ouen** (29) along the north side of the church, **Impasse de l'Épée** (9), **Cour Canel** (the name of a former mayor) have kept fine examples.

On the corner of Rue des Cordeliers and Rue Notre-Dame-du-Pré stands an attractive turreted house, half-timbered but resting on a stone ground-floor.

Bridge over the Risle (B). – South of Rue de la République, the bridge affords a charming view of the river lined with picturesque old houses.

Ⓒ **St Germain Church (Église).** – *Access by N 175 to the south.* This very old church, parts of which date back to the 11C, was considerably remodelled in the 14C and truncated in the 19C. The arches of its squat Romanesque tower have been rebuilt in the Gothic style.

PONT-DE-L'ARCHE   Pop 2 456

Michelin map 🟦55🟦 southeast of fold 6 or 🟦231🟦 south of fold 23

This little township is most pleasantly located in the valley on the edge of the Forest of Bord, whose glades of pine trees give it a southern note on a fine summer's day. It takes its name from the first bridge built across the lower Seine, before even Rouen had a bridge.

Ⓒ **Notre-Dame-des-Arts Church (Église).** – The doorway and southern side of this Flamboyant church are much decorated. Inside, the nave is lit by 16 and 17C stained glass windows (restored). The second window of the south aisle represents the town boat hauliers, pulling a boat under an arch of the bridge. The Louis XIII retable of the high altar, the 16C baptismal fonts and the organ are the most remarkable items in the church. Also note the 18C choir stalls and a *Pietà* standing by the first column in the north aisle.

A 14C statue of the Virgin stands on the north side of the nave and a 16C polychrome St Peter on the south side. Notice the 16C canvass depicting the Birth of the Blessed Virgin in the sacristy.

PONT-L'ÉVÊQUE Pop 3 802

Michelin map 54 folds 17, 18 or 231 fold 20 – Local maps pp 39 and 128 – See town plan in the current Michelin Red Guide France

Pont-l'Évêque, famous since the 13C for its cheese, was badly damaged during the Second World War. Only a few old houses remain mostly in Rue St-Michel and Rue de Vaucelles. No 68 in the latter, now the picturesque Aigle d'Or Hotel, was a staging post in the 16C and still has the Norman courtyard of the period.

SIGHTS

St-Michel Church (Église). – A fine Flamboyant structure flanked by a square tower. The modern stained glass windows (1963-64) are by François Chapuis.

Former Convent of the Dominican Sisters of the Island (Ancien Couvent). – The building, at the end of the Place du Palais de Justice, has an interesting wooden balcony.

Hôtel Montpensier. – Louis XIII style. Exhibitions are held during the tourist season.

Hôtel de Brilly. – This 18C mansion, the birthplace of the dramatist Robert de Flers (1872-1927), houses the town hall and the Tourist Information Centre.

Leisure Centre (Centre de Loisirs). – South of the town a 59 ha - 146 acre lake and woodland surroundings offer windsurfing, boating and camping facilities.

EXCURSION

St-André-d'Hébertot. – Pop 244. *8.5km - 5 miles to the northeast. Leave Pont-l'Évêque by the N 175. At St-Benoît, turn right into the D 140 and after the church, take the La Gohaigne road on the left; 200m further on is the access road to St-André-d'Hébertot, on the right.*
This small village is located in a particularly attractive setting. The **château** surrounded by a moat stands in a park with centuries old lime trees. A fine 17C corbelled tower abuts on the graceful 18C façade. The **parish church** has a Romanesque chancel with pointed arch vaulting.

You will find a selection of
touring programmes on pp 6 and 7.

Plan your route with the help of
the map of principal sights on pp 4 and 5.

QUILLEBEUF Pop 1 100

Michelin map 54 fold 9 or 231 fold 21 – Local map p 137

The one time Viking port of Quillebeuf retained its importance until the 19C. It was here that boats waited for high tide to make the crossing. The *Télémaque* sank offshore in 1790 with, reputedly, the crown jewels on board. Today the port is overshadowed by the petroleum installations of Port Jérôme on the far bank of the river and is scarcely in use. The town, however, has kept its seaport atmosphere.

Quillebeuf Point (Pointe de Quillebeuf). – From the lighthouse on the point at the end of the angled promontory separating the disused Vernier Marsh *(qv)* and the Old Port, there is a good view up and down river, across to Port-Jérôme and the Tancarville Bridge.

Notre-Dame-de-Bon-Port Church (Église). – The church, surmounted by a fine but incomplete Romanesque tower, has a 12C door. The nave is purely Romanesque in style with archaic capitals, the upsweeping chancel is 16C.

The RISLE Valley

Michelin map 54 folds 8, 18, 19, 20 or 231 folds 20, 21, 33, 34

The Risle, a river whose waters run cold and swift, rises west of the town of l'Aigle and flows first through the dark Ouche Region.

Ouche Region. – This well-wooded plateau, drained by the Risle but also by the Charentonne *(p 56)*, forms a lonely-looking region in contrast with the flat and predictable landscape south of the Seine. The land is difficult to exploit and industry no longer plays the important rôle it once did. However the presence of **grison,** or red iron agglomerate once used for building, recalls the natural richness of the area and although the small family forges no longer exist, the factories of **Rai, Rugles, Bonneville-sur-Iton, St-Sulpice-sur-Risle,** together with the foundries and pin-manufacturing plants of the Aigle region, employ several thousand workers.

Conches-en-Ouche *(qv)*, although located on the eastern edge of the Ouche Region, is considered as the capital.

The river, augmented by the waters of the Charentonne, goes on to divide the Lieuvin Plateau in the west from the Neubourg Plain and Roumois Plateau in the east *(map p 13)*, before flowing into the Seine above Honfleur. Its total length is 150km - 93 miles.

1 FROM HONFLEUR TO PONT-AUDEMER

26km - 16 miles – about 3/4 hour – Local map p 128

From Honfleur to Pont-Audemer, follow drive 3 p 128 in reverse direction.

2 FROM PONT-AUDEMER TO LA FERRIÈRE-SUR-RISLE

77km - 48 miles – about 4 hours

★ **Pont-Audemer.** – *Description p 106.*

Leave Pont-Audemer by ②, the D 130.

From Pont-Audemer the road follows the Risle Valley except for a short section in the Bec-Hellouin Valley.

Corneville-sur-Risle. – Pop 1 068. The **carillon** at the Hôtel des Cloches was instituted following the runaway success of a 19C operetta, *Les Cloches de Corneville.*

Appeville-Annebault. – Pop 725. The large church was rebuilt in the 16C, conserving the 14C chancel, when the Governor of Normandy laid plans to make the river navigable up to this point. Inside, note the keystones in the nave and the fine collection of Brothers of Charity staffs.

Montfort-sur-Risle. – Pop 885. The village lies close to the rolling Montfort Forest.

★★ **Le Bec-Hellouin.** – *Description p 41.*

Brionne. – *Description p 48.*

The sugar refining factory of Nassandres stands by the road leading out of la Rivière-Thibouville.

Beaumontel. – Pop 763. The belfry on the well sited church is 16C.

Beaumont-le-Roger. – Pop 2 738. The ruins of the former 13C Trinity Priory, with its impressive buttresses visible from the road, stand on a terrace. Access is by a ramp leading under a porch.
St Nicolas' Church, built in the 14 and 16C, has been restored following war damage. Modern stained glass windows supplement those of the 15 and 16C.

Drive south towards Grosley-sur-Risle.

The road runs alongside Grosley Lake (rowing and fishing facilities). Thereafter it becomes narrow and winding.

★ **Le Val Gallerand.** – Superb old Norman farm buildings in a woodland setting.

Continue south and turn right at the crossroads. Turn right again onto the D 35.

La Ferrière-sur-Risle. – Pop 309. The small village has a remodelled 13 and 14C church. Inside note a large 17C oak altarpiece with gilt carvings. The centrepiece is a Descent from the Cross by a pupil of Leonardo de Vinci. There is an interesting collection of statues: a Virgin and Child (14C), St Anne in polychrome stone (16C), a St Michael (17C) and a polychrome wooden *Pietà*. The picturesque village square is completed by a number of old houses and a restored 14C covered market.

3km - 2 miles west on the D 35, **Risle Valley Park** has plenty to offer: train, slides, swings, crazy-golf, a street in the "wild west" etc.

★ ROBERT THE DEVIL'S CASTLE (CHÂTEAU DE ROBERT LE DIABLE)

Michelin map **55** fold 6 or **231** fold 22 – Local map p 129

Robert the Devil's Castle is a popular site in the Seine Valley near Rouen with a fine view of the river.
Robert the Devil, who by tradition built the fortress, is a purely fictitious character vaguely inspired by Robert the Magnificent, father of William the Conqueror. In fact the castle was the work of the early dukes of Normandy and destroyed by John Lackland in 1204. Rebuilt by Philippe-Auguste, King of France, it was probably destroyed again by the French in the 15C to prevent its falling into the hands of the English.

Viking Museum (Musée des Vikings). – Beyond the drawbridge in the courtyard stands the reconstruction of a *drakkar* (a Viking boat). 21.4m - 70 feet long and 5.5m - 18 feet wide, the vessel could carry 40 men. A gallery of wax figures retracing the Norman epic has been laid out in the basement.
Two towers may be visited, the Bourgtheroulde Tower with scale model of the castle as it was in 1418, and the Rouen Tower (wax figures evoking the life of William the Conqueror). From the top of the latter there is a magnificent **panorama★** over the bend in the Seine and Roumare Forest.

Join us in our never endling task of keeping up to date.

Send us your comments and suggestions, please.

**Michelin Tyre Public Limited Company
Tourism Department
Davy House – Lyon Road – HARROW – Middlesex HA1 2DQ**

Michelin map 55 fold 6 or 231 folds 22, 23 – Local maps pp 127 and 129 – See town plans in the current Michelin Red Guide France

Rouen, capital of Upper Normandy, numbers approximately 400 000 inhabitants in twenty-two communes if one includes the surrounding built-up areas. The Museum Town, burnt in 1940 and bombed in 1944, has since rebuilt and restored its famous monuments. Visitors flock to see the remarkable old town and witness the evolution of architectural styles over the centuries.

The Site. – The town has been developing since the Roman Rotomagus was established at the first point on the river at which a bridge could be built. The site is in many ways similar to that of Paris, being at the start of a bend protected by encircling hills and where valleys provide access to the hinterland; it is also above the floodwater mark and provides easy access to this stretch of the river where there are a number of islands.

The hills surrounding Rouen, however, are higher and therefore afford better views looking down on the city *(p 119).*

HISTORICAL NOTES

Rollo the Forerunner. – After the St-Clair-sur-Epte Pact *(p 17),* Rollo was baptised at Rouen, the capital of the new Duchy, and took the name Robert. This administrator proved himself to be a far-sighted planner: he narrowed and deepened the river bed, built up unused marshlands, linked the downstream islands to the mainland and reinforced the banks with quays. His constructions lasted until the 19C, unrivalled for their efficiency.

The Goddons. – Rouen was hard hit during the Hundred Years War: in 1418 Henry V besieged the town which capitulated, famine stricken, after six months. Alain Blanchard, who was the heart and soul of the resistance, was captured and swiftly hanged.

Revolts and plots followed against the Goddons – the nickname for the English derived from their common swear word "God damned". Terror reigned until hope was reborn in the hearts of the Normans by the exploits of Joan of Arc and the coronation of Charles VII.

But Joan was taken prisoner at Compiègne by the Burgundians. The English threatened the Duke of Burgundy with economic sanctions and through the mediation of Cauchon, Bishop of Beauvais, Joan was handed over against a payment of 10 000 gold ducats. On Christmas Day, 1430, she was imprisoned in one of the towers – "the Tower of the Fields" – in the castle of Philippe-Auguste. The Captain of Rouen, Lord Warwick, organised widespread military presence in the city in order to deter all attempts at a popular uprising.

Meanwhile Joan was closely guarded night and day.

The Trial of Joan of Arc. – Bishop Cauchon promised "a fair trial" and opened the first session on 21 February 1431. An amazing dialogue began between Joan and her judges: bold but "without pride or concern for herself, thinking only of God, her mission and the King", the Maid replied to all the tricks and subtleties of the churchmen and lawyers.

The questioning went on for three months. The charge declared Joan to be "heretical and schismatic". On 24 May, in the cemetery of the Abbey of St Ouen, tied to a scaffold, Joan was pressed to recant; she finally gave way, was granted her life but condemned to life imprisonment.

The English were furious and threatened the judges; Cauchon replied "We will get her yet." On Trinity Sunday the guards took away Joan's woman's clothes which she had promised to wear, and gave her men's clothing instead. At noon "for the necessities of the body, she was constrained to go out and indulge in the said habit". She was thus said to have broken her promise and was condemned to the stake. On 30 May she was burned alive in the Place du Vieux Marché. Her heart, not consumed by the fire, was thrown in the Seine. The English, afraid, murmured that they were lost as they had burned a saint.

In 1449 Charles VII entered Rouen; in 1456 Joan was rehabilitated and in 1920 she was canonised and made Patron Saint of France.

The Golden Century. – The period situated between the French reconquest and the Wars of Religion was a golden century for all Normandy and particularly for the city of Rouen. Cardinal d'Amboise *(see under Gaillon, p 78),* Archbishop and patron, introduced the Renaissance style to the city. Local dignitaries began to build sumptuous stone mansions and carved woodwork adorned the façade of burgesses' houses. The Law Courts built by Louis XII for the Exchequer were transformed into a parliament by François I.

Rouen businessmen in cooperation with Dieppe navigators *(p 61)* traded all the main maritime routes: the coat of arms of the powerful merchant haberdashers' guild showed three ships built and masted of gold and the device "O sun, we will follow you to the ends of the earth".

The former linen weaving town now wove silk and cloth of silver and gold. In 1550 the first Colonial Exhibition was mounted in the town.

Industrial Upsurge. – Early in the 18C a rich merchant unable to sell his stock of cotton, used up to then to make candlewick, spun and wove the fibre into a cloth that had an immediate success: dyed indigo blue and known as *Rouennerie,* it outstripped all others. In 1730 came the first velveteen and twill.

Dyeing made equal progress, keeping pace with textile production, transformed by mechanisation. Finishing, bleaching and textile printing followed. Some 26 000 tonnes of material were treated a year, and a multitude of different items were manufactured from the same cloth.

Industrialisation called for changes in the port: in the 19C docks were constructed, the railway brought to the harbour; the old city on the right bank spread to the tributary valleys and hillsides.

The Modern City. – Industrial expansion accelerated at the beginning of the 20C and Rouen's urban development increased considerably with the creation of industries associated with its port.

The Second World War destroyed the old quarter between the Seine and the cathedral, razed the bridges and partially destroyed the industrial zone on the left bank. The people of Rouen rebuilt their city, removing damaged factories to industrial zones and converting the centre of the left bank into a residential area with a population nearly equal to that of the right bank, and an administrative centre with a semicircular Préfecture (1966) flanked by a 80m - 262ft tower.

Lacroix Island, formerly industrial, has become residential with parks and open spaces which include sports grounds, a skating rink, a swimming pool and a pleasure boat harbour.

The right bank has remained the centre of modern Rouen and has rediscovered its business and tourist character.

THE PORT

Rouen is France's fifth busiest port after Marseilles, Le Havre, Dunkerque and Nantes-St-Nazaire, and the country's third most important river port. It has a considerable advantage in being located between Paris and the sea.

ROUEN

*For a pleasant stroll
in a town
look for the
pedestrian streets
indicated
on the town plans.*

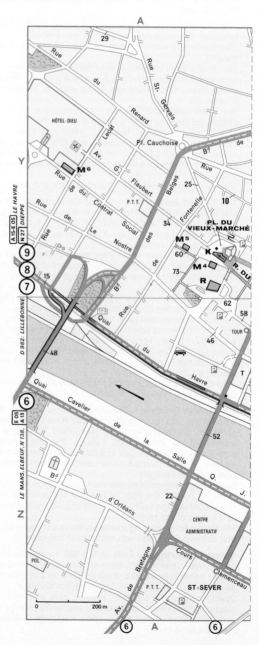

Due to improved means of access – Rouen can accommodate 140 000 tonne ships and container carriers loading 1 500-2 000 containers – modernisation of port équipment and facilities (cranes, gantries...), and the building of silos and new terminals, the growth of the port has been constant.

Each year Rouen receives around 3 500 ships flying the flags of sixty different countries. It is the country's number one port for exports, especially agricultural produce, and stands in third place for container traffic. Wood, pulp and paper are unloaded for the nearby presses and the industries in or near the port are the cause of traffic as diversified as phosphates, sulphur, chemical products, fertilizers, coal and by-products of refined oil.

The port stretches from Rouen to Tancarville north of the Seine and from Rouen to Honfleur on the south side.

Right Bank Quays. – The quays north of the river stretching to Val-de-la-Haye (12km - 7 1/2 miles west) are equipped with facilities for receiving and processing (wood, chemical products...), a winestore, semolina factory, three silos and a container terminal.

Left Bank Quays. – South of the river from Rouen to Moulineaux stand the cereal processing plant of the Elie peninsula with its three silos, the Rouen-Quevilly container terminal, wood and paper terminals, a shipyard and so on. Upstream industrialisation has reached Oissel.

Industries include chemical processing, metallurgy, mechanical engineering and paper processing.

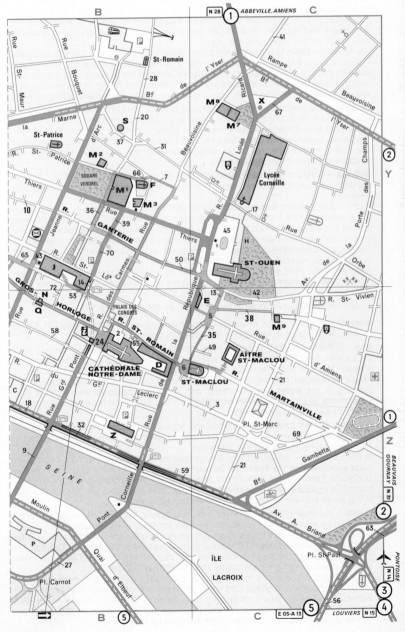

★★★ NOTRE-DAME CATHEDRAL (BZ) *time: 1 1/2 hours*

The cathedral of Rouen is one of the most beautiful examples of French Gothic architecture. Construction began in the 12C, but after a devastating fire in 1200 it was reconstructed in the 13C. In the 15C the cathedral took on its final appearance under the master builder Guillaume Pontifs and in the 16C under Roulland le Roux. In the 19C it was crowned with the present cast iron spire. Badly damaged during the Second World War, the cathedral conducts services but the enormous restoration work started over forty years ago continues.

Exterior. – The attraction of Rouen Cathedral lies in its infinite variety including an immense façade bristling with openwork pinnacles and framed by two totally different towers: the St Romanus Tower on the left and the Butter Tower (Tour de Beurre) on the right.

West façade. – This façade was used in a series of paintings by Monet to study the effects of lighting at different times of the day on the same subject. The **St John** (left) and **St Stephen** (right) doorways have each a delicately carved semicircular arch crowned by a small colonnade: note the workmanship of the foliage scrolls which surround the door leaves. The two tympana are 13C, that of St Stephen (badly damaged) shows Christ Enthroned and the Stoning of St Stephen; that of St John shows the Martyrdom of St John the Baptist and the Feast of Herod. The latticework window gallery (1370-1420) above the two portals is in the Flamboyant style; the long and narrow niches decorated with statues and topped by openwork gables are 14 and 15C.

The **central doorway** (early 16C) was done by Roulland le Roux; it is flanked by two powerful pyramid buttresses reinforcing the façade whose embrasures are decorated with statues of the Prophets and Apostles and were formerly topped by a series of archbishops. The tympanum is decorated with a Tree of Jesse, destroyed by the Huguenots and restored in 1626. An immense elegant gable cut along a superb latticework gallery surmounts the portal.

The **St Romanus Tower,** to the left, is the oldest tower (12C), and in the early Gothic style. The sumptuous **Butter Tower** (Tour de Beurre) was thus named in the 17C when it was believed that it had been paid for by dispensations granted to those who did not wish to fast during Lent but on the contrary drink milk and eat butter. It never received a spire but was surmounted by an octagonal crown. Inside is a carillon of fifty-six bells.

South side. – The **central lantern tower** with its spire is the tallest in France (151m - 495ft) and Rouen's glory. Built in the 13C it was raised in the 16C. The present spire, in cast iron, replaced in 1876 the wooden spire covered in gilded lead which had been built in 1544.

The **Calende Doorway** which opens between two 13C square towers is a 14C masterpiece. The lower embrasures, its most original feature, are decorated with four leaf medallions inspired by French ivories.

North side. – On skirting the **Albane Court** closed to the east by the cloister gallery, one can see the north side, the lantern tower and spire and the upper section of the Booksellers' transept.

A little further on the **Booksellers' Court** (Cour des Libraires) is closed by a magnificent stone gateway in the Flamboyant style. At the end of the court is the **Booksellers' Doorway** (Portail des Libraires) which opens on to the north side aisle. It is topped by two tall gables between which are a large rose window and a clerestory with a fine balustrade. The sculpted decoration is exquisite, the lower embrasures are ornamented with medallions representing beasts of the Middle Ages.

The tympanum (end of the 13C) is decorated by a Last Judgment with, in the lower register, the Resurrection of the Dead and, in the upper register, the Separation of the Saved and the Damned depicted in terrifying detail.

Return to the parvis to enter the cathedral by the main door.

Interior. – An impression of simplicity and harmony reigns in this cathedral in spite of the differences of style found in the nave and chancel.

Nave. – In the early Gothic style, the nave is made up of eleven bays four storeys high: tall arcades, false tribunes, triforium and clerestory, the capitals are crocketed and leaf shaped. The side aisles are very high because the tribunes were to appear at mid-height, as is shown by the curiously clustered small columns. Dominating the transept crossing is the **lantern tower** (1) rising with incredible boldness 51m - 167ft from pavement to keystone on enormous piles which in groups of no fewer than 27 columns sweep upward in a simple thrust.

Transept. – On the back of the Calende and Booksellers' doorways are attractive 14C carvings, the decoration is the same for the two gables: four large windows topped by crocketed gables frame and line the walls.

In the north arm – embellished by a large rose window restored with its 14C stained glass windows – is the **Booksellers' Stairway★** (Escalier de la Librairie) (2), the work of Guillaume Pontifs; from a charming little balcony – where there is a door elegantly topped by a gable – rise the two flights of the staircase (the first is 15C, the second 18C). In the south arm are lovely 14 and 16C stained glass windows.

Chancel. – The choir of finest 13C style is of great beauty. It is the most noble part of the cathedral by reason of its simple lines and the lightness of its construction.

It presents a level of very high and pointed arcades, a triforium and a clerestory. Three of them are decorated with 15C stained glass representing the scene at Calvary. The pillars supporting the arcades have massive circular capitals (13C) with charming stylised plants which are crowned by abaci held by carved heads.

The high altar is made of a marble slab from the Valle d'Aosta, and dominated by a Christ (3) by Clodion in gilded lead (18C). On either side of the altar are two angels in adoration by Caffiéri which come from the Church of St Vincent destroyed in 1944. Opening off the south arm is the apsidal chapel dedicated to Joan of Arc (4) and embellished with modern stained glass windows by Max Ingrand.

⊘ **Crypt, ambulatory, Lady Chapel.** – The 11C ring-shaped **crypt** preserves its altar and its curb stone well (5m - 16ft deep). On display are fragments of columns, and Roman capitals found during excavations. The heart of Charles V is preserved in a coffer embedded in the east end wall.

The **ambulatory** *(access south arm – exit north)* which is made up of three apsidal chapels (one the Lady Chapel) holds the recumbent figures of Rollo, Richard the Lionheart (late 13C), Henry (second son of Henry II of England) the Young King (13C), and William Longsword, Duke of Normandy and son of Rollo (14C). Also shown are five 13C **stained glass windows★**, the bottom one of which, depicting St Julian the Hospitaller, was presented by the Fishmongers' Guild and inspired Flaubert to write a tale. The fine windows representing the history

NOTRE-DAME CATHEDRAL

0 — 30 m

Lady Chapel
8 / 6 / 7
5
Ambulatory
3
CHANCEL
4
Calende Doorway
1
TRANSEPT
Booksellers' Court
2
NAVE
Archbishop's Palace
St-Romain
Rue des Bonnetiers
Rue du Change
Albane Court
St Romanus Tower
Rue
R. Georges Lanfry
St John Doorway
Central Doorway
St Stephen Doorway
Butter Tower

of Joseph (5) are signed by Clément, a glassmaker from Chartres and then, finally, come those of the Passion and Good Samaritan with their remarkable colours.

The **Lady Chapel** (14C) contains two admirable 16C tombs. To the right the **tomb of the Cardinals of Amboise★★** (6) of the early Renaissance (1515-25) was carved according to drawings by Roulland le Roux. The two cardinals – Georges d'Amboise (left), Minister under Louis XII and Archbishop of Rouen and his nephew, also Georges (right) – are shown kneeling. In the base, the Four Cardinal Virtues (Justice, Strength, Temperance and Prudence) and two of the Theological Virtues (Charity and Faith); the third (Hope) occupies a niche on the left upright; on the right upright is Chastity. The background of the monument is occupied by the Virgin, St John the Baptist, St Romanus and various prelates; the frieze round the top is decorated by Sibyls, Prophets and Apostles. Note the head of Roulland le Roux carved in the right hand corner. On the

left, stuck on the recess of the Gothic tomb of Pierre de Brézé (15C) is the **tomb of Louis de Brézé★** (7), Seneschal of Normandy and husband of Diane of Poitiers, which was built between 1535 and 1544. The design of the monument and the decoration of the lower part are said to be by Jean Goujon. The mausoleum consists of two parts: below, the body of the Seneschal is treated in the pathetic style favoured in the 16C; at the foot of the recumbent figure stands the Virgin, while Diane of Poitiers is portrayed weeping at the head. The upper part of the tomb is irregular in style: the caryatids are extremely fine but the effigy of Louis de Brézé on horseback is too solemn and the rider too small in relation to the size of his mount.

In addition, the chapel possesses 14C stained glass windows representing the Archbishop of Rouen and a fine picture by Philippe de Champaigne, *The Adoration of the Shepherds,* which is framed in a rich altarpiece (8) of 1643.

Tomb of the Cardinals of Amboise, Rouen

★★★ OLD ROUEN

Restoration. – Bristling with spires and bell towers the old city lies along the right bank of the Seine. Originally commercially dependent on the river, it has now become isolated because of the large quays. In spite of the vast destruction it was subjected to in the Second World War this area is today almost entirely restored: the narrow and tortuous streets are reappearing in their original state lined by more than 700 half-timbered houses. These old Rouen houses exemplify half-timbered houses from the Middle Ages to the end of the 18C. Oak, light and easy to work and at one time found in abundance, was chosen as ideal material in which to construct these houses.

Peaking out amidst this harmonious architectural complex are the three jewels of Gothic architecture in Rouen: the Cathedral, the Church of St-Maclou and the Church of St-Ouen.

More than 3km - 2 miles of pedestrian streets are decorated with flowers and fountains.

Half-timbered Houses. – These old houses also found in such towns as Caen, Lisieux, Bayeux, Honfleur are called as such because their external and internal walls were built of timber frames and the spaces between the structural members were filled with brick plaster or

Half-timbered houses at Rouen

wattle and daub. This type of construction was used at a time when the climate was moderate; large quantities of wood, particularly oak, were obtainable and the craftsmen available (quite possible in this area with its long-standing tradition of boatbuilding).

In this binding of beam and plaster there were two types of construction – either the vertical posts extended to the full height of the house or they just reached the first floor. This second system had the upper storeys hanging over the ground floor, protecting the lower part of the house from inclement weather and so reducing the light of day on the streets that they resembled covered passageways.

These houses had a simple interior plan with usually a shop at street level and a kitchen behind. A corridor, running the entire width of the house from the street to the courtyard, terminated in a spiral staircase which provided access to the first floor where there was a large room. The upper storeys held the bedrooms.

The exterior was usually devoid of any decoration until in the second half of the 15C Gothic and Italianate carvings appeared – usually the ground floor posts were carved with images while the other framing elements were enriched with delicate repeating patterns.

TOUR *time: 3 hours*

Cathedral Parvis (Place de la Cathédrale) (BZ). – Opposite the cathedral on the corner of Rue du Petit-Salut stands the former **House of the Exchequer** (Bureau des Finances) (BZ *Tourist Information Centre*), an elegant Renaissance building erected in 1510 by Roulland le Roux.

★★ **Rue St-Romain.** – One of Rouen's most fascinating streets with its beautiful 15 to 18C half-timbered houses and at the end the spire of the church of St-Maclou. Note no 74, a Gothic house with 15C bay windows.

Archbishop's Palace (Archevêché) (BZ D). – *(not open to the public)* Just after the Booksellers' Court stands the 15C palace (altered in the 18C) with its vigorous façade and its almost military-like towers. A gable pierced by the remains of a window in whose opening one can see the outline of the cathedral spire is all that remains of the chapel in which was held the solemn session of the trial of Joan of Arc on 29 May 1431, and where her rehabilitation was proclaimed in 1456. The doorway on Rue Bonnetiers leads to the courtyard where you can view the interior façade of the building.

Cross Rue de la République to reach **Place Barthélemy** bordered with picturesque half-timbered houses where the Church of St-Maclou stands.

★★ **St-Maclou Church (Église)** (CZ). – This beautiful building of Gothic-Flamboyant style is remarkable for its homogeneity. It was built between 1437 and 1517. It is a remarkable fact that in the heyday of the Renaissance style, the purest Gothic was preserved. Only the spire of the belfry is modern.

The west façade, the finest part of this building, is preceded by a large five panelled porch set like a fan. Two of the three doorways, the central one and that on the left, are celebrated for their Renaissance **panels★★**, some of which are attributed to Jean Goujon.

These panels are divided into two parts: the leaf of the door has charming little bronze heads of lions or other animals and designs in semi-relief of pagan inspiration, while the upper panel, which is a little heavy, has a carved medallion. The medallions on the central door represent the Circumcision on the left and the Baptism of Christ on the right; the upper part of the door represents on the left God the Father before the Creation; on the right, God the Father after the Creation.

The "Door of the Fonts" on the left has only one panel. The medallion represents the Good Shepherd entering the pasture from which he has driven out the thieves. This motif is maintained by four statues which seem to represent Samson, David, Moses and Solomon; beautiful figures of men and women outlined in the background represent Sin in the triple guise of Graeco-Roman paganism, Egyptian idolatry and the Muslim faith.

Inside the **organ case★** (1521) is remarkable for its Renaissance woodwork, supported by marble columns which are attributed to Jean Goujon. The **spiral stairs★** (1517), magnificently carved, are from the choir screen.

The chancel, severely damaged by bombing raids on 4 June 1944, has been restored: note the Chapel of Notre-Dame-de-Pitié (left) with its 18C panelling, as well as the Christ and two Angels, elements in the *Glory* adorning the 18C apse.

★ Rue Martainville (CZ). – The street has kept some marvellous 15-18C half-timbered houses. At the corner of the St-Maclou façade is a lovely Renaissance fountain. The north door of the church has attractive panels depicting scenes from the life of the Virgin: on the left the Ark of the Covenant; on the right her death.

★★ St-Maclou Cloister (Aître St-Maclou) (CZ). – *184-186 Rue Martainville.* This 16C agglomeration is one of the last examples of a mediaeval plague cemetery. The half-timbered buildings which surround the yard were built from 1526 to 1533, however the south side was built in 1640 and never served as a charnel house.

The ground floor of these buildings is made up of galleries which were once open – as in a cloister. On the column shafts (formerly door frames) are carved figures (damaged) portraying the Dance of Death; they support a double frieze decorated with macabre motifs: skulls, crossbones, grave diggers' tools, etc.

Above the ground floor the "attic" was used as a charnel house until the 18C when it was transformed into its present state.

These buildings now house the School of Fine Arts (École des Beaux-Arts).

Return to the façade of St-Maclou and turn right.

★ Rue Damiette (CZ 35). – The street is lined by half-timbered houses and offers a nice vista of the central tower of St-Ouen Church. Note on the right the picturesque blind alley of the Hauts-Mariages.

On Place du Lieutenant-Aubert bear left into Rue d'Amiens to the 17C **Hôtel d'Étancourt** (CZ **E**) and admire its façade embellished with large statues.

Return to Place du Lieutenant-Aubert so as to turn left into Rue des Boucheries-St-Quen. Rue Eau-de-Robec is on the right.

Rue Eau-de-Robec (CZ 38). – Old houses, their façades restored, line this street where a little stream flows, recalling the time when the Robec's waters ran alongside the dwellings to which access was by footbridge.

Museum of Education (Musée de l'Éducation) (CZ **M⁹**). – The museum is housed in a fine timber-framed and slate-shingled **residence★** with two corbelled upper floors. The district was once ill-frequented and the house had a regular clientèle of hardened drinkers. It was then known under the name of "The Marriage House" owing to the activities that went on inside.

The museum is a true place of learning with temporary exhibitions such as the history of the Revolution for children, the education of young girls a hundred years ago, child and machine etc. Original documents and a reconstruction of a classroom illustrate the different themes.

In Rue Ruissel, note an attractive 16C house with carved wooden columns and other stone columns decorated with statues.

Return to the Rue des Boucheries St-Ouen.

★★ St-Ouen Church (Église) (CY). – Remarkable for its proportions and the purity of its lines this former abbey church is one of the jewels of French Gothic architecture. The construction which began in 1318 and slackened during the Hundred Years War was terminated in the 15C.

Exterior. – On the south side is the beautiful door of the Ciriers (named after the wax candle merchants who held their market here). The **east end★★** is beautiful with delicate flying buttresses and pinnacles and individually roofed radiating chapels. At the transept crossing the square **central tower★** flanked by small towers rises two tiers before ending decoratively in a ducal coronet. On the façade of the south transept, above the great rose window in the Flamboyant gable, are statues of kings and queens of Judah; below is the strange arching or **Marmousets Door** in which the arching, on one side, rests disconcertingly on false keystones.

Interior. – The nave, of light construction, is above all striking for its magnificent proportions. The organ (19C) is among the largest in France. The choir is perhaps even more beautiful. Above the great arcades, as in the nave, there is a magnificent double clerestory of great delicacy. Higher again rise the great windows, which have once more their 14C stained glass, with the exception of the axial bay which has a modern Crucifixion. The choir is closed off by 18C grilles. The ambulatory is enclosed by absidal chapels which are noteworthy.

Take Rue de l'Hôpital opposite the church.

At the corner of Rue des Carmes stands the attractive Gothic fountain, Crosse fountain (restored) and further on at the corner of Rues Beauvoisine and Ganterie is a handsome half-timbered house.

Continue on Rue Beauvoisine which crosses Rue Thiers, one of Rouen's most commercial and animated streets.

On Rue Beauvoisine note no 55, a carved half-timbered house with courtyard: no 57 is a Renaissance house. Turn to the left on Rue Belfroy, bordered at the beginning by 15-16C half-timbered houses, to reach Place St-Godard.

★ **St-Godard Church (Église)** (BY F). – This late 15C church contains wonderful **stained glass** windows★, in particular a 16C one on the right side showing the Tree of Jesse.
Near it is the window of the Virgin which is made up of six 16C panels. Above the three naves is a 19C plastered wood vaulting pierced with skylights.
Beside the church stand Rouen's two most fascinating museums: the Fine Arts Museum and the Secq des Tournelles Museum *(pp 117 and 118)*.
Cross Rue Thiers, in front of Square Verdrel, into Allée Eugène Delacroix, then turn left into the charming **Rue Ganterie★** (BY) lined by old half-timbered houses.

Turn right into Rue des Carmes and right again into Rue aux Juifs which leads to the Law Courts.

★★ **Law Courts (Palais de Justice)** (BY J). – Built to house the Exchequer of Normandy this splendid 15 and early 16C Renaissance building is said to be the work of Roulland le Roux. Rebuilt in the 19C it was badly damaged in August 1944.
The main court – excavations have revealed a 12C **synagogue** – is flanked by two wings, the **façade★★** (1508-26) of which is exquisite.
The decoration of the façade, which is the most beautiful part of the building, is typical of the Renaissance, infinite care being taken to enrich the ornament at each level – the base is therefore quite plain, but the crest line is a forest of chiselled stone with pinnacles, turrets, gables and flying buttresses above a rich balustrade. The main turret is delicately carved.
The left wing stone staircase leads to the **Prosecutors' Room** (Salle des Procureurs). This large room has a splendid modern panelled ceiling. Leave the room by the door at the end which leads to stairs which will take you to the Place Foch and the monument to the dead.

Cross Rue Jeanne d'Arc and take Rue Rollon.

★ **Place du Vieux-Marché** (AY). – This modern architectural complex made up of a small covered market, church and national monument is the work of Louis Arretche, the architect who was responsible for the restoration of St-Malo. In the Middle Ages the square was the scene of public mockery and executions.

St Joan of Arc Church (Église) (AY K). – The spacious interior, its ceiling reminiscent of a ship's hull, contains superb 16C **stained glass windows★★**. These ancient windows were originally in St Vincent's Church which was destroyed in 1944. The 500m² - 10 764sq ft tapestry of glass is believed to have been done by the workshops of Arnould de Nimègue and Le Prince de Beauvais.
The windows which have been placed at eye level, capture the light of day and thus display exquisite coloration and tonality: for example the Triumph of the Virgin or the Chariot Window. Other windows such as the Childhood of Christ, the Passion, the Crucifixion are illustrated in a wealth of colours which combine with the beauty of the figures, their attitudes and expressions.
A statue of Joan of Arc leans against the church and faces the stake. It announces the beginning of the Remembrance Gallery devoted to Joan of Arc and the history of the square.

National Monument. – This "Cross of the Rehabilitation" *(Croix de la Réhabilitation)*, 20m - 65ft high, stands at the spot where Joan of Arc was burned on 30 May 1431.
North of the stake excavations have uncovered the foundation of the pillory and, to the south, the ruins of the Church of St Saviour (destroyed during the Revolution) and the tribunes belonging to the judges of Joan.

★★ **Rue du Gros-Horloge** (ABYZ). – Connecting Place du Vieux-Marché to the cathedral this picturesque scene is the most evocative of old Rouen. Bristling with tradespeople during the Middle Ages the street was the seat of local government from the 13 to 18C. Once again with its large cobblestones and attractive 15-17C half-timbered houses, Rue du Gros-Horloge has recaptured its original commercial role as a bustling pedestrian street and is nowadays one of the city centre's major tourist attractions.

The Gros-Horloge (BZ N). – This is the most popular monument in Rouen. The clock, formerly placed in the belfry *(p 117)*, was raised to its present location above the arch because in 1527 the people of Rouen wished to

The Gros-Horloge, Rouen

see it better. The hour signs on the face of this single handed clock, made at the same time, are completed by those of the upper "bull's eye", giving the phases of the moon, with weekly signs appearing in the lower opening.

Go under the arch, decorated with a sculptured scene of the Good Shepherd and his flock – an allusion to the lamb of St John the Baptist, who figures in the Rouen coat of arms.

Belfry (Beffroi) (BZ **Q**). – This small tower is topped by a dome which was added in the 18C to replace the one removed by Charles VI in 1382 to punish the citizens of Rouen who organised a revolt, known as la Harelle, against the taxes levied by the Duke of Anjou.

Go up to the belfry by the spiral staircase (1457). Several rooms contain wrought iron work, bronze bells, 16 and 17C clock needles and the movement of the St Vivien clock (15C). Note also the two bells (13C) which sounded the start of the Harelle uprising: on the right the "Rouvel" (not operated since 1903) which was to ring out the alarm (from 1724 it rang the curfew); on the left, the Cache-Ribaud which replaced it (in 1903), it sounds the curfew every night at 9pm. The dome houses the movement of a 14C clock said to be one of the oldest in France by Jehan de Félains.

From the top of the belfry there is a majestic **vista★★** of the city, its port and the surrounding countryside: note just in front Rue du Gros-Horloge, the cathedral and on the left the Church of St-Ouen, the Law Courts, the Joan of Arc Tower and the Church of St-Godard.

Abutting on the belfry is the Renaissance loggia where the Great Clock keeper used to stand as well as a beautiful 18C fountain.

Continue down Rue du Gros-Horloge to the corner of Rue Thouret where the old town hall (1607) stands.

ADDITIONAL SIGHTS

★★ **Fine Arts Museum** (Musée des Beaux Arts) (BY **M**[1]). – The ground floor contains to the right on entering, a room devoted to the Rouen painter Jacques-Émile Blanche (1861-1942), displaying portraits of famous writers of his time: Mauriac, Bergson, André Maurois, Paul Valéry, André Gide and so on.

On the first floor the altarpiece of the Virgin and the Saints (1523) by **Gérard David** is considered to be one of the masterpieces of Flemish primitive painting. Note the delicate finish of the clothes and hair. Admire the works of the 16 and 17C Italian painters Veronese, Guercino and Caravaggio; the Spanish master Velázquez's *Democritus* or *Man with Mappemonde;* the Dutch and Flemish artists Teniers, Van de Velde, Van Goyen and N. Berchem; the 16 and 17C French painters Clouet *(Diana Bathing),* Regnier and particularly the Normans Poussin *(Venus Arming Aeneas)* and Jouvenet. The 18C is represented by the French school (Hubert Robert, Oudry, Fragonard), and also by a fine collection of portraits by the Normans Jean Restout and Deshayes.

A room is devoted entirely to Géricault, who was born in Rouen (1791-1824) and another to *The Justice of Trajan* by Delacroix. The 18C galleries also contain works by David, Ingres *(Portrait of the Beautiful Zélie),* Huet and Corot and portraits by Joseph Court.

The François Depeaux Room (after the name of the donator) has a collection of Impressionist paintings by Monet *(Mist on the Seine),* Sisley, Lebourg, Renoir. Contemporary art follows with works by Marinot, sculpture by Duchamp-Villon including a bust of Baudelaire. The artists Soulages, Viera da Silva and Dufy are also represented.

The second floor is mainly devoted to 17C painting. Works include those by Philippe de Champaigne *(Concert of Angels)* and Mignard *(Portrait of Madame de Maintenon).*

★★ **Ceramics Museum** (Musée de la Céramique) (BY **M**[2]). – Housed in the 17C Hôtel d'Hocqueville, the museum presents the history of Rouen pottery with outstanding faience collections.

Rouen Faience. – The word ceramics covers all aspects of terra cotta (baked clay) whereas faience is a type of ceramic made of compound clay covered with a tin-based enamel. White in colour, faience can be decorated. Two types of earth went into the making of Rouen faience: St Aubin (from the Boos Plateau), clayey and bright red, and earth from Quatre-Mares (between Sotteville and St-Étienne-du-Rouvray), a light, sandy alluvial soil. Mixed in the right proportions, 1/3-2/3 – the result was ground, washed, dried, powdered, sifted and placed in decantation containers. When sufficiently consistant the mixture was placed near an oven to finish evaporating, and then trodden to extract fermentation gases and add the sand needed for a ceramic compound. Finally there were the different processes of shaping, casting, glazing, painting and curing.

Collections. – First we see the works of pioneer Masséot Abaquesne, mid – 16C, which consist of paving flags and portrait vases. Secondly the works of the Edme and Louis Poterat workshop (17C) consist mainly of blue and white ornamental tableware probably of Chinese inspiration. Red made its appearance around 1670 owing to the influence of the Dutch ceramists working in the Poterat shops.

At the beginning of the 18C new factories cropped up and production developed. Polychrome colours began to appear – the Brument salad bowl of 1699 decorated in five colours on blue background. Notice the heavenly sphere by Pierre Chapelle in the room devoted to polychrome decoration. At around the same time motifs began to diversify with the *style rayonnant* – arabesques inspired by embroidery and metalwork – and in the mid 18C came the Rococo style with its amorous pastoral scenes surrounded by elaborate borders composed of flowers, birds and insects.

Examples of other French and foreign faiences on display show the influences undergone by the Rouen "school".

★★Wrought Ironwork Museum (Musée le Secq des Tournelles) (BY M³). – The museum is installed in the former St-Laurent Church, a fine Flamboyant building, and is exceptionally rich (3C to 19C).

The nave and transept contain large items such as balconies, signs, railings etc and in the display cabinets locks, door-knockers and keys. Their evolution can be studied from Gallo-Roman times.

The north aisle includes displays of locks, belts and buckles from the 15 to 19C, together with glass from St-Vincent church (15C Last Judgement), statues and a 17C gilt wooden altar.

The south aisle exhibits a large variety of domestic utensils and tools, such as knives, grills, irons.

The north gallery on the first floor is devoted to accessories such as jewels, clasps, combs, and smoking requisites.

A rare 16-19C collection of professional tools is housed in the south gallery, concerning areas as varied as hairdressing, woodwork, watch-making, gardening and surgery.

Bourgtheroulde Mansion (Hôtel de Bourgtheroulde) (AY R). – *No 15 Place de la Pucelle.* This famous building (pronounced Boortrood) inspired simultaneously by Gothic and the first precepts of the Renaissance, was built in the first half of the 16C by Guillaume le Roux, Counsellor to the Exchequer and Lord Bourgtheroulde.

Stand back a little to look at the façade and then enter the justifiably well-known inner court.

The end building is pure Flamboyant, with gable pinnacles and an octagonal staircase tower. The left gallery is entirely Renaissance with six wide basket handle arches. It is surrounded by friezes: the upper one, disfigured, shows the Triumphs of Petrarch, the lower, the Field of the Cloth of Gold (1520) at which, besides Henry VIII and François I, Abbot Aumale, son of Guillaume le Roux, was also present. It was he who later erected the mansion.

Joan of Arc Museum (Musée Jeanne d'Arc) (AY M⁴). – Posters, manuscripts (facsimiles), models, wax museum, etc. A vaulted cellar houses a model of the castle where Joan was imprisoned.

Corneille Museum (Musée Corneille)(AY M⁵). – This house where Pierre Corneille (1606-84) was born and lived for fifty-six years, contains drawings and engravings recounting the story of his life. Often considered the father of French Classical tragedy he wrote, among others, *Mélite* (1629; first performed in Rouen), *Le Cid, Horace* and *Cinna.*

On the first floor is his writing room; on the second floor the library contains first editions of his works. Also displayed are 17C models and engravings of old Rouen, including the Old Market Square.

Flaubert Museum (History of Medicine) (Musée Flaubert) (AY M⁶). – The Hôtel-Dieu (17-18C) on Place de la Madeleine has a Classical façade. The museum is set in the home (one of the pavilions) where Gustave Flaubert (1821-80) was born. His father worked as a surgeon. On display are souvenirs of Flaubert, 19C surgical instruments and 17 and 18C documents concerning Rouen hospitals.

Rue des Bons-Enfants (ABY 10). – Several half-timbered houses (some are 15C) stand on this street; no 22 *(Imprimerie Le Cerf)* has carved figures on the façade.

St-Patrice Church (Église) (BY). – This Gothic church is remarkable for its **stained glass windows★** made between 1538 and 1625. The windows on the north side of the chancel depict the Triumph of Christ, in the adjoining chapels are Sts Faron, Fiacre, Louis and Eustache, and an Annunciation in Italian Renaissance style as well as a Nativity scene. In the north aisle are the stories of St Barbara and St Patrick and Job. An 18C gilt baldachin crowns the altar.

Joan of Arc Tower (Tour Jeanne d'Arc) (BY S). – This is the former keep in Philippe-Auguste's 13C castle where Joan was subjected to torture on 9 May 1431. A facsimile of the manuscript relating to her trial is displayed on the ground floor from which a spiral staircase leads up to the first floor where models and documents evoke the history of the castle.

The second floor is devoted to the life of Joan of Arc.

St-Romain Church (Église) (BY). – The former 17C Carmelite chapel, restored in the 19C and again in 1969, contains interesting Renaissance **stained glass.**

★★Antiques Museum (Musée des Antiquités de la Seine Maritime) (CY M⁷). – Located in an old 17C convent, this museum displays objects from prehistory to the 19C.

Representing the Middle Ages and the Renaissance are tiles, stained glass windows, capitals, altarpieces, English alabaster altarpieces (15C), stunning religious gold and silver plate (12C Valasse Cross), 12-13C **enamels★**, 5-16C **ivories★** (a 14C seated Virgin) as well as a collection of arms and Moorish and Italian majolicas. In a long gallery is an interesting series of Gothic and Renaissance **carved façades★** from half-timbered houses of old Rouen. A separate gallery set aside to display tapestries contains the 15C **Winged Deer tapestry★★** and Renaissance furnishings.

There is, in addition to a display of local prehistory, Egyptian, Oriental, Greek and Etruscan departments, also a rare collection of Merovingian objects. There is an important **Gallo-Roman exhibit★** noteworthy for its bronzes and glassware. In the centre of the lapidary gallery is the famous **Lillebonne mosaic★★** (4C; restored 19C), the largest signed and illuminated mosaic to be found in France – note especially the scenes depicting the deer hunt.

Near the museum gardens is the large **St Marie Fountain** (CY X) by Falguière.

Natural History, Ethnography and Prehistory Museum (CY M⁸). – Next to the Antiques Museum, the collection includes scenes of the Normandy coast, forests, marshes and farms, stuffed animals, prehistoric and ethnographic exhibits.

Lycée Corneille (CY). – The school is in the former 17-18C Jesuit college and was attended not only by Corneille but later also by Corot, Flaubert, Maupassant and Maurois.

Fierte St-Romain (BZ Z). – An original Renaissance building. The stone canopy used to contain the relics of St Romanus.
The building adjoins the **Linen Hall** (Halle aux Toiles), a partly modern construction with exhibition, conference and banquet rooms. The façade looking out onto the Place de la Haute-Vieille-Tour has nicely arranged windows under a high slate roof.

SIGHTS BEYOND THE TOWN CENTRE

★★★ **The Corniche.** – *10km - 6 miles – plus 1/4 hour sightseeing. Preferably at sunset. Starting from Place St-Paul (southeast of plan p 111, CZ), drive along Rue Henri-Rivière and its continuation Rue du Mont-Gargan. Branch right into Rue Annie-de-Pène.*
The road climbs by a hairpin bend to the top of Ste-Catherine Hill, a chalk spur separating the Robec and Seine Valleys.

★★★ **Ste-Catherine Hill** (Côte Ste-Catherine). – Leave the car on a terrace in a sharp bend to the left. There is a strikingly beautiful **panorama** *(viewing table)* over the river bend and the town with all its belfries.

> *Continue along the D 95 which meets the N 14 bis by a school. Turn left and 200m later turn right before the Café de la Mairie.*

★★ **Bonsecours.** – Pop 6 108. The Neo-Gothic Basilica of Bonsecours (1840) which crowns the Mount Thuringe spur is a popular place of pilgrimage and also an excellent belvedere from which to see the shipping and industrial Rouen. From the monument to Joan of Arc located on a terrace there is a **view** that includes Rouen and the Seine Valley.
The bell, the Great Lion, at the cemetery entrance is rung on solemn occasions. From the foot of the Calvary *(viewing table)* there is a **panorama** straight down to the river bend with the left bank and its industry, the port and the bridges going away downstream and on the right bank, the cathedral.

Continue along the N 14 going towards Paris but turn off right into the N 14 which brings you back to Rouen along a fine *corniche* stretch of road.

★ **Croisset; Canteleu.** – *9km - 6 miles – plus 1/4 hour sightseeing. Leave Rouen by ⑦, going towards Duclair. Take the D 51 on the left towards Croisset.*

⊙ **Croisset.** – The **Pavillon Flaubert,** now a museum, is all that remains of the house in which Flaubert wrote *Madame Bovary* and *Salammbô.* The museum contains mementoes of the great writer whose library is housed in the town hall.

> *Turn back towards Rouen along the same road and the D 982 on the left which climbs picturesquely to Canteleu.*

★ **Canteleu.** – Pop 18 851. There is an interesting but limited **view** of the port and part of the town from the church terrace.

Botanical Gardens (Jardins des plantes). – *2.5km - 2 miles. Leave Rouen by ⑥, bear left into the Rue des Murs St-Yon.*
⊙ Planted in a beautiful park of 10 ha - 25 acres is a large variety of trees and shrubs and a multitude of colourful flower beds. The **greenhouses** contain tropical vegetation (orchids especially); the giant "Victoria Regia" is astonishing with its leaves which can grow to be 1m - 3ft in diameter in the summer. The pavilion is 17C, the wrought iron gate 18C.
Notice the cider press in a half-timbered building and two 19C greenhouses.

University Centre (Centre Universitaire). – *5km - 3 miles. Leave Rouen by Rue Chasselièvre* (AY) *northwest on the plan.*
From the road which ends on the Mont-aux-Malades Plateau on which the University Centre has been built, there is a good **panorama**★★ of the city, the port and the curve in the river.

⊙ **Pierre-Corneille Manor House** (Manoir Pierre-Corneille). – *In Petit-Couronne, 8km - 5 miles. Leave Rouen by ⑥ the N 138* (AZ), *turn right by the first houses of Petit-Couronne into Rue Pierre-Corneille. Leave the car before no 502.*
The "house in the fields" was bought in 1608 by the poet's father. When his father died Corneille inherited the house, in 1639, and continued to stay there. The Norman house is now a museum and evokes the writer's family life with 17C furniture and numerous documents. At the bottom of the garden is a thatched bakery reconstructed to look as it did in the 17C.

Verte Forest (Forêt Verte). – *23km - 14 miles – about 3/4 hour. Leave Rouen by Rue Bouquet* (BY).
The road crosses the forest, a favourite spot for the people of Rouen.

> *At the intersection of the D 121 and D 66, turn right to Isneauville.*

Turn round and drive back to the D 66 which skirts the forest.

> *Turn left on the D 43 and return to Rouen by Mont-St-Aignan and Bois Guillaume.*

Discover the other Normandy of the Armorican Massif, the "mountains" of the Suisse Normande, the D-Day Beaches, the Mont-St-Michel, the famous Bayeux Tapestry and Caen with its abbeys.
*These sights are described in the **Michelin Green Guide** Normandy Cotentin and the Channel Islands.*

RY

Michelin map 55 fold 7 or 231 fold 23 – 20km - 12 1/2 miles northeast of Rouen

This village with its pretty half-timbered and brick houses is said to be the "Yonville-l'Abbaye" where **Gustave Flaubert** (1821-80) placed the action of *Madame Bovary*.
A monument has been erected in front of the post office with a medallion of Flaubert.
The personality of Emma Bovary is said to have been inspired by the life of Delphine Couturier, wife of a Doctor Delamare; she died in 1848 in the "house of the doctor", now occupied by the village chemist's shop, while the chemist's shop where M. Homais used to pontificate is today the Lagarde dry cleaners and trinkets shop.

Museum of Animated Puppets (Musée d'automates). – Located on the bank of the Crevon River in an old 18C cider factory (restored), the museum houses a collection of automata, 300 of which represent scenes from Flaubert's *Madame Bovary*. The exhibition includes a reconstitution of the Homais chemist's shop.

Church (Église). – The 12C church has a charming carved wood Renaissance **porch★**. The interior is decorated with an attractive wooden framework; in the chancel is a fine Renaissance carved altarfront; in the south chapel note the angry faces carved at the end of the beams.
The whole is surmounted by a lantern tower with corbelled cornice.

ST-ÉVROULT-NOTRE-DAME-DU-BOIS

Michelin map 60 north of fold 4 or 231 folds 32, 33

The town, which lies near the source of the Charentonne, is named after the most famous abbey of the Ouche Region.

Abbey (Abbaye). – The abbey, founded by St Évroult in the 6C, laid waste by wars in the 10C, re-arose to find its greatest glory in the 11C when it became an influential centre of learning. In the 13C it was rebuilt in the Gothic style and today is once more a ruin. A statue was erected on the church site in 1912 to Orderic Vital, one of the abbey's great men and a historian and chronicler of Normandy in the 12C (1075-1142).
Go through the late 13C porch behind the monument to see the abbey ruins on the left.
Large-scale restoration work has been in progress since 1966. A **museum** has been installed between the porch and the abbey church to house the various works of art originating from the abbey.
An artificial pond has been created opposite the abbey, offering canoeing, boating and windsurfing facilities.

★ ST-GERMAIN-DE-LIVET Château

Michelin map 54 fold 17, 18 or 231 folds 32 – Local map p 39

This delightful 15 and 16C château has a highly original stone and brick chequered decoration. The façade is flanked by a 15C half-timbered wing. The south and southwest wings were demolished in the 19C although this is not immediately apparent on arrival.
Inside the courtyard has an Italian-style gallery with four basket arches.

TOUR *time: about 1/2 hour*

In the 15C wing is the Guards' Room with 16C **Frescoes** (battle scene) and a dining room, both with ornamental fireplace and Empire style furniture. In the hall two rooms have been furnished in the styles of Louis XV and Louis XVI.
On the first floor of the 16C wing are two beautifully tiled rooms in terracotta from the Auge Region, the so-called bedroom of Eugène Delacroix with photo of the painter, the gallery decorated with paintings by the Riesener family (19C) and a small Louis XVI salon located in the south turret, with Louis XIV furniture in ebony and copper.

The château at St-Germain-de-Livet

★ ST-GERMER-DE-FLY

Michelin map 55 folds 8, 9 or 237 fold 4 – 8km - 5 miles southeast of Gournay-en-Bray

This little town of the Bray Region is the site of an abbey founded in the 17C.

★ **Church (Église).** – The vast church, completely dominating the humble village crouched at its feet, is the finest religious edifice in the Bray. It was an abbey church and was built from 1150 to 1175 in early Gothic style. Go through the 14C fortified gateway (now the town hall) to enter the nave which was mutilated during the Hundred Years War. The chancel, the most interesting part of the building, has galleries with round arched windows and a triforium with square lintels. A Romanesque altar decorated with blind arcades stands in one of the apsidal chapels; a vaulted passage from the apse leads to an elegant Holy Chapel built in the 13C on the model of the famous Paris original.

Times and charges for admission to sights described in the guide are listed at the end of the guide.

The sights are listed alphabetically in this section either under the place-town, village or area-in which they are situated or under their proper name.

Every sight for which there are times and charges is indicated by the symbol ⊘ in the margin in the main part of the guide.

★ ST-MARTIN-DE-BOSCHERVILLE

Michelin map 54 fold 10 or 231 fold 22 – Local map 129

The Benedictine Abbey was founded in 1144 by William of Tancarville on the site of a college church built around 1050 by his father Raoul, Grand Chamberlain to William the Conqueror. Raoul of Tancarville had installed a community of Canons Regular of St Augustine who were later replaced by the Benedictines of St-Évroult *(détails p 120)*. No more than forty monks were ever present and they were driven out during the Revolution.

★★ FORMER ABBEY CHURCH OF ST-GEORGES *time: 1/4 hour*

⊘ The Abbey church, which became the St Martin parish church at the time of the Revolution and so was saved from destruction, is now one of the Seine Valley's finest small monuments.

Church (Église). – The building, which was constructed from 1080 to 1125, apart from the vaulting in the nave and transept which is 13C, has a striking unity of style and harmony of proportion.
The façade is plain: the ornament on the main door archivolts geometric, in typical Norman Romanesque fashion *(p 22)*; the capitals which are remarkably delicately carved are by craftsmen from the Ile-de-France or the Chartres region.

Interior. – The nave of eight bays with aisles on either side, has Gothic vaulting and a false triforium in place of galleries. A big open gallery supported by a monolithic round column ends either transept. The low reliefs inlaid in the wall beneath the balustrade illustrate, on the left, the Bishop giving his blessing, on the right, warriors fighting. The monumental confessional in the south transept is 18C.
Groined vaulting covers the chancel and side aisles and a heavier version the oven vault over the apse. The black marble pavement stone near the high altar is to Antoine the Red, nineteenth Abbot of St George's, who died in 1535.

Chapter House (Salle capitulaire). – The tour affords the opportunity first of letting you see the north face of the church which was reconstructed in the 14C – the cornice modillions are outstanding – and, even more interesting, the massive lantern built over the transept.
The chapter house which is 12C and surmounted by a 17C building used to open on the former cloister by way of three Romanesque arches supported on groups of slender columns with now mutilated historiated capitals. On the right are statue columns. Inside, a fine decorative frieze runs above where the monks' stalls once stood.
Excavations in the cloister have uncovered pavings from Gallo-Roman temples and a Merovingian funerary church.

EXCURSION

Roumare Forest. – *Round tour of 36km - 22 1/2 miles – about 2 hours.*
Oaks, beeches and hornbeams populate the land around the Seine between Rouen and Duclair.

Leave St-Martin-de-Boscherville eastwards and take the D 982 towards Canteleu. At the crossroads in Leu, 2km - 1 mile further on, take the first road on the right and after 500m - 1/3 mile turn left.

The road winds through the forest.

At the Treize Chênes crossroads take the D 351 across the forest to Sahurs.

Sahurs. – Pop 870. The 16C Marbeuf Chapel, which stands in a manor, was made famous by the vow of Anne of Austria who promised the chapel a silver statue equal in weight to the child she desired. The 5.5kg - 12lb silver statue despatched on the birth of Louis XIV disappeared during the Revolution.

Take the D51 to the left.

Sahurs Church (Église). – Off of the road that goes from Sahurs to Hautot is a shaded roadway that leads to the church, overlooked from the far bank by the ruins of Robert the Devil's castle.

Go back to the D 51 along the banks of the Seine.

Le Val-de-la-Haye. – Pop 715. *5km - 3 miles from Sahurs.* The column on the right, facing the Grand Couronne Ferry as you leave the village, commemorates the return of Napoleon's body to France.

Return to Sahurs and follow the D 51 which follows a bend in the Seine. Then continue on the D 67 to Quevillon, passing through St-Pierre-de-Manneville.

Quevillon. – Pop 506. Transformed into a rest home, the castle of La Rivière-Bourdet, on the left at the entrance to the village, is a sumptuous 17C building. The monumental dovecote remains and is well preserved.

The D 67 leads back to St-Martin-de-Boscherville.

ST-VALERY-EN-CAUX
Pop 5 814

Michelin map **52** fold 3 or **231** fold 9 – Local map p 55 – Facilities

St-Valery is a fishing and coastal trading port as well as a popular seaside resort. The harbour is connected to the sea by a fairway and can shelter a large number of pleasure boats.
A promenade overlooks the long shingle beach.

SIGHTS

★ **Aval Cliff** (Falaise d'Aval). – Leave the car at the Quai du Havre and a little further on turn left into the Sentier des Douaniers. The steps lead up to the monument commemorating the battles of June 1940 (51st Highland Division and the French 2nd Cavalry Division).
The view stretches eastwards to Ailly lighthouse and on a clear day to Dieppe.

Henri IV House (Maison Henri IV). – *Quai du Havre.*
Beautiful Renaissance house with carved beams.

Amont Cliff (Falaise d'Amont). – A stairway leads to the 51st Highland Division Monument which overlooks the town, harbour and beach of St-Valery.
Nearby stands a modern monument in memory of Coste and Bellonte who were the first to fly from Paris to New York on board their aeroplane *Point d'Interrogation* (literally "Question Mark") in 1930.

★ ST-WANDRILLE
Pop 1 184

Michelin map **54** fold 9 or **231** fold 22 – Local map p 129

St-Wandrille Abbey and the renascent Abbey of Le Bec-Hellouin are a moving testimony to the continuity of the Benedictine Order in Normandy since the earliest times.
Today the monks live mainly on the manufacture of furniture polish and household products.

HISTORICAL NOTES

God's Athlete (7C). – All at King Dagobert's court were celebrating the marriage of the wise and handsome Count Wandrille who seemed brilliantly destined when, by common accord, the young newly weds decided to consecrate their lives to God. The bride entered a convent and Wandrille joined a group of hermits. The King ordered Wandrille to return to court but the new hermit placed his cause in the hands of God and, in time, Dagobert enlightened by a miracle resigned himself to the loss of his subject. Wandrille, after staying in far off monasteries, returned to St-Ouen in Rouen where he was ordained.
His saintliness and his magnificent physique earned him the nickname of God's True Athlete.

The Valley of the Saints (7 to 9C). – In 649 Wandrille founded a monastery in the Fontenelle Valley. The monks cleared the forest and planted the first vines. **Fontenelle** library and schools became famous (the abbey had not yet taken the name of its founder). A succession of learned men were appointed as abbots: Einhard, Charlemagne's historian and Ansegise who organised the first collection of the Emperor's capitulary ordinances. In 831 the *Epic of the Abbots of Fontenelle* appeared – the first history of a Western monastery. But even more important, Fontenelle, "where saints flourish as rose trees in a greenhouse", became for the people living locally the Valley of the Saints and St Wandrille remains to this day the only monastery in Christendom to celebrate its own feast of All the Saints of the Monastery.

Benedictine Continuity. – In the 10C some monks began to rebuild the ruined abbey, destroyed by the fury of the Northmen. The new abbey, which took the name of its original founder, became one of the most flourishing centres of the Benedictine Order which spread widely throughout Normandy in the 11C *(details p 125)*. The Wars of Religion brought only a temporary decline; the Maurian Reform sustained its influence but the Revolution led to the dispersal of the monks and the buildings fell into ruin. In the 19C the abbey passed successively into the hands of a textile mill owner and the English peer, the Marquess of Stacpoole. In 1894 the Benedictines returned, but seven years later were again dispersed. For several years the author Maurice Maeterlinck lived in the abbey. In 1931, however, Gregorian Chant began once more to be heard in the church.

★THE ABBEY *time: 3/4 hour*

The monumental gateway was erected in the 19C by the Marquess of Stacpoole, shortlived owner of the premises. The entrance to the abbey is through a 15C door surmounted by a symbolical pelican (the pelican piercing its side so that its offspring may feed on its blood is the symbol of Christ). The porter's lodge and its twin are 18C; the gate between the two is known as the Jarente Gate.

Jarente Gate (Porte de Jarente). – This imposing 18C structure leads to the main courtyard, accessible on guided tours only. It was built by Abbot Louis-Sexte de Jarente, Bishop of Orléans, from whom it took its name.
At the back of the courtyard are the monks' workshops (woodwork, baking, laundry).

The Abbey Church Ruins. – The bases of the columns which supported the main arches of the 14C nave can be seen rising out of the grass. The only parts still standing are the tall columns in two groups of massive and slender pillars which stood at the opening of the north transept. The 13C chancel, with six bays, was circled by an ambulatory and fifteen chapels.

★ **Cloister (Cloître).** – All four galleries of the cloister remain. The 14C south gallery (the only one open to the public), parallel with the nave, was linked to it by a fine door surmounted by a now mutilated tympanum illustrating the Coronation of the Virgin. A niche, in a wall at right angles, contains the deeply venerated and graceful 14C statue of Our Lady of Fontenelle. On either side lie the tombstones of Jean, Bailiff of Fontenelle in the 13C, and Abbot Jean de Brametot in the south gallery, where a small lapidary museum has been installed.
The remaining three galleries are 15C; in the north gallery, beside the highly ornate refectory door, is a half Gothic, half Renaissance **lavabo**. Above is a gable decorated with a fretwork of leaves and a blind arcade with six sections each containing a tap. Scenes from the New Testament are illustrated in an exquisitely delicate Flamboyant decoration.

Church (Église). – The church is an old 13C tithe barn, the Canteloup Barn, which was transported piece by piece in 1969 from La Neuville-du-Bosc in the Eure and re-erected at St-Wandrille by the monks themselves. The beams and uprights of the roof are assembled with dowels and enhanced by discreet lighting.
The Chapel of the Holy Sacrament, which is characterised by its wood beams, is the barn's one time porch.
To the right of the chapel's opening is a 1970 shrine containing the head of St Wandrille.

Notre-Dame-de-Callouville Chapel (Chapelle). – Built by the monks, it was the wish of the Abbot after a 1944 bombing.

WALK TO ST-SATURNIN CHAPEL

Allow about 3/4 hour Rtn – if you go by car follow the signs.

As you come out of the abbey take the path downhill on the right which passes by a 16C Entombment beneath a sort of porch. Skirt the wall for 150m - 164 yards, go round a field and take the path along the abbey wall to the chapel.

St-Saturnin Chapel *(not open to the public)* built at the edge of the abbey park is a small trefoil plan oratory, rebuilt in the 10C on what were probably Merovingian foundations. The façade was remodelled in the 16C but the building has preserved its thickset appearance with three apsidal chapels dominated by a heavy square tower.
The building has been restored inside. The tops of three pillars embedded in the base of the tower and decorated with roses, palms and fantastic animals come, no doubt, from an earlier construction probably of the Carolingian period.

The current **Michelin Guide France**
offers a selection of pleasant quiet and well situated
hotels. Each entry includes the facilities provided
(gardens, tennis courts, swimming pool and equipped beach)
and annual closure dates.

Also included is a selection of establishments recommended for their cuisine:
– well prepared meals at a moderate price, stars for good cooking.

The current **Michelin Guide Camping Caravaning France**
indicates the facilities and recreational amenities offered
by each individual site.
Shops, bars, laundries, games room, tennis courts,
miniature golf, children's play area, paddling pool, swimming pool... etc.

The Seine River, which rises in Burgundy, flows successively through Champagne, the Ile-de-France and finally Normandy on its 776km - 485 mile course to the sea. The valley's history, natural beauty, the castles and other monuments built upon its banks and its ever increasing economic importance make it Normandy's greatest inland tourist feature.

GEOGRAPHICAL NOTES

The Winding River. – The name Seine is said to derive from the Latin *sequana* from the Celtic *squan,* meaning to curve or bend – the river being likened to a coiled snake. The Seine has almost no fall being only 16m - 52ft above sea level at Vernon although still more than 100km - 50 miles, as the crow flies, from the Channel. It is almost certain that originally it flowed over the countryside, following the lie of the land and progressing capriciously, possibly by wide curves. The volume gradually hollowed out the valley we know today with its enclosed bends which, in their turn, have greatly influenced Norman topography.

Concave Banks and Convex Promontories. – The concave river banks have an almost uniform appearance. At point (a) the river flows with all its force into a bank topped by steep slopes or even by cliffs extraordinarily similar to those along the coast. These relative heights with sheer drops to the river make good defensive positions and several were crowned with such fortresses as Gaillard and Robert the Devil's castles. These concave areas were also, by the river's flow, the deepest parts and where a tributary entered the mainstream, good sites for river ports. Les Andelys, Duclair, Caudebec, Lillebonne and finally Rouen which is particularly well placed *(p 109)* were all established and developed apace. In contrast, at (b) the current flows more slowly along the convex stretch of bank, depositing part of the debris collected upstream. The land behind the bank slopes only gently upward. The convex promontories (L) are often

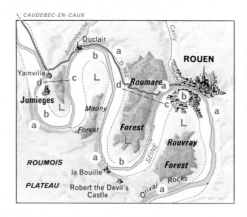

stony and have, therefore, been left over the centuries as forest areas.

The Spread of the Valley. – If one takes the line **c d** one notices that at **c** the river is flowing swiftly, driving against the promontory and undercutting the bank ever more steeply whereas at **d** the current is slack and much of the alluvium caught upstream can be deposited, making the river bed ever more shallow.

Over the centuries the stream's cutting away of the banks and depositing of silt have thus moved the river's course downstream a considerable way at the bends and produced an ever-expanding alluvial arc *(the white area on the map above).*

Finally, near the estuary *(map p 128)*, the promontories have been reduced to triangular headlands as at Quillebeuf and La Roque and further on to hillocks such as Cape Le Hode and Tancarville Point. In the Vernier Marshland one can see the semicircle of hills which once formed the outer bank of a bend in the river.

At Duclair there is an unusual example of "river capture". The tributary Austreberthe originally entered the Seine at Yainville, but owing to the westward movement of the Duclair bend suddenly found itself flowing into the mainstream at Duclair, leaving a dead valley between Duclair and Yainville. This disused course is now used by the D 982.

The Bore. – When the great tides are running, the seas entering the estuary are trapped between the river banks and, as they rush forward, meet the normal river flow. The sea current prevails, reversing the stream and causing a bore or, as it is called in Normandy, *le mascaret.* The phenomenon, which used to be seen at its most impressive at Caudebec during the equinoctial tides, and which caused the death by drowning, when they were suddenly caught in the rushing waters, of Victor Hugo's daughter and her husband at Villequier in 1843, is now seldom seen and then much diminished, having been "tamed" by engineering work on the river banks *(see p 125: The embankment of the Seine).*

HISTORICAL NOTES

Highway to the sea, highway to Paris – such has been the dual role of the Valley of the Seine, together with that of cradle of the Duchy of Normandy, throughout its history.

The Tin Road. – In the Bronze Age – *c 2500 BC* – rivers provided the only possible thoroughfares through densely wooded country. Boats sailed upstream to river sources; where the bed was too shallow, boats and goods were carried overland to the next deep water. Gradually all those sending ships across the Channel to Cornwall for tin to alloy with copper and make bronze, congregated on the banks of the Seine.

With the Roman occupation, the paths of Gaul became the glorious roads of Caesar – the road beside the Seine from Troyes was extended to the great base at Juliobona (Lillebonne) and on to Caracotinum (Harfleur).

The Castles of God. – Christianity penetrated in the 3C to the Second Lyonnaise, a Roman province with Rouen as its capital.

From the 6C, the first monasteries developed into centres of learning and intellectual life as well as religion, and also of economic development. Merovingians and Carolingians supported the monastic surge with concessions of land, bringing about the foundation of abbeys such as Fontenelle (now St-Wandrille) and Jumièges. Monastic discipline was inspired equally by the Rule of St Benedict and that of St Columban.

Churches were built in honour of the saints and to contain their relics; every abbey established a school where children learnt "reading the psalter, counting, singing and how to write".

The Vikings. – From the 9 to the 11C the Northmen, intrepid navigators and warriors from Scandinavia, voyaged to wherever there were riches, pillaging and ravaging *(p 15)*. These pirates or **Vikings** were a race apart. Setting sail in their *drakkars* they harassed western Europe, landed on the coast of Africa and even entered the Mediterranean. For a hundred years they dominated the Atlantic, colonising Iceland and Greenland and landing in America four centuries before Columbus.

The Valley of the Seine with its prosperous towns, rich churches, abbeys and monasteries, offered an open invitation to the plunderers: at the beginning of the 9C the *drakkars* advanced up river under sail and oar. Each ship was 24m long by 5m broad with a draught of 2m - 79×16×7ft; they lacked superstructures but had graceful lines, boldly carved prows and each carried some sixty warriors.

On land these Normans, as they came to be called, proved to be good horsemen and redoubtable fighters, masters at guerrilla warfare, ambush and surprise attack. They massacred, pillaged and burnt. Caught in a tight corner, they negotiated a truce, had themselves baptised – some would boast of as many as twenty baptisms! – and promptly joined another band of marauders.

Terror reigned: the monks fled with their precious relics; the peasants abandoned their houses amidst the fields to group together in villages around local seignorial castles where the chapel became the parish church.

No king could stop these devastating raids which recurred with sinister regularity, threatening the countryside as far as Paris and Chartres. Eventually, however, the Normans lost their passion for plunder as booty became scarce. King Charles the Simple, who was in fact far from simple, decided to neutralise the pirates he could not overcome by getting them to settle down. In 911, the King met the Viking, Rollo, at St-Clair-sur-Epte *(p 17)* and conceded to the "Normans on the Seine" the lands they were occupying; the Duchy of Normandy had been born; Rollo was the first Duke.

Normandy's Great Century. – The country, within a century, became a well ordered State – the first to emerge in the Middle Ages – so adept did the former pirates prove as administrators. A wonderful civilisation began to flourish.

Rollo and his descendants made it a point of honour to repair the damage caused by the Vikings and outrivalled each other in their generosity towards the Church. It was through this contact with the Church that the Scandinavians first mixed with and began to be absorbed by the native Gallo-Franks.

The 11C was the century of epic deeds of war: of the adventures of the sons of Tancrede de Hauteville in southern Italy and Sicily and of the undertaking of William the Bastard, the Conqueror who gathered his knights at Lillebonne to set out on the "great Norman adventure", the conquest of England *(p 17)*. In the spiritual compass, it was the time of Benedictine flowering, quickened by the Cluniac Reform introduced at Fécamp by Guglielmo da Volpiano *(qv)* and encouraged by the dukes.

St George's Abbey was constructed at Boscherville and Jumièges was gloriously rebuilt.

Finally the Norman style was to develop and dominate religious architecture for more than a century and influence architecture abroad from Sicily to England *(p 22)*.

THE MARITIME SEINE

A Difficult Street to Cross. – Napoleon declared "Le Havre, Rouen and Paris are but a single town of which the Seine is the main street." The phrase depicts exactly the Seine Valley, the vital artery which links Paris to the sea but also the barrier which, throughout history, has separated the Caux from the Roumois. Today, however, the bridges at Tancarville *(qv)* and Brotonne *(qv)* join the north to the south and Caux has ceased to be an isolated "peninsula".

The Embankment of the Seine. – The sight of a cargo boat gliding between the banks of the river, a complete stranger to the surrounding countryside, is the result of the efforts of engineers over the last hundred years to open up the Seine to high capacity ships.

The appearance of large steamers at the beginning of the 19C posed many a problem. Between 1830 and 1852 105 vessels ran aground between Quillebeuf and Villequier alone! To get as far as Rouen it took sailing ships four days at the best of times. Six hours are needed nowadays as a result of embanking started in 1848.

The undertakings of the last century have included the extension of the alluvial plain between Rouen and the sea by 15 000 ha - 59sq miles; the construction in 1887 of the 25km - 15 1/2 mile long Tancarville Canal to enable river barges to reach Le Havre without entering the estuary; the completion in 1960 of a new channel between the confluence of the Risle and the region of Honfleur between two dikes converging upstream, the north dike connected to the existing one upstream of the former Le Hode ferry, and the new south bank extended downstream by a 7km - 4 1/2 mile submersible dike. The result is that the new channel has been deepened enabling boats of 50 to 60 000 tonnes laden to sail up to Rouen.

The Economy of the Lower Seine. – The Seine Valley has been developing apace industrially since 1900 with the two ports of Rouen and Le Havre playing a capital role in the general scheme.

The textile industry, the oldest in the region, has severely declined due to competition from the third world countries; nevertheless cotton has remained faithful to the area around Rouen. The Norman mills represent more than 8 % of the national cotton production, and the cotton market remains, as always, at Le Havre.

The metallurgy industry owes its expansion, albeit slowed down since the 1974 oil crisis, to the three great shipyards, two at Le Havre and one at Quevilly. The growth of foundries, wire-drawing mills, metal construction shops in the suburbs of Le Havre and Rouen have also made their contribution, together with the Renault works at Sandouville and Cléon and the electrical and electronic equipment manufacturing plants.

The cheminal industry, born of a need for finishing and dyeing products for textiles, has diversified and now includes chemical fertilisers. The *département* of Seine-Maritime is the first producer of compound fertilizers. Around Rouen there are large papermills producing paper for domestic consumption and newsprint, factories making acid and pharmaceutical products, bleach, etc; the first synthetic rubber factory outside the USA was built at Port-Jérôme; two plastics factories and a sulphur recovery works have also been built.

The nuclear power station at Paluel and the Le Havre thermal power station produce electricity for the area. The plant under construction at Penly will help to meet the ever-increasing need for energy.

The most spectacular activities now, however, derive from the oil refining industry and its by-products in petro-chemistry including large hydrocarbon factories.

The River of Petrol. – The capacity of the Seine-Maritime's four great refineries at Gonfreville, Port-Jérôme, Notre-Dame-de-Gravenchon and Petit-Couronne now amounts to 37 million tons a year or nearly 30 % of the total French refining capacity. Production includes car petrol, high octane fuels and the gamut of products from liquid gas to bitumens and primary products for the petro-chemical industry which, in turn, produces detergents and solvents, man-made fibres and synthetic rubber and plastics. The refineries and factories can be seen from afar, their aluminium painted storage tanks and superstructures clearly visible by daylight and floodlit at night. The transport to Paris of petroleum products refined or stored in Le Havre or further refined or manufactured in the Seine-Maritime works, is undertaken by four pipelines (total length of 1 330km - 798 miles), with a monthly capacity of 2 500 000 tons. The network's ramifications serve the storage and distribution centres of the Paris area such as the dépôts of Roissy and Orly airports, Orléans, Tours, Rouen and Caen. Products such as car petrol, aeroplane fuel and domestic oil are transported at a speed of 7 to 10km - 4 to 6 miles per hour. Their flow is uninterrupted and it is possible at any given time to localise the different fuels as they are transported along the pipeline.

★★THE NORMANDY VEXIN

① From Vernon to Rouen

100km - 63 miles – about 5 hours – Local map p 127

The road in the main runs parallel to the right bank of the Seine, sometimes at a distance through the farmlands of the alluvial plain, sometimes close at hand between the bank's edge and the bare escarpment to be found at each hollow bend.

★**Vernon.** – *Description p 138.*

> *Leave Vernon by ③, the D 313.*

Between Pressagny-l'Orgueilleux and Port-Mort, the D 313 crosses a plain ringed by a semicircle of hills. As you approach the junction with the D 10 look out on the right for a dolmen, known as Gargantua's Pebble (Gravier de Gargantua), standing in a field.

Gaillon. – *Description p 78.*

Before Tosny, arriving at Villers-sur-le-Roule, the best **view**★ is had from the D 176 deviation. Les Andelys is reached by a suspension bridge with Gaillard Castle behind *(p 34)*, superbly sited on the concave cliff of the meander.

★★**Les Andelys.** – *Description p 33.*

From Les Andelys to Muids, the D 313 runs at the foot of strangely jagged chalk escarpments bordering the river. The La Roque Rock has an almost human profile. From the D 65 one can see how the escarpment has changed banks, or rather the river altered course, so that the cliff now dominates the concave left bank. There are fine private properties between the Herqueville crossroads and Amfreville-sous-les-Monts.

★★**Deux Amants Hill** (Côte des Deux Amants). – *Description p 60.*

★**Amfreville Locks** (Écluses d'Amfreville). – *Description p 32.*

Le Manoir. – Pop 990. The new church preceded by a detached belfry is a plain, modern building. A vast composition in glass by Barillet makes up the pierced façade which also gives a warm light to the interior.

The N 15 cuts away from the river at Igoville and across the base of the Elbeuf Promontory by two valleys which almost meet, to come out at Port-St-Ouen.

⊘ **Les Authieux.** – Pop 155. The **church** has a fine series of Renaissance stained glass windows.

Industrial plants on the outskirts of Rouen appear on the left facing Port-St-Ouen. The D 7 beyond St-Adrien climbs rapidly to the plateau at Belbeuf.

St-Adrien Chapel (Chapelle St-Adrien). – This 13C chapel lies in the hollow of a cliff.

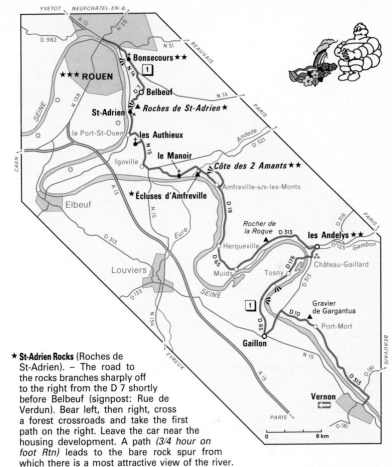

★ **St-Adrien Rocks** (Roches de St-Adrien). – The road to the rocks branches sharply off to the right from the D 7 shortly before Belbeuf (signpost: Rue de Verdun). Bear left, then right, cross a forest crossroads and take the first path on the right. Leave the car near the housing development. A path *(3/4 hour on foot Rtn)* leads to the bare rock spur from which there is a most attractive view of the river.

Belbeuf. – Pop 1 681. The small church guarded by its old yew tree is pleasantly situated. The château is 18C.

A stupendous **panorama**★★ opens out as the N 14, below the Bonsecours Church, descends *corniche* fashion to the river which at this point contains islands covered with greenery. Rouen lies ahead in its unique setting, the cathedral spire tall and slender against the sky.

★★ **Bonsecours.** – *Description p 119.*

★★★ **Rouen.** – *Description p 109.*

★★★ THE LOWER SEINE

② From Rouen to Le Havre

109km - 68 miles – about 4 1/2 hours – Local map pp 128 and 129

This road is the sightseeing one – it is the **abbey road.** Another of its attractions is the variety of views one gets of the meanderings of the Lower Seine.

★★★ **Rouen.** – *Description p 109.*

Leave Rouen by ⑦, the D 982.

A **view**★ of Rouen can be glimpsed to the east through a small valley.

★ **Canteleu.** – *Description p 119.*

The D 982 crosses Roumare Forest from which you emerge to a view once more overlooking the Seine Valley with St-Martin-de-Boscherville Church in the foreground.

★ **St-Martin-de-Boscherville.** – *Description p 121.*

The road between La Fontaine and Mesnil-sous-Jumièges follows the outer side of the bend for several miles skirting the river bank and the cliff.

Duclair. – *Description p 66.*

Shortly after Duclair turn left on the D 65.

The drive across the end of the Jumièges Promontory is through typically Norman scenery and is at its best at apple blossom time.

There is a succession of elegant houses. The road is part of the picturesque **route des fruits,** where blackcurrants, redcurrants, cherries etc are sold directly to the public, and is very popular on summer weekends.

Le Mesnil-sous-Jumièges. – Pop 556. It was in the 13C manor house at Mesnil that Agnès Sorel, the favourite of Charles VII, died in 1450. There is an attractive covered well in the courtyard.

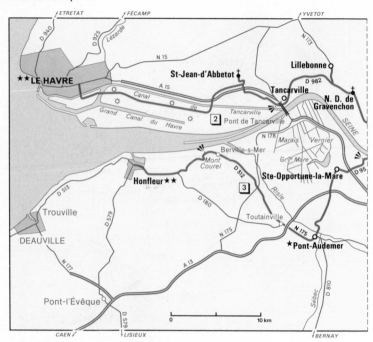

The road runs past the **country park** and **open-air leisure centre** (windsurfing, canoeing, swimming, tennis, camping), part of the Brotonne Regional Nature Park.

★★★ **Jumièges.** – *Description p 91.*

Yainville. – Pop 1 246. The square church tower and nave are 11C. A factory of the Christofle goldsmith's has been operating here since 1971.

⊘ **Le Trait.** – Pop 5 917. The 16C parish **church** in this industrial town includes some delightful alabasters *(Adoration of the Magi* and *Coronation of the Virgin)* on the pedestals beneath the statues surrounding the altar. In a recess on the north side there is a 16C restored Entombment.

    Turn off from Caudebecquet for St-Wandrille.

★ **St-Wandrille.** – *Description p`122.*

Monument "To the Latham 47 Company". – The monument is a memorial to the fatal expedition made by Amundsen, with Guilbaud and others, to the Arctic in 1928 to rescue the crew of the dirigible *Italia,* shipwrecked on an ice-floe.

★ **Caudebec-en-Caux.** – *Description p 51.*

After Caudebec-en-Caux, the wooded countryside gives way to the open of the reclaimed alluvial plains. The stretch from Caudebecquet to Villequier affords views of the ever-widening river.

★ **Villequier.** – *Description p 139.*

The villages of Norville and St-Maurice-d'Ételan come into view, each with an attractive stone belfry.

★ **Etelan Château.** – Built on the site of a former fortress, this remarkable Gothic-Flamboyant
⊘ edifice dominates the Seine Valley. The elegant pavilion standing at the angle formed by the wing and the main building is lit by nine bays. Interesting 16C wall paintings and fine woodwork are to be found in the chapel. Some of the furnished rooms are reserved for temporary exhibitions or chamber music concerts.

From the terrace the delightful **view** stretches over the Petitville and Norville marshes in the foreground and thereafter over Brotonne Forest. The boats on the Seine glide as if on dry land and form a truly unexpected sight.

Notre-Dame-de-Gravenchon. – Interesting modern church with a lead and copper composition on the façade of St George slaying the dragon.

Lillebonne. – *Description p 92.*

The whitish cliffs around Tancarville emerge in the distance; the road bridge suddenly comes clearly into view; the alluvial plain extends even further.

Tancarville. – *Description p 130.*

Below Tancarville, the D 892, which passes at the foot of northern pylon of the suspension bridge, continues to hug the cliff until it reaches Le Hode. There are views of the southern shore of the estuary and then of the industrial zone lying south of the Tancarville Canal.

St-Jean-d'Abbetot. – The **church,** which dates from the first half of the 11C, contains 12, 13 and 16C **frescoes★**, the most remarkable being in the crypt.

    Return to Le Havre through the industrial zone.

Between the Tancarville Canal and the Central Maritime Canal the petroleum plants, refineries and industrial complexes are quite spectacular.

★★ **Le Havre.** – *Description p 80.*

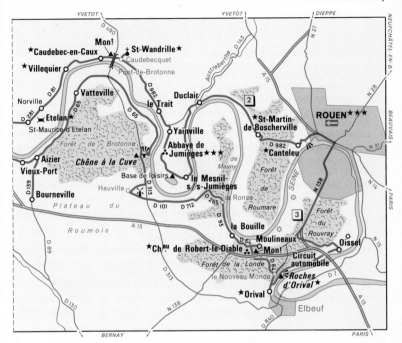

★★ THE SOUTH BANK

③ From Rouen to Honfleur

130km - 81 miles – about 5 hours – Local map above.

The road goes through several woodland areas and the bird's eye views of the river are most attractive.

★★★ Rouen. – *Description p 109.*

Leave Rouen by ⑥, the N 138.

The Rouvray Forest on the outskirts of Rouen with its groves of pine trees and extensive bare acres resembles a heath rather than a forest in places.

Leave the N 138 and take the D 13 to the left.

Oissel. – Pleasant public gardens.

The picturesque D 18 runs alongside the Seine.

★ Orival Rocks (Roches d'Orival). – *1 hour on foot Rtn.* On the D 18, park the car at the signpost *Sentier des Roches* and walk up the steep and difficult path on the left (slippery if wet). The path passes in front of some caves hollowed out of the rock, improves, runs at the foot of a cliff on the right and about 300m from a grass covered crest, affords an open **view** of the Seine and the rock escarpment along which the path continues as a grass *corniche.*

★ Orival. – Pop 926. The chalky escarpment whose curious rocks hang over the road from Oissel to Orival overlooks a river countryside, which tourists will appreciate. The church is a curious 15C half-troglodyte structure.

Return northwards to the crossroads of the D 64 and the N 138.

Turning right, the road leads to the **Rouen-les-Essarts car circuit,** 5 543m - almost 3 1/2 miles – of forest track.

Turning left, the drive (D 64) through the La Londe Forest and along a *corniche* road above a deep wooded valley is briefly reminiscent of mountain country.

At the crossroads at the top of the road turn right on the D3.

⊘ Moulineaux. – Pop 838. The **church** with its slender spire dates from the 13C. Inside there is an attractive woodwork group formed by the pulpit and rood screen (one side of the latter is Gothic and the other Renaissance). In the apse is the 13C **stained glass window**★ the gift of Blanche de Castille. Note also the 16C tableau of the Flemish School depicting the Crucifixion and a monk in prayer. There is a far-reaching view of the Seine Valley from the cemetery.

Turn round.

★ Robert the Devil's Castle (Château de Robert-le-Diable). – *Description p 108.*

Qui Vive Monument. – *At the D 64 and D 67ᴬ crossroads.* There is a remarkable **view** *(viewing table)* of the Seine as it curves round to encircle the Roumare Forest.

The D 64 goes down to the Seine so that one gets a view of the river bend commanded by Robert the Devil's Castle and the Rouen industrial suburbs.

La Bouille. – Pop 550. La Bouille has a most attractive setting at the foot of the wooded slopes of the Roumois Plateau on the first concave bend of the Seine below Rouen. The village was a favourite with Monet and has remained so with the citizens of Rouen.

Between La Bouille and La Ronce the road follows the river course.

Take the D 265 to the left which crosses Mauny Forest.

As the road goes up there are views of Jumièges Forest and the Seine.

Turn right on the D 712 which later becomes the D 101.

🕐 **Hauville Mill** (Moulin d'Hauville). – This 13C mill is one of the few surviving stone mills in Upper Normandy and once belonged to the monks of Jumièges Abbey. Its roof can be orientated according to the direction of the wind and is supported by oak beams. The stone tower and large sails are most impressive. If the weather allows one can see the mill in operation.

Return to the crossroads with the D 313 and bear left.

La Cuve Oak Tree (Chêne à la Cuve). – *100m from the D 913, opposite the 11km post.* Four oak trunks growing from a single bole form a kind of natural cup, 7m - 23ft in circumference.

300m – about 330 yards further down, stop on the right at the La Mailleraye lay-by.

★ **Viewpoint.** – *Picnic area.* Viewing table. To the right can be seen the towers of Jumièges Abbey, particularly impressive at sunset, and to the left the Seine Valley.

The D 143 runs alongside the river between the Jumièges and Yainville ferries.

Follow the signposts "Route des Chaumières".

Running alongside the Seine to the right, the road offers views of typical Norman thatched cottages half-hidden by trees.

The D 65 to the right leads to La Mailleraye (ferry).

Vatteville. – Pop 144. An emblazoned mourning band can be seen where it was painted on the death of a local lord in black on the walls of the church nave which dates from the Renaissance. The chancel is Flamboyant, the windows 16C.

Between Le Quesney and Aizier the D 65 and the D 95 cross the Brotonne Forest *(qv).*

Aizier. – Pop 117. The stone bell tower of the 12C church looks very old. Near the church there is a manhole slab – the remains of a covered way dating from around 2 000 BC.

Drive south on the D 139.

🕐 **Bourneville.** – Pop 680. The **House of Crafts and Trades** (Maison des Métiers) is a group of craftsmen's workshops: pottery, weaving, cabinet-making. The **museum** inside presents the traditional professions of Upper Normandy: metalwork, woodwork, glasswork... Temporary exhibitions are held each year.

Return to Aizier.

Vieux-Port. – Pop 56. The thatched village cottages stand half hidden by their orchards.

Ste-Opportune-la-Mare. – *Description p 137.*

From the fine *corniche* section between Vieux-Port and Le Val-Anger, the Seine Valley reappears. Then the road goes down the Roumois Plateau.

★ **Pont-Audemer.** – *Description p 106.*

The road follows the course of the Lower Risle Valley *(qv).* The landscape is particularly attractive in the spring when the apple orchards are in blossom, especially around Toutainville. Between Berville and Honfleur there are many views of the estuary; the best **view★** appears as you round Mount Courel and after you have passed La Pommeraye Castle.

★★ **Honfleur.** – *Description p 87.*

TANCARVILLE
Pop 1 139

Michelin map 52 fold 12 or 231 fold 21 – Local maps pp 128 and 137

Tancarville Castle, built upon the last promontory of the chalk cliffs constricting the Seine before its estuary finally splays out into the Channel, commands the fine panoramic view of the right bank of the river. The great suspension bridge over the Seine springs from the same cliff.

★ **Road Bridge (Pont routier).** – *Toll bridge: for rates see the current Michelin Red Guide France.*

Until 1959 no bridge spanned the Seine between Rouen and Le Havre – a distance of 127km – 79 miles. Large boats sailed upstream to Rouen and communication between the two banks was maintained by a number of ferries. It became clear, however, that ferry-crossings were inefficient: difficulties in embarking large vehicles, queues, no crossings at night etc. The idea of a permanent structure connecting the two banks without affecting shipping was finally born.

Begun in 1955 it was opened to the public in July 1959. One of the largest suspension bridges in Europe, its vital statistics are:

Length: 1 400m - 4 943ft; height above water at high tide: 48m - 156ft; height of pylons: 125m - 410ft; central span: 608m - 1 995ft.

There is a fine **view★** of the Seine Estuary from the bridge *(leave the car at one end).* A spectacular view of the bridge itself can be had from the south bank or from the D 982 on the north bank passing the base of the north pylon.

Feudal Castle (Château féodal). – The Eagle Tower is the only part intact of the castle, some of whose buildings date back to the 10C. The tower, with its base in the form of a spur, stands to the left of the terrace and is 15C. On the other side of the terrace stands a square 12C tower.

The castle was part of a strategic defence commanding the Seine Estuary. It was granted a certain number of privileges by William the Conqueror, Raoul of Tancarville being his private tutor and chamberlain. The entrance is flanked by two round towers. In the courtyard the ruins of the main building were entered through three pointed archways. The side looking out over the valley has been rebuilt and is now a restaurant.

Michelin map 52 fold 5 or 231 folds 11, 12 – Facilities

Le Tréport, a small fishing port at the mouth of the Bresle near the border with Picardy, is a seaside resort which owes much of its popularity to its being so near Paris. During the summer gay crowds round the harbour turn the town into a fair. The long shingle beach, backed by tall cliffs, is crammed with visitors at weekends, but is wide enough to take them all.

Mers-les-Bains, on the right bank of the Bresle, is less commercial than Le Tréport and has many devotees, as has Ault, a beach further north.

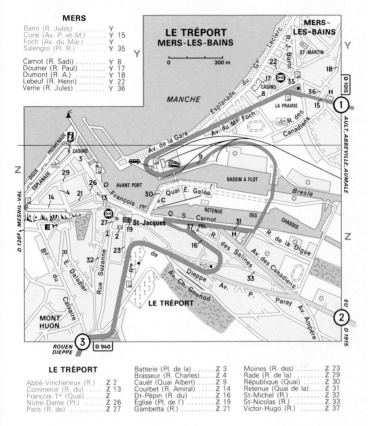

MERS		
Barni (R. Jules)	Y	
Curie (Av. P.-et-M.)	Y	15
Foch (Av. du Mar.)	Y	
Salengro (Pl. R.)	Y	35
Carnot (R. Sadi)	Y	8
Doumer (R. Paul)	Y	17
Dumont (R. A.)	Y	18
Lebeuf (R. Henri)	Y	22
Verne (R. Jules)	Y	36

LE TRÉPORT								
Abbé-Vincheneux (R.)	Z 2	Batterie (Pl. de la)	Z 3	Moines (R. des)	Z 23
Commerce (R. du)	Z 13	Brasseur (R. Charles)	Z 4	Rade (R. de la)	Z 29
François-1er (Quai)	Z	Cauët (Quai Albert)	Z 9	République (Quai)	Z 30
Notre-Dame (Pl.)	Z 26	Courbet (R. Amiral)	Z 14	Retenue (Quai de la)	Z 31
Paris (R. de)	Z 27	Dr-Pépin (R. du)	Z 16	St-Michel (R.)	Z 32
		Église (Pl. de l')	Z 19	St-Nicolas (R.)	Z 33
		Gambetta (R.)	Z 21	Victor-Hugo (R.)	Z 37

SIGHTS

★**Ascent to the Terrace Calvary** (Calvaire des Terrasses) (Z E). – *About 1/2 hour Rtn.* The Calvary on the top of the cliff is linked to the town hall, a brick and flint construction, by a 378 step stairway. To go up by car take Rue St-Michel and Boulevard du Calvaire.

From the terrace on which the Cross stands, there is a **view** which extends north beyond the last of the Caux Cliffs to Hourdel Point, the Somme Estuary and inland, along the Lower Bresle Valley to Eu and over the lower town's slate roofs, beach and harbour.

St-Jacques Church (Église) (Z). – The building, which stands halfway up the hill, dates from the second half of the 16C although it has been extensively restored. The modern porch shelters a Renaissance doorway.

Inside are several interesting 16C features including remarkable hanging keystones, a *Pietà* in the Chapel of Our Lady of Mercy (north aisle) and a low relief above the altar showing the Virgin encircled by Biblical emblems. At the far end of the church, in which the chancel is on a lower level than the nave, is the fine statue of Our Lady of Tréport.

MICHELIN GUIDES

The Red Guides (hotels and restaurants)

    **Benelux – Deutschland – España Portugal – Main cities Europe – France –
Great Britain and Ireland – Italia**

The Green Guides (beautiful scenery, buildings and scenic routes)

    **Austria – Canada – England: The West Country – Germany – Greece – Italy –
New England – Portugal – Scotland – Spain – Switzerland
London – New York City – Paris – Rome**

...and 6 guides on France.

Michelin map **54** fold 17 or **231** fold 19 – Local maps pp 39 and 128 – Facilities

Trouville, situated where the cliffs of the Normandy Corniche slope away as they approach the mouth of the Touques River, to be replaced on the far bank by a wonderful beach of find golden sand, has all the latest amenities and so maintains its reputation as the seaside resort which, as long ago as the start of the Second Empire (1852), launched the Fleurie Coast.

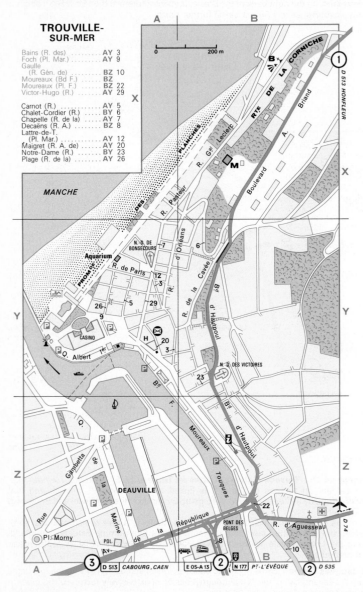

TROUVILLE-SUR-MER

Bains (R. des)	**AY** 3
Foch (Pl. Mar.)	**AY** 9
Gaulle (R. Gén. de)	**BZ** 10
Moureaux (Bd F.)	**BZ**
Moureaux (Pl. F.)	**BZ** 22
Victor-Hugo (R.)	**AY** 29
Carnot (R.)	**AY** 5
Chalet-Cordier (R.)	**BY** 6
Chapelle (R. de la)	**AY** 7
Decaëns (R. A.)	**BZ** 8
Lattre-de-T. (Pl. Mar.)	**AY** 12
Maigret (R. A. de)	**AY** 20
Notre-Dame (R.)	**BY** 23
Plage (R. de la)	**AY** 26

The Resort. – As at Deauville *(qv)*, the wooden plank promenade, the *Planches,* which lines the entire length of the beach, is the main gathering place for all holidaymakers. Opposite the swimming pool in the right wing of the Casino thermal baths offer a marine "cure".

Trouville is a lively place even during the off-season thanks to its local population-fishermen and others. The harbour quaysides make a bustling centre of attraction especially during the summer season.

⊙ **Aquarium** (AY). – Different species of fish are displayed in a reconstitution of their natural setting. Fresh and salt water fish together with equatorial forest reptiles provide a colourful and sometimes surprising spectacle.

⊙ **Montebello Museum (Musée)** (BX M). – A fine 19C brick and stone villa houses a museum containing engravings, paintings, sketches and watercolours by artists such as Boudin, Isabey, Truffault and Mozin who introduced Trouville to the Parisians. One of the rooms is devoted to the history of bathing in Trouville. Also of note is a display of 19C Bayeux lace.

⊙ **Exhibition Gallery** (Galerie d'exposition). – The gallery belongs to the museum and is located in the premises of the tourist office. Temporary exhibitions are held on a specific theme or the works of a local artist.

★ **The Corniche.** – *Make for the Corniche road on the left by way of the Boulevard Aristide-Briand.* On the way down there is a magnificent **view** of the Trouville and Deauville beaches and the Fleurie Coast.
Stop at the Bon Secours Calvary (BX B). From the viewing table the view is equally breathtaking.

EXCURSIONS

★★ **The Normandy Corniche.** – *15km - 9 1/2 miles. Leave Trouville by ③, the D 513. Description p 59.*

★★ **The Fleurie Coast.** – *19km - 12 miles. Leave Trouville by ③, the D 513. Description p 60.*

VALASSE Abbey

Michelin map 54 fold 8 or 231 fold 21 – 6km - 4 miles northwest of Lillebonne

This Cistercian abbey was founded as a result of two distinct wishes expressed by Walerian of Meulan, who escaped from a shipwreck safe and sound, and Empress Mathilde, granddaughter of William the Conqueror and who fled from her enemies during her fight against her cousin Etienne of Blois for the English throne.
The abbey was consecrated in 1181 in the presence of Henri II (son of Mathilde) and numerous bishops and lords.
Until the 14C the abbey was prosperous with possessions in more than a hundred parishes, but ruin came about with the Hundred Years War and the Wars of Religion. Under the auspices of Prior Dom Orillard the abbey was transformed in the 18C. Sold as national property during the Revolution, it had a series of different owners including a dairy and cheese factory.

⏱ **TOUR** *time: about 1 hour*

The main façade is an elegant 18C pedimented construction with two wings. The central pediment bears the arms of Empress Mathilde: three Norman leopards (relationship to William) and an eagle (she was married to the German Emperor Henry V).
The tour also includes the chapter house dating from the 13C (gadrooned capitals decorated with palmettes), lay brothers' quarters, the different rooms and living quarters on the first floor housing an exhibition on the Cistercian order and the history of the abbey.

VALMONT   Pop 860

Michelin map 52 fold 12 or 231 fold 9 – 11km - 7 miles east of Fécamp

Located in the very heart of the Caux Region and dominated by a castle built on a rocky spur, the little town of Valmont possesses the ruins of a Benedictine abbey.
The town grew in importance with the arrival of the Estouteville family, probably of Viking origin and very successful in the 12C. Robert I d'Estouteville took part in the Battle of Hastings in 1066 beside William the Conqueror.

SIGHTS

★ **Abbey (Abbaye).** – Founded in the 12C, the Benedictine Abbey of Valmont was rebuilt
⏱ in the 14C following a fire and was radically altered in the 16C. The conventual buildings (1680) were rebuilt by the Maurists (a congregation of Benedictine monks). After the Revolution the abbey became a private residence and in the 19C it belonged to cousins of Delacroix – the artist visited here several times. Of the old abbey church, only the Renaissance choir remains and its roof has fallen in. The Flamboyant influence dominates the aisles and the remains of the transept.
The **Lady Chapel★**, or "six o'clock chapel (the monks celebrated mass every day at this time), which has remained intact among the ruins, has an overall effect of great grace. The highly decorated arches are very delicate. The five 15C windows are devoted to the life of the Virgin Mary. Above the altar is a tiny room which has exquisite decorations and also a picture of the Annunciation attributed to Germain Pilon.
Notice on the right the tomb and recumbent figure of Nicolas d'Estouteville, founder of the abbey, and a low relief depicting the Baptism of Christ.
The altar is made of one large stone resting on columns from the triforium which was partly destroyed. The 12C altar cross dominated the former monks' cemetery. To the right, a high relief over a fountain portrays the Baptism of Christ in Jordan.
Recently restored, the Renaissance sacristy has windows of the period and 18C panelling.

⏱ **Castle (Château).** – Property of the Estoutevilles, lords of Valmont, this former military fortress preserves a Romanesque keep flanked by a Louis XI wing, crowned by a covered watchpath, and a Renaissance wing. Only the keep and the Louis XI wing are open to visitors. Certain rooms are reserved for temporary exhibitions.
The charter or archives room, 9m - 29 feet high, is decorated with the arms of the lords and barons of Valmont. A wooden gallery runs round the upper part. The garret with its fine woodwork contains tools used in farming and other professions in the Caux Region.

Park. – With an area of 90 ha - 222 acres – the park consists of lawns and various species of trees. There is also a large games and amusement area.

Michelin map 52 fold 4 or 231 fold 10 – Local map p 55

Varengeville, a seaside resort in a beautiful setting, has always attracted artists. The village houses lie scattered in small groups along the roadsides in a typical Norman countryside of hedges and half-timbered houses.

SIGHTS

★ **Moustiers Park.** – Situated in a pretty valley with a view of the coast, the park is an ⊙ ornamental and botanical garden (9 ha - 22 acres) with a profusion of flowering plants including rare species and giant rhododendrons 6 to 8m, 20 to 26ft high and in bloom from April to June. The darker shades of the trees form an appropriate backcloth.
A number of paths lead to "tableaux" formed by the most beautiful trees and flowers.
⊙ The **house** in the middle of the park was built in 1898 by an English architect Edwin Luytens and is certainly original (Luytens designed the Viceroy's palace in New Dehli). Temporary exhibitions are held there.

Church (Église). – Dating from the 11, 13 and 15C the church has a beautiful **setting**★ overlooking the sea, and is surrounded by a small cemetery where one can discover the graves of the artist Georges Braque, the dramatist Georges de Porto-Riche (1894-1930) and the musician Albert Roussel. The church has a 16C porch and two naves. The stained glass in the chancel of the large nave is by Ubac, whereas the glass in the south nave depicting the Tree of Jesse is by Braque.

⊙ **St-Dominique Chapel (Chapelle).** – At the edge of the village, to the left of the Dieppe road, the chapel houses a number of stained glass windows by Braque and a tableau by the Granville painter Maurice Denis. The chapel was once a barn.

⊙ **Ango Manor House (Manoir d'Ango).** – Located in a pleasant landscape, this lovely Renaissance home was constructed by Italian craftsmen from 1533-45. It was once the summer home of ship-owner Jean Ango (qv) who received François I on the premises.
The buildings are grouped round a vast interior courtyard. Entrance to the ground floor of the south building is by a loggia, with four arches, which was originally decorated with frescoes by the school of Leonardo da Vinci. Pierced with windows, its stone walls are ornamented in the Renaissance style with finely sculpted foliage, shells and medallions.
The imposing seignorial **dovecot**★ is a colourful brick and stone structure beyond which stand the other outbuildings.

EXCURSIONS

★ **Ailly Lighthouse (Phare d'Ailly).** – *1km - 2/3 mile on the D 75^A starting from the D 75.*
⊙ A modern lighthouse with a range of 80km - 50 miles has replaced the two 18 and 19C lighthouses, destroyed in 1944. From the upper platform the **view** extends over the Caux cliffs for more than 60km - 40 miles.

Valleuses. – *For an explanation of this term see p 53.*
Vasterival and Petit Ailly Gorge *(access signposted)* are among the most characteristic examples of this kind of formation on the coast.

VASCŒUIL   Pop 317

Michelin map 55 fold 7 or 231 fold 24 – 11km – 7 miles northwest of Lyons-la-Forêt – Local map p 97

This little village in the Eure Region is famous for its castle which has become a true centre of culture.

⊙ **Castle (Château).** – Framed by the confluence of the Andelle and Crevon Rivers, the castle (14, 15 and 16C) where **Michelet** wrote part of his **Histoire de France** (1833-67), is surrounded by gardens where reconstructions of half-timbered thatched cottages evoke old Normandy.
Temporary exhibitions are held in the restored rooms of the castle.
The **Michelet House** contains important mementoes of the historian and his family (portraits, notes, correspondance...).
The main courtyard is decorated with carvings and mosaics by Braque, Dali, Vasarely and Folon. An attractive 17C brick dovecot stands in the yard, complete with its original spiral staircase.

Church (Église). – The church contains the tomb of the 12C Blessed Hugues de Saint-Jovinien. Note also the 17C statues of the Holy Virgin and Saint Martial in polychrome stone.

EXCURSIONS

Crevon Valley. – *8km - 5 miles to the northwest on the D 12.*
The road winds its way up the charming valley.

Ry. – *Description p 120.*
Blainville. – *Description p 46.*

Le Héron Valley. – *21km - 13 miles to the north on the D 46.*

Héronchelles. – Pop 91. A pretty village with a 16C manor house.

Yville. – Notice the lovely thatched roofs.

At Buchy take the D 919 to the right.

Bosc-Bordel. – Pop 385. The 13C church is a pleasing rustic construction with a 16C wooden porch.

★ VERNEUIL-SUR-AVRE

Pop 6 926

Michelin map **60** fold 6 or **231** fold 46

Verneuil is divided into three quarters with, respectively, the Madeleine, Gambetta and Notre-Dame Streets as their main arteries, and formerly a fortification surrounding each ending, like the city wall which encircled them all, in a moat filled from the Iton River.
The town has kept a number of beautiful half-timbered houses and restored *hôtels*. Place de la Madeleine is the traditional centre.

HISTORICAL NOTES

Verneuil is the descendant town of a fortified city created in the 12C by Henri I Beauclerc, Duke of Normandy, second son of William the Conqueror. Together with Tillières and Nonancourt it formed the Avre defence line on the Franco-Norman frontier, and before it was finally won by the French in 1449, therefore, saw many bloody battles including that of 1424 when Charles VII was defeated.
As the River Avre flowed through French territory, Henri had a canal dug out in order to divert the Iton, about 10km - 6 miles to the north, and thereby supply Verneuil. The town became French in 1204 under Philippe Auguste, who granted a charter and built the Grise Tower and its defence system.
In the battle of 1424 the French army with its Italian, Breton and Scottish mercenaries suffered heavy losses through lack of strategy and discipline. The French victory of 1449 was achieved thanks to the guile of miller Jean Bertin who helped the front line of the troops to enter the town.

SIGHTS

★ **La Madeleine Church** (Église). – *Enter by the south doorway.*
⊙ The **tower**★ dates from the late 15 – early 16C. Built onto the church it consists of four tiers with pierced bays decorated on all sides with statues. The third tier is surmounted by a richly ornamented belfry. The different materials used at each reconstruction, particularly during the Gothic period, can be clearly seen as you walk round the church. The Renaissance style porch is flanked to right and left by mutilated but still beautiful 16C statues of the Virgin and of St Anne.
Some 15 to 19C works of art worth noting: near the door, St Crispin patron saint of shoemakers, St Teresa of the Child Jesus with a surprisingly grave countenance, in the south transept; across from it is a 16C Holy Sepulchre, the tomb of Count de Frotté (one of the last leaders of the Chouans in Normandy) by David d'Angers (1783-1856); finally at the end of the south aisle and left of the altar to the Holy Sacrament, a 15C polychrome statue of the Virgin with an Apple.
St John the Baptist stands near the font. A 16C *Pietà* stands at the end of the south aisle next to the large 18C organ. In the nave covered with barrel vaulting there stands a fine wrought iron pulpit.

⊙ **Notre Dame Church** (Église). – The church, which was built of the red agglomerate stone known as *grison* in the 12C *(p 107)* and has been remodelled, possesses a number of 16C **statues**★ carved by local sculptors.

1) St Denis (14C)
2) St James the Greater
3) St Christopher
4) St Christine
5) St Fiacre
6) St Susanna
7) St Barbara
8) St Francis of Assisi
9) St Benedict
10) Joan of Arc, as a Lorraine countrygirl
11) Renaissance Pietà
12) St Lawrence
13) St Augustine
14) St Denis with open skull
15) St Louis (17C)
16) Two Prophets (Renaissance woodwork)
17) St Sebastian (17C woodwork).
18) 15C chest and altar base
19) 11C font
20) 14C Trinity (early Norman Renaissance, 14C)
21) Virgin at the Calvary (13C)
22) St John

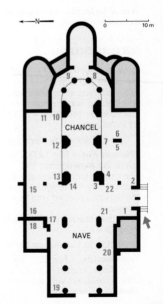

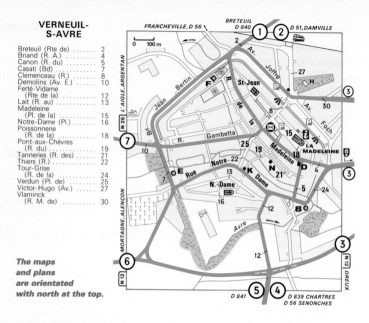

The maps and plans are orientated with north at the top.

Grise Tower (Tour Grise) (B). – The walk round this 13C tower commands the town and surrounding countryside. Like the church, it is built of red agglomerate.

To the south of the tower cross the small bridge over one of the arms of the Iton to view the building together with a charming little house at its base. The pleasant and relaxing Fougère Park lies near the bridge.

St Jean Church (Église). – This partly ruined church has kept its 15C tower and Gothic doorway.

The "Promenades". – The term refers to Boulevard Casati and the continuing streets.

Remains of several of the old outer fortifications can be seen, notably the ruins of the Tour Gelée (**E** – Boulevard Casati) and Jean Bertin's Mill (**F** – Boulevard Jean Bertin). Interesting views of the town can be had from Avenues Maréchal Joffre and Maréchal Foch.

Old Houses. – They are extremely well restored and undeniably add to Verneuil's charm.

Corner of Rue de la Madeleine and Rue du Canon. – 15C house (**D**) with chequered walls and angle turret.

Rue de la Madeleine. – Between Rue Canon and Rue Thiers stand a number of attractive stone or timbered houses. The 18C Bournonville Hôtel has wrought iron balconies.

Note also the houses at nos 532, 466 and 401. No 532 stands behind a courtyard.

Rue des Tanneries. – A Renaissance house (**N**) stands at no 136, with a carved wooden door surmounted by wooden statues.

Corner of Rue Notre Dame and Rue du Pont-aux-Chèvres. – A 16C town house with chequered wall and decorated turret (**K**).

Place de Verdun, Place de la Madeleine, Rue de la Poissonnerie. – Other picturesque old wooden houses can be seen.

EXCURSIONS

Avre Valley. – *Round tour of 25km - 16 miles – about 3/4 hour. Leave Verneuil by ④, the D 839 and turn left into the D 316 which continues as the D 102.*

The road runs along the pleasantly shady right bank of the Avre. On your way you will see the water catchment works of the aquaduct which was built in 1892 and still conveys 160 000m³ - 35 million gallons of drinking water daily to Paris 102km - 63 miles away.

Go to Tillières by Montigny-sur-Avre and Bérou-la-Mulotière.

Tillières-sur-Avre. – Pop 1 233. Tillières was the first Norman fortified town built (1013) to guard the Avre defence line.

The church, with its Romanesque nave and panelled vault was rebuilt in the 16C. Badly damaged by fire in 1969, restoration work has been carried out. Note the carvings on the beautiful pointed arch vaulting of the chancel (16C), the work of the school of Jean Goujon.

From the garden known as the *Grand Parterre* there is a fine view of the village and the Avre Valley.

Return to Verneuil on the N 12.

Francheville. – Pop 839. *9km - 5 1/2 miles northwest on the D 56.*

The village, located in an attractive setting beside the Iton River, has a pretty country church, restored, with interesting folk statues. On the square stands a small **metalwork museum.**

VERNIER Marsh (LE MARAIS VERNIER)

Michelin map ██ folds 8, 9 or ███ folds 20, 21

The Vernier Marsh, once a bend in the River Seine, cuts a vast bay of 5000 ha - 20 square miles – out of the Roumois Plateau between Quillebœuf and Roque Point. It forms part of the Brotonne Regional Nature Park.

FROM QUILLEBŒUF TO ROQUE POINT

23km - 14 miles – about 1 hour

Quillebœuf. – *Description p 107.*

The drive will take you from the Seine Valley to that of the Risle. Between Quillebœuf and Ste-Opportune-la-Mare, the road overlooks the wide Seine Valley. On the other side of the river, the Port-Jérôme refineries and petro-chemical factories can be seen.

Ste-Opportune-la-Mare. – Pop 339. Within the context of the Lower Seine regional open-air "museum" *(p 49)* this small village boasts in the ⊘ former presbytery the **Apple House** (Maison de la pomme), an exhibition on apples and their varieties together with an audio-visual explanation of the cider-making process.

⊘ An old **forge** presents the blacksmith's tools which can be seen in operation on certain days.

Follow the signs *Panorama de la Grande Mare* to a viewpoint over the Great Marsh and beyond to the reclaimed Marshland.

⊘ **Mannevilles Nature Reserve** (Réserve Naturelle des Mannevilles). – The area is protected and enables the visitor to discover the flowers and animals of the marsh and to approach Camargue horses and highland cattle.

Beyond Bouquelon, from a hairpin bend to the left on the D 103 (viewing table), there is a good view over the marsh to Tancarville Bridge. Between the fork with the D 100 and Foulbec the D 90 continues as a corniche road with a view down into the Risle Valley.

Take the D 39 north to St-Samson-de-la-Roque.

Beyond the village a narrow, winding road leads to Roque Point.

★ **Roque Point** (La Pointe de la Roque). – *Picnic area.* From the lighthouse on the cliff the **panorama** extends over the Seine Estuary to Cape Hève and the Côte de Grace. Tancarville Cliffs and Bridge can be seen to the right.

Roque Point, Vernier Marsh

Michelin map 55 folds 17, 18 or 231 fold 36 – Local map p 127

Vernon, on the bank of the Seine, close to the forest of the same name, was created by Rollo, first Duke of Normandy, in the 9C. It became French during the reign of Philippe-Auguste early in the 13C and is now an extremely pleasant residential town.

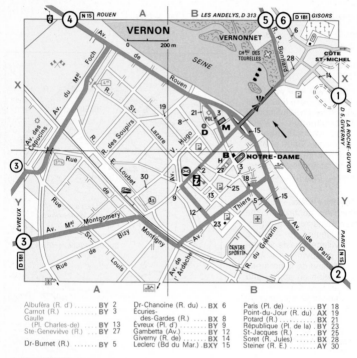

Albuféra (R. d') .... **BY** 2	Dr-Chanoine (R. du) .. **BX** 6	Paris (Pl. de) .... **BY** 18
Carnot (R.) .... **BY** 3	Écuries-	Point-du-Jour (R. du) **AX** 19
Gaulle	des-Gardes (R.) .... **BX** 8	Potard (R.) .... **BX** 21
(Pl. Charles-de) ... **BY** 13	Évreux (Pl. d') .... **BY** 9	République (Pl. de la) . **BY** 23
Ste-Geneviève (R.) .. **BY** 27	Gambetta (Av.) ...... **BY** 12	St-Jacques (R.) ...... **BY** 25
	Giverny (R. de) ...... **BX** 14	Soret (R. Jules) ...... **BX** 28
Dr-Burnet (R.) .... **BY** 5	Leclerc (Bd du Mar.) .**BXY** 15	Steiner (R. E.) .... **AY** 30

SIGHTS

★ **Notre-Dame Church (Église) (BY).** – This 12C collegiate church was remodelled several times before the Renaissance. The 15C west front has a beautiful rose window flanked by galleries. The nave, also 15C, is higher than the transept and chancel, its triforium and tall windows having considerable beauty of line. The Romanesque arches in the chancel were superimposed by an upper tier in the 16C, the period also of the organ loft and the windows in the second chapel off the south aisle.

Half-timbered Houses (BY B). – An attractive 15C house stands to the left of the church. There are others in Rue Carnot and Rue Potard.

⊙ **A.-G. Poulain Museum (Musée) (BX M).** – A wrought iron door opens on to the courtyard of the museum which is arranged in several buildings dating from the 15 to the 19C. The collections concentrate on prehistory, paintings and drawings and include works by Monet, Rosa Bonheur, Maurice Denis, Vuillard and Steinlen (1859-1923).

Archives Tower (Tour des Archives) (BX D). – The tower was the keep of the 12C castle built by Philippe Auguste. The ground floor, first and second floors and the watchpath are accessible by a spiral staircase. The first floor room has quadripartite vaulting supported by four carved capitals and is decorated with the arms of the four Governors of the castle between the 14 and the 17C.
The windows of the top floor look out onto the former ramparts. From the watchpath there is a view over the town and its surroundings.

Bridge Viewpoint (BX). – From the bridge you get a view of Vernon, the wooded islands in the Seine and the ruined piles on which the 12C bridge stood.
On the right bank amidst the greenery can be seen the towers of Tourelles Castle which formed part of the defences of the old bridge.

★ **St-Michel Hill (Côte St-Michel) (BX).** – *1 hour on foot Rtn.*
There is a good view of Vernon and the Seine Valley.

EXCURSIONS

★ **Giverny.** – *2km - 1 1/4 miles. Leave Vernon by ①, the D 5. Description p 79.*

★ **Bizy Château.** – *2km - 1 1/4 miles. Leave Vernon by ③, the D 181. Description p 45.*

Coutumes Beacon (Signal des Coutumes). – *Leave Vernon by ②, the N 15. 5km - 3 miles further, on entering Port-Villez, turn right on the D 89.*

Notre-Dame-de-la-Mer Chapel. – There is a most entertaining **aerial view★** of the right bank of the Seine from Bonnières to Villez from the belvedere on the chapel forecourt.

> *Follow the D 89. Turn sharp left at Jeufosse town hall, leaving a surfaced road on the right. On leaving Coutumes take a surfaced road on the right.*

Coutumes Beacon. – From the hill's lower slopes there is a wide and pleasant **view★** of the Bonnières bend in the river.

Villequier stretches out in a beautiful **setting**★ along the banks of the Seine, at the foot of a wooded hill crowned by a castle.

The Villequier Tragedy. – Victor Hugo's daughter, Léopoldine, and her husband, Charles Vacquerie were drowned in the Seine at Villequier six months after their marriage in 1843. The village was brought literary fame when the poet expressed his sorrow in his volume of poems, *Les Contemplations.*

The tomb of Charles Vacquerie and Léopoldine, Victor Hugo's statue on the Caudebec road and the Victor Hugo Museum are all reminders of the tragedy.

SIGHTS

★ **Victor Hugo Museum (Musée).** – *Access by Rue Ernest Binet.*

The museum is in the house once owned by the Vacqueries, a rich family of boat builders from Le Havre. It evokes the life of Léopoldine Hugo, her family and friends. Letters exchanged between Léopoldine and her relatives, portraits and furniture once belonging to the family together with landscapes of Normandy bring to life those peaceful moments preceding the fateful day of September 4th 1843. Also on display are Hugo's *Contemplations,* handwritten letters and sketches drawn by the poet.

Church (Église). – 15 and 16C. The church has a fine timberwork roof and 16C stained glass windows. One is known as the "naval battle". To the right, in the small cemetery, among the tombs of the Hugo family, are the tombs of Charles Vacquerie and Léopoldine as well as that of Victor Hugo's wife, Adèle.

Quays along the Seine. – As you walk along the quayside you can watch the boats on their way upstream and downstream. In the past it was here that estuary pilots took over from upstream pilots and vice versa.

The White House (Maison Blanche). – This late 15C stone manor house stands just outside the town on the Caudebec road. The staircase is located in a turret alongside the façade looking out onto the courtyard.

Temporary exhibitions by local artists are held in the nicely restored cellars and first floor rooms.

VIMOUTIERS   Pop 5 063

Michelin map **55** fold 13 or **231** fold 32

The small town of Vimoutiers is tucked away in the valley of the River Vie between hills covered with apple trees which supply the local cider factories. Vimoutiers has close ties with Marie Harel, who gave us the famous Camembert cheese. A statue to her memory, offered by an American cheesemaker, stands on the town hall square.

Camembert Museum (Musée du Camembert). – 10 Avenue du Général de Gaulle, on the premises of the Tourist Information Centre.

The exhibition includes the history and different stages in the manufacturing process *(p 29),* from the arrival of the milk to the dispatching of the final product, with the aid of explanatory documents. Note the impressive collection of Camembert labels.

EXCURSION

Camembert. – Pop 177.

According to the legend, **Marie Harel** (1761-1812) hid a refractory priest during the Revolution. By way of thanks he gave her the secret of his cheese recipe. Camembert was born. At first covered with a bluish rind which turned grey on maturing, it took on the appearance we know today by the addition of white mildew from the *bondons* (cylindrical cheese) of the Bray Region.

A few farms can be visited where cheese is still made in the traditional way.

The Bayeux Tapestry illustrates
with fascinating detail the Norman Conquest of England.

For further details consult
*the **Michelin Green Guide Normandy Cotentin and the Channel Islands.***

YVETOT

Michelin map 52 fold 13 or 231 fold 22 – Local map p 55 – See town plan in current Michelin Red Guide France

Legendary capital of an imaginary kingdom made famous in a song by Béranger, Yvetot is in fact a large market town on the Caux Plateau.

St-Pierre Church (Église). – This is a modern structure (1956) with remarkably large **stained glass windows**★★ by Max Ingrand. The effect is dazzling. The colours, soft at the entrance, become more brilliant towards the centre where the Virgin and Apostles can be seen around the Crucified Christ. Other panels show the saints of France, founders of religious orders and great saints of the Rouen diocese.

Behind the altar the Lady Chapel is illuminated by stained glass windows relating episodes in the life of the Virgin.

EXCURSION

★ **The Caux Plateau.** – *Round tour of 24km - 15 miles – about 1 hour. Leave Yvetot to the south on the Caudebec road and then take the by-pass to the right. Further on, take the D 34 on the left.*

Allouville-Bellefosse. – Pop 903. This village is well known for its **oak tree** (chêne), which rises in front of the church, the most famous tree in Normandy and, at 1 300 years, one of the oldest in France. To keep it standing the trunk and biggest branches have had to be supported. Two superimposed chapels have been built into the hollow trunk and are accessible by stairs and galleries.

⊙ The **Nature Museum,** approximately 1 1/2km - 1 mile away *(signposted),* is located in an old Caux farmhouse. Two diorama displays show local bird families and a reconstitution of the Normandy countryside (marsh, plain, forest, farmyard and coastline). Notice the coastline before and after the effects of pollution.

Return to Allouville and take the D 33 to the right. After the crossroads with the D 131, turn left into the D 37 leading back to Yvetot.

Fine examples of Caux farmhouses surrounded by trees can be seen beyond Touffreville-la-Corbeline.

Practical Information

The French Government Tourist Offices at 178 Piccadilly, London WIV OAL, ☎ (01) 49 76 22 and 610 and 628 Fifth Avenue, New York, ☎ (212) 757-1125 will provide information and literature.

How to get there. – You can go directly by scheduled national airlines, by commercial and package tour flights, possibly with a rail or coach link-up or you can go by cross-Channel ferry or hovercraft and on by car or train.

The following companies operate cross-Channel services direct to Normandy:

Brittany Ferries: Wharf Road, Portsmouth PO2 8RU ☎ 0705 827701.

P & O European Ferries: Channel House, Channel View Road, Dover CT17 9TJ ☎ 0304 203388.

Sealink: Charter House, Park Street, Ashford, Kent TN24 8EX ☎ 0233 47047.

Enquire at any good travel agent and remember if you are going during the holiday season or at Christmas, Easter or Whitsun, to book well in advance.

CUSTOMS AND OTHER FORMALITIES

Visa for U.S. citizens. – An **entry visa** is required for all U.S. citizens visiting France in accordance with a French security measure.

Apply at the French Consulate (visa issued same day; delay if submitted by mail).

Papers and other documents. – A valid national **passport** (or in the case of the British, a Visitor's Passport) is all that is required.

For the car a valid **driving licence, international driving permit, car registration papers** (log-book) and a **nationality plate** of the approved size. Insurance cover is compulsory and although the Green Card is no longer a legal requirement for France, it is the most effective form of proof of insurance cover and is internationally recognized by the police.

There are no customs formalities for holidaymakers importing their caravans into France for a stay of less than 6 months. No customs document is necessary for pleasure boats or outboard motors for a stay of less than 6 months but you should have the registration certificate on board.

Motoring regulations. – The minimum driving age is 18 years old. Certain motoring organizations run accident insurance and breakdown service schemes for their members. Enquire before leaving. A **red warning triangle** or hazard warning lights are obligatory in case of a breakdown. In France it is compulsory for the front passengers to wear **seat belts.** Children under ten should be on the back seat.

The **speed limits,** although liable to modification, are: motorways 130kph – 80mph (110kph when raining); national trunk roads 110kph – 68mph; other roads 90kph – 56mph (80kph – 50mph when raining) and in towns 60kph – 37mph. The regulations on speeding and drinking and driving are strictly interpreted – usually by an on the spot fine and/or confiscation of the vehicle. Remember to **cede priority** to vehicles joining from the right. There are tolls on the motorways.

Medical Treatment. – For EEC countries it is necessary to have Form E III which testifies to your entitlement to medical benefits from the Department of Health and Social Security. With this you can obtain medical treatment in an emergency and after the necessary steps, a refund of part of the costs from the local Social Security offices (Caisse Primaire d'Assurance Maladie). Comprehensive insurance cover is still advisable. Nationals of non-EEC countries should make enquiries before leaving.

Currency. – There are no restrictions on what you can take into France in the way of currency. To facilitate export of foreign notes in excess of the given allocation, visitors are advised to complete a currency declaration form on arrival.

Your passport is necessary as identification when cashing cheques in banks. Commission charges vary with hotels charging more highly than banks when "obliging" non-residents on holidays or at weekends.

DULY ARRIVED

Embassy: British – 35 Rue du Faubourg-St-Honoré, 75008 Paris, ☎ 42 66 91 42.
American – 2 Avenue Gabriel, 75008 Paris; ☎ 42 96 12 02.

Tourist Information Centres or *Syndicats d'Initiative* 🛈 are to be found in most large towns and many tourist resorts. They can supply large scale town plans, timetables and information on entertainment facilities, sports and sightseeing.

Poste Restante. – Name, Poste Restante, Poste Centrale, *département's* postal code number, followed by the town's name, France. The Michelin Red Guide France gives local postal code numbers.

Postage via air mail to: UK letter 2.50F; postcard 1.90F
US aerogramme 3.90F; letter (20g) 6F; postcard 3.35F.

Where to stay. – In the Michelin Red Guide France you will find a selection of hotels at various prices in all areas. It will also list local restaurants again with prices. If camping or caravaning consult the Michelin Guide Camping Caravaning France.

Electric Current. – The electric current is 220 volts. European circular two pin plugs are the rule – remember an electrical adaptor.

Public holidays in France. – National museums and art galleries are closed on Tuesdays. The following are days when museums and other monuments may be closed or may vary their hours of admission:

New Year's Day
Easter Sunday and Monday
May Day **(1 May)**
Fête de la Libération **(8 May)**

Ascension Day
Whit Sunday and Monday
France's National Day **(14 July)**

The Assumption **(15 August)**
All Saints' Day **(1 November)**
Armistice Day **(11 November)**
Christmas Day

In addition to the usual school holidays at Christmas, Easter and in the summer, there are week long breaks in February and late October-early November.

SPORTS AND OUTDOOR ACTIVITIES

Sailing. – Apply to: the Fédération Française de Voile, 55 Avenue Kléber, 75084 Paris Cedex 16, ☎ 45 53 68 00.

Windsurfing. – The sport is subjected to certain regulations. Apply to sailing clubs. Permitted on lakes and in sports and leisure centres. Boards can be hired on all major beaches.

Landsailing. – Apply to the Offices Départementaux du Tourisme: 2 bis Rue du Petit Salut, 76008 Rouen, ☎ 35 88 61 32; Place du Canada, 14000 Caen, ☎ 31 68 53 30; 35 Rue du Docteur Oursel. 27000 Évreux, ☎ 32 38 21 61.

Freshwater fishing. Whatever the area the regulations must be observed. Contact the fishing associations and tourist information centres. A useful document is the brochure *Pêche en France* (in French only) published by the Conseil Supérieur de la Pêche, 10, Rue Péclet, 75015 Paris, ☎ 48 42 10 00.

Hunting. – For all enquiries apply to « Saint-Hubert Club de France », 10 Rue de Lisbonne, 75008 Paris, ☎ 45 22 38 90.

Outings on horseback. – Apply to the Fédération des Randonneurs Équestres, 16 Rue des Apennins, 75017 Paris, ☎ 42 26 23 23; or to the Fédération Équestre Française Ligue de Normandie, 235 Rue Caponière, 14063 Caen Cedex, ☎ 31 73 31 35.

Rambling. – Short, medium and long distance footpath Topo Guides are edited by the Fédération Française de la Randonnée pédestre/Comité national des Sentiers de Grande Randonnée.
If you are interested in this document, apply to 64 Rue de Gergovie, 75014 Paris, ☎ 45 45 31 02.

Cycling. – The Fédération Française de Cyclotourisme, 8 Rue Jean-Marie Jégo, 75013 Paris, ☎ 45 80 30 21, supplies itineraries covering most of France, mentioning mileage, difficulties and sights to see. Apply also to the Ligue Haute-Normandie de la FFCT represented by M. Andrieu Julien, 21 Rue de l'Enseigne Renaud, 76000 Rouen, ☎ 35 89 45 06; the Comité Départemental de Cyclotourisme, 50 Rue de la Libération, 27380 Fleury-sur-Andelle, ☎ 32 49 00 87.
Three types of bicycles to rent are proposed in the railway stations (Gare SNCF) – racing, traditional or "cross-country". They may be hired for 1/2 day, a day or several days, with special rates for longer periods. Apply in particular to the following railway stations: l'Aigle, Dieppe, Dives-sur-Mer, Dreux, Fécamp, Forges-les-Eaux, Gisors, Neufchâtel-en-Bray, Nogent-le-Rotrou, Le Tréport-Mers, Trouville-Deauville, Vernon. Tourist Information Centres generally have addresses where bicycles may be hired.

Canoeing. – Apply to the Fédération Française de Canoë-kayak, 17 Route de Vienne, 69007 Lyon, ☎ 78 61 32 74. A guide is edited annually indicating schools and places where canoeing may be practised.

Country accommodation. – Apply to the Fédération Française des gîtes ruraux, 35 Rue Godot-de-Mauroy, 75009 Paris, ☎ 47 42 25 43, for a list of useful addresses.

Brotonne Regional Nature Park. – For information on rambling or other activities, apply to the Maison du Parc, 2 Rond-Point Marbec, 76580 Le Trait, ☎ 35 37 23 16. Jumièges-le-Mesnil country park is open from March to October ☎ 35 37 93 84.

Crafts. – Apply to Maison des Métiers, 27500 Bourneville, ☎ 32 57 40 41.

Tourism and the handicapped. – A number of sights described in this guide are accessible to the handicapped. They are listed in a work edited by the National Committee for the Reinsertion of Handicapped People (Comité National Français de Liaison pour la Réadaptation des Handicapés) 38 Bd Raspail 75007 Paris, entitled *Touristes quand même! Promenades en France pour les voyageurs handicapés*. More than 90 towns in France are listed with abundant practical information to facilitate the physically handicapped and those with defective sight or hearing.

The **Michelin Red Guide France** and the **Michelin Guide Camping Caravaning** France indicate respectively bedrooms for the physically handicapped and specially equipped sanitary arrangements.

BOOKS TO READ

Blue Guide to France by Ian Robertson *(A and C Black)*.

A Holiday History of France by Ronald Hamilton *(Chatto and Windus)*.

Normandy, Brittany and the Loire Valley *(Benn Blue Guides)*.

Normandy by Nesta Roberts *(Collins)*.

Claude Monet: Life at Giverny by Joyes *(Thames and Hudson)*.

The Impressionists by William Gaunt *(Thames and Hudson)*.

Food Lover's Guide to France by Patricia Wells *(Eyre and Spottiswoode)*.

PRINCIPAL FESTIVALS (1)

25 March

Janville Chapel .... Pilgrimage

30 April to I May

Rouen .... 24 hours boat race: international competition grouping a hundred motor boats around the Ile Lacroix

Whit Sunday and Whit Monday

Honfleur .... Seamen's Festival – Sunday: blessing of the sea Monday morning: seamen's pilgrimage

Whit Monday

Bernay .... Pilgrimage to Notre-Dame-de-Couture

Sunday nearest 30 May, except Whit Sunday

Rouen .... Joan of Arc Festival

End of May to early June

Houlgate .... European festival of folk dancing

Early June to late September

Lisieux .... Son et lumière at the Basilica, every evening at 9.30 pm. From 13 to 30F. Apply to the Tourist Information Centre (syndicat d'initiative) ☏ 31 62 08 41

Last Sunday in June

Villedieu 55 fold 8 .... Festival of St John the Baptist. Procession particularly for dignitaries of the Order of St John of Malta

July

Le Havre .... International Regatta

Sunday nearest 15 July

Lisieux .... Consecration of the Basilica

16 July

La Haye-de-Routot .... St Clair Bonfire

Last weekend in July

La Heuze Chapel 52 fold 15 ..... Pilgrimage to St Christopher – Outdoor festival Saturday evening. Sunday morning mass

Early August

Ste-Marguerite-sur-Mer .... Fishing competition

15 August

Lisieux .... Procession to the Smiling Virgin

Last weekend in August

Cabourg .... Historical procession "William the Conqueror"

Last Sunday in August

Deauville .... Grand Prix: horseracing. Polo championship cup.

Early September

Deauville .... American Film Festival

Last Sunday in September

Lisieux .... St Thérèse Festival. On the previous evening and the day itself: procession with shrine containing the relics of the saint.

Last Sunday in September (next event 1990)

Caudebec-en-Caux .... Cider Festival (every other year)

---

(1) For localities not described in this guide, the Michelin map and fold numbers are given.

FRENCH WORDS APPEARING
ON THE MAPS AND PLANS

For words and expressions used in hotels and restaurants see the annual Michelin Red Guide France.
See also architectural terms pp 20-21.

abbatiale	abbey church	gorges	gorge
aéroport	airport	halles	covered market
ancien (ne)	former, old	hôtel	mansion, town house
barrage	dam	hôtel de ville	town hall
belvédère	belvedere	jardin	garden
bois	wood	lycée	secondary school
bureau de P.T.T.	post office	mont	mount
calvaire	wayside cross	moulin	mill
caserne	barracks	musée	museum
cathédrale	cathedral	parc des expositions	exhibition ground
chapelle	chapel		
château	castle, château	phare	lighthouse
cirque	amphitheatre	police	police
cité administrative	municipal or administrative centre	pont	bridge
		pont tournant	swing bridge
donjon	keep	remparts	ramparts
écluse	lock	réserve naturelle	nature reserve
école	school	rocher	rock
église	church	signal	beacon
enclos	enclosure	site	site, setting
étang	pool, pond	stade	stadium, sports ground
falaise	cliff	table d'orientation	viewing table
foirail	fair-ground, agricultural market place		
		tour	tower
forêt	forest	usine	factory, power station
gare	railway station	vallée	valley
gare maritime	ferry terminal	vers	towards
gare routière	bus station	vieux (vieille)	old
gisement	deposit	vélodrome	cycle racing track

Times and charges for admission

As times and charges for admission are liable to alteration, the information below is given for guidance only.

The information applies to individual adults. However, special conditions regarding times and charges for parties are common and arrangements should be made in advance. In some cases admission is free on certain days, eg Wednesdays, Sundays or public holidays.

Churches do not admit visitors during services and are usually closed from 1200 to 1400. Tourists should refrain from visits when services are being held. Admission times are indicated if the interior is of special interest. Visitors to chapels are accompanied by the person who keeps the keys. A donation is welcome.

Lecture tours are regularly organised during the tourist season in Bernay, Dieppe, Eu, Evreux, Honfleur, Louviers, Pont Audemer, Rouen, Verneuil-sur-Avre and Vernon. Apply to the Tourist Office (syndicat d'initiative).

When guided tours are indicated, the departure time of the last tour of the morning or afternoon will be up to an hour before the actual closing time. Most tours are conducted by French speaking guides but in some cases the term "guided tours" may cover group visiting with recorded commentaries. Some of the larger and more frequented sights may offer guided tours in other languages. Enquire at the ticket office or book stall. Other aids for the foreign tourist are notes, pamphlets or audio guides.

Enquire at the Tourist Office for local religious holidays, market days etc.

Every sight for which there are times and charges is indicated by the symbol ⓥ in the margin in the main part of the guide.

A

L'AIGLE 🛈 place Fulbert de Beina, 61300. ☎ 33 24 12 40.

Marcel-Angot Museum. – Guided tours (time: 30 min) from 0830 to 1200 and from 1430 to 1800; closed Saturdays, Sundays and public holidays; no admission charge; ☎ 33 24 44 99 (Town Hall).

"June 1944: Battle of Normandy" Museum. – Guided tours (time: 30 min) Palm Sunday to 11 November from 1000 to 1200 and from 1400 to 1800; closed Mondays; 13F; ☎ 33 24 19 44.

AILLY

Lighthouse. – Guided tours (time: 15 min) daily in season from 1000 to 1200 and from 1400 to 1900.

ALLOUVILLE-BELLEFOSSE

Nature Museum. – Open daily from 0900 to 1200 and from 1400 to 1900; closed 1 January and 25 December; 15F; ☎ 35 96 06 54.

Les ANDELYS 🛈 24, rue Philippe-Auguste, 27700. ☎ 32 54 41 93.

Gaillard Castle. – Open 15 March to 15 November from 0900 to 1200 (except Wednesdays) and from 1400 to 1800; closed Tuesdays and 1 May; 15F; ☎ 32 54 04 16 extn 213.

St-Sauveur Church. – Open afternoons only.

ANET

Château. – Guided tours (time: 45 min) 1 April to 31 October daily from 1430 to 1830; also Sundays and public holidays from 1000 to 1130 and from 1430 to 1830; otherwise open Sundays and public holidays from 1000 to 1130 and from 1400 to 1700, and Saturdays from 1400 to 1700; closed Tuesdays; 32F; ☎ 37 41 90 07.

Funerary Chapel of Diane of Poitiers. – Same times as for the château.

AUBE

Ségur-Rostopchine Museum. – Open 15 June to 15 September from 1400 to 1800; closed Tuesdays, Wednesdays, Thursdays; 8F; ☎ 33 24 01 68 (Town Hall).

Les AUTHIEUX

Church. – Open for services only.

B

BAILLEUL

Château. – For information, contact; ☎ 35 27 77 87.

BARENTIN

Church. – Closed Sundays after services and public holidays.

Local History Museum. – Open from 0830 (0900 Saturdays) to 1200 and from 1300 to 1800; closed Saturday afternoons, Sundays and public holidays; ☎ 35 94 90 20.

BEAUFICEL-EN-LYONS

Church. – To visit ring ☎ 32 49 66 66 or 32 49 62 51.

BEAUMESNIL

Castle. – Open Easter to 30 September, Fridays, Saturdays, Sundays, Mondays and public holidays from 1430 to 1800; in October on Sundays only at the same time; 25F; gardens only: 10F; gardens open all year round every day except Tuesdays; ☎ 32 44 40 09.

Le BEC-HELLOUIN

Abbey. – Guided tours (time: 45 min) June to September at 1000, 1100, 1500, 1600 and 1700 (no tour at 1700 on Saturdays), Sundays and public holidays at 1200, 1500, 1530, 1600 and 1800; otherwise daily tours at 1100, 1515 and 1630, Sundays and public holidays at 1200, 1500 and 1600; closed Tuesdays; 20F; ☎ 32 44 86 09. Concerts take place five or six times a year. Apply to the abbey.

Car Museum. – Open from 0900 to 1200 and from 1400 to 1900; closed Wednesdays and Thursdays between 1 November and 31 March; 25F.

BERNAY
🛈 29, rue Thiers, 27300. ☎ 32 43 32 08.

Former Abbey Church. – Same opening times and charges as for Municipal Museum, which is where the keys are kept.

Municipal Museum. – Open Easter school holidays and 1 July to 31 August from 1000 to 1200 and from 1400 to 1900; otherwise from 1000 to 1200 and from 1400 to 1730 (Sundays and public holidays from 1500 to 1730 only); closed Tuesdays: 15F (ticket valid for Abbey Church also); ☎ 32 46 63 23.

Norman Museum. – Open from 1000 to 1200 and from 1500 to 1900 (1800 between 30 September and Easter); Sundays by appointment only; closed Mondays; 10F; ☎ 32 43 05 48.

Ste-Croix Church. – Closed Sunday afternoons.

BEUVREUIL

Church. – For information, contact the Town Hall.

BIZY

Château. – Guided tours (time: 30 min) 1 April to 1 November from 1000 to 1200 and from 1400 to 1800; 2 November to 31 March weekends only from 1400 to 1700; closed Fridays, 24 to 26 December, 31 December and 1 January; 26F; ☎ 32 51 00 82.

BLAINVILLE

Castle. – Guided tours (1 hour) from 15 July to 31 August from 1400 to 1800; otherwise on request; no admission charge; ☎ 35 34 00 53.

BOCASSE

Park. – Open 27 April to 9 September daily from 1000 to 1800; also Easter to 26 April and 10 September to 20 October on Wednesdays and Saturdays from 1300 to 1800, and on Sundays and public holidays from 1100 to 1800; 28F (32F Sundays and public holidays).

BONNEVILLE-SUR-TOUQUES

Castle (Fortified enclosure and moat). – Guided tours (time: 45 min) Easter to last weekend in October from 1400 to 1800 only, on Saturdays, Sundays and public holidays; 15F, children: 7F50; ☎ 31 88 00 10.

BOUQUETOT

Church. – Apply to the presbytery of Routot (M. Christian Duval); ☎ 32 57 30 46.

BOURNEVILLE

House of Crafts and Trades. – Open 1 February to 31 December daily from 1400 to 1830 (November and December open at weekends only); closed Tuesdays; Patchwork section open same times, but closed Mondays not Tuesdays; 20F; ☎ 32 57 40 41.

BOURY-EN-VEXIN

Château. – Guided tours (time: 30 min) Easter to mid-October on Saturdays, Sundays and public holidays from 1430 to 1830; in July and August at these times daily except Tuesdays; groups by appointment please; 30F; ☎ 32 55 15 10 or ☎ (1) 42 61 22 62 (evenings only).

BRIONNE

ℹ place de l'Église, 27800. ☎ 32 45 70 51.

Normandy House (Exhibitions). – Open mornings and afternoons; closed Wednesdays except from early June to late September; ☎ 32 44 81 09.

BULLY

Church. – Apply to the presbytery; ☎ 35 93 06 24.

BURES-EN-BRAY

Church. – Apply to Mme Marie Jourdain; ☎ 35 93 29 28.

C

CANAPVILLE

Manor of the Bishops of Lisieux. – Guided tours (time: 30 min) 15 June to 31 August daily (except Tuesdays) from 1400 to 1800; otherwise open Fridays, weekends and public holidays from 1400 to 1800; 20F; ☎ 31 65 24 75.

CANY

Château. – Guided tours (time: 45 min) from 1 July to 1 September from 1000 to 1200 and from 1500 to 1800; closed Fridays and the 4th Sunday in July; 24F; ☎ 35 97 70 32.

CANY-BARVILLE

Church. – Open during services only.

CAUDEBEC-EN-CAUX

ℹ place Charles-de-Gaulle, 76490. ☎ 35 96 20 65.

Templars' House. – Open 1 June to 30 September from 1500 to 1800; 15F; ☎ 35 96 00 21.

Seine Maritime Museum. – Open 15 March to 31 October from 1400 to 1830; 1 November to 3rd Sunday in December weekends only at these times; closed Tuesdays (except July and August); 16F; ☎ 35 96 27 30.

CHAMP DE BATAILLE

Château. – Open Easter to 1 November daily from 1000 to 1900; 30F; there is an 18-hole golf course in the castle grounds, for further information contact; ☎ 32 34 84 34.

CLÈRES

Zoo. – Open 1 May to 30 September daily from 0900 to 1830; in March, April, October and November from 0900 to 1200 and from 1330 to 1800; sale of tickets stops 1 hour before closing time; 25F, children: 15F; ☎ 35 33 23 08.

Car and Military Museum. – Open daily 1 January to 20 December from 0900 to 1800; 20F; ☎ 35 33 23 02.

CLERMONT-EN-AUGE

Church. – Open Ascension to 30 September daily from 0800 to 2000; 1 October to 1 November and Palm Sunday to Ascension open at weekends only; ☎ 31 79 23 50.

COQUAINVILLIERS

Moulin de la Foulonnerie Distillery. – Guided tours (30 min) from 0800 to 1900; closed at weekends and from 16 September to 30 March; free admission and tasting; ☎ 31 62 29 26.

CORNEVILLE-SUR-RISLE

Carillon. – Open daily from 1000 to 1130 and from 1530 to 1800; closed Mondays and public holidays; 10F; ☎ 32 57 01 04.

COUPESARTE

Manor. – Visitors are allowed in the grounds only.

COURGEON

Church. – Key to the church is kept at the Café de la Place; ☎ 33 25 18 00.

La COUTURE-BOUSSEY

Museum of wind instruments. – Open from 1400 to 1700 (guided tours, time: 45 min); closed Tuesdays, 1 January, 1 May and 25 December; 10F; ☎ 32 36 28 80.

CRÈVECŒUR-EN-AUGE

Crèvecœur Manor and Schlumberger Museum. – Open 15 February to 30 September daily from 1300 to 1900; 1 October to 15 November at these times at weekends only; 1 July to 31 August from 1000 to 1900; closed from 16 November to 15 February; 20F, 25F for guided tour (1 hour); ☎ 31 63 02 45.

CROISSET

Pavillon Flaubert. – Guided tours (time: 30 min) from 1000 to 1200 and from 1400 to 1800; closed Wednesday mornings, Tuesdays and public holidays; 2F; ☎ 35 36 43 91.

La CROIX-ST-LEUFROY

Church. – Contact the Town Hall; ☎ 32 67 75 20.

D

DANGU

Church. – Apply to the presbytery.

DEAUVILLE
🛈 place Mairie, 14800. ☎ 31 88 21 43.

Air trips. – All year by appointment; ☎ 31 88 00 52.

DIEPPE
🛈 boulevard du Général-de-Gaulle, 76200. ☎ 35 84 11 77.

Museum. – Open from 1000 to 1200 and from 1400 to 1800 (1700 weekdays October to May); closed Tuesdays from 1 October to 31 May; also closed 1 January, 1 May, 1 November, 25 December; 12F; ☎ 35 84 19 76.

DREUX
🛈 4, rue Porte-Chartraine, 28100. ☎ 37 46 01 73.

Belfry. – Open Wednesdays and weekends from 1400 to 1800, also weekends from 1000 to 1200; July and August open daily (except Tuesdays) from 1000 to 1200 and from 1400 to 1800; 8F; ☎ 37 46 01 73.

St-Louis Royal Chapel. – Guided tours from 0900 to 1200 and from 1400 to 1900 (1745 or at dusk during February, March, October, November and December); closed in January and during family ceremonies; 20F; ☎ 37 46 07 06.

Marcel-Dessal Art and History Museum. – Open 1 July to 31 August from 1500 to 1800 (from 1400 to 1800 Saturdays and from 1400 to 1900 Sundays and public holidays); closed Tuesdays; otherwise open Wednesdays, weekends and public holidays from 1400 to 1800 (1900 Sundays and public holidays); closed 1 January, 1 May, from Easter to Whitsun, 14 July and 25 December; 8F (free on Wednesdays); ☎ 37 50 18 61.

E

ÉCAQUELON

Church. – Apply to the Town Hall (mairie).

ELBEUF
🛈 ☎ 32 96 90 10 (Town Hall).

St-Stephen's Church. – Restoration work in progress; open at weekends from 0900 to 1100 and from 1600 to 1900; closed Sunday afternoons December to March; ☎ 35 77 04 81.

St-John's Church. – Closed Wednesdays.

Natural History Museum. – Open Mondays and Saturdays from 1400 to 1800; Wednesdays from 1000 to 1800; closed on public holidays; admission free; ☎ 32 96 90 15.

ÉTELAN

Château. – Guided tours July and August from 1430 to 1830; closed Tuesdays; 15F; otherwise groups by appointment; ☎ 35 39 91 27.

ÉTRETAT   ⓑ place M.-Guillard, 76790. ☎ 35 27 05 21.

Nungesser and Coli Museum. – Open 15 June to 15 September daily, and weekends only from Easter to 15 June, from 1000 to 1200 and from 1500 to 1900; 4F70; ☎ 35 27 07 47 or 35 27 01 23 (Town Hall).

Cape Antifer Lighthouse. – Guided tours (time: 1 hour) by request from 1000 to 1200 and from 1400 to 1900 (1600 between 1 October and 30 April); ☎ 35 27 01 77.

EU   ⓑ 41, rue P.-Bignon, 76260. ☎ 35 86 04 68.

Notre-Dame and St-Laurent Church Crypt. – Open from 0900 to 1130 (except Sundays) and from 1400 to 1800 (1600 1 November to 31 March); closed on public holidays.

Louis-Philippe Museum. – Open Palm Sunday to 1 September from 1000 to 1200 and from 1400 to 1800; closed Tuesdays; 10F; ☎ 35 86 44 00.

College Chapel. – Open daily 1 May to 30 November from 1000 to 1200 (except Sundays) and from 1400 (1500 Sundays) to 1800; ☎ 35 50 16 73.

ÉVREUX   ⓑ 1, place du Général-de-Gaulle, 27000. ☎ 32 24 04 43.

Museum. – Open from 1000 to 1200 (except Sundays) and from 1400 to 1800 (1700 October to March); closed Mondays, 1 January, 1 May, 1 and 11 November, 25 December; ☎ 32 31 52 29.

Former Capuchin Cloister. – Open daily July and August from 0900 to 1200 and from 1400 to 1700; otherwise open Wednesdays, Saturdays, Sundays and public holidays only from 1400 to 1700.

F

FÉCAMP   ⓑ 113, rue Alexandre-le-Grand, 76400. ☎ 35 28 51 01.

Benedictine Museum. – Guided tours (time: 1 hour) between 4 July and 13 September from 1000 to 1800, and between 21 March and 3 July, also 14 September and 11 November from 1000 to 1200 and from 1400 to 1730; otherwise one guided tour daily at 1030 and one at 1530; 24F; ☎ 35 28 00 06.

Museum of Local Art. – Open from 1000 to 1200 and from 1400 to 1730; closed Tuesdays and 1 January, 1 May and 25 December; 20F (ticket valid also for Terre Neuvas Museum); ☎ 35 28 31 99.

Terre Neuvas and Deep Sea Fishing Museum. – Open from 1000 to 1200 and from 1400 to 1730 (1830 July and August); closed Tuesdays (except July and August) and 1 January, 1 May and 25 December; 20F (ticket valid also for Museum of Local Art); ☎ 35 28 31 99.

La FERRIÈRE-SUR-RISLE

Risle Paradise Valley Park. – No information available at time of going to press (closed for renovation work); contact ☎ 32 30 71 80.

FERVAQUES

Château. – Open by appointment; apply to AMARCH-Le Kinnor; ☎ (1) 46 27 75 93 or 31 32 33 96.

FEUGERETS

Château. – Grounds only open to the public; early March to late October; 5F.

FILIÈRES

Château. – Guided tours (time: 30 min) July and August daily from 1400 to 1900; Easter to 30 June and 1 September to 1 November on Wednesdays, Saturdays and Sundays from 1400 to 1900; 25F; ☎ 35 20 53 30.

FLEURY-LA-FORÊT

Château. – Guided tours (time: 45 min) Easter to 1 November from 1400 to 1800; otherwise open Sundays and public holidays at these times; 30F, gardens only: 20F; ☎ 32 49 54 34

FONTAINE-GUÉRARD

Abbey. – Open (guided tours: 1 hour) 1 April to 31 October from 1400 to 1800; closed Mondays; 15F; ☎ 32 49 03 82.

FONTAINE L'ABBÉ

Church. – Open during services.

FOUCARMONT

Church. – Closed Sundays and Mondays.

FRANCHEVILLE

Metalwork Museum. – Open from 1 June to 30 September at weekends and on public holidays from 1100 to 1230 (except Saturdays) and from 1500 to 1900; 1 March to 31 May and 1 October to 15 November Sundays and public holidays only from 1500 to 1800.

G

GISORS
🛈 place Carmélites, 27140. ☎ 32 27 30 14.

Castle. – Open 1 April to 30 September daily from 1000 to 1200 and from 1400 to 1800; 1 October to 1 April at weekends only from 1000 to 1200 and from 1400 to 1700; otherwise open by appointment only; closed Tuesdays; 20F; ☎ 32 27 30 14.

GIVERNY

House of Claude Monet. – Open 1 April to 31 October daily from 1000 to 1800; closed Mondays; 30F (house and gardens); the gardens are open throughout the day during the same period; 20F (gardens only); ☎ 32 51 28 21.

Musée Américain Giverny. – Open daily 1 April to 1 November from 1000 to 1800; closed Mondays; 30F; guided tours can be booked in advance; ☎ 32 51 94 65.

H

HARCOURT

Castle. – Open 16 June to 8 September daily from 1000 to 1900; 3 March to 15 June and 9 September to 17 November from 1400 to 1900; closed Tuesdays; 20F; ☎ 32 56 29 70.

Church. – Apply to M. le Curé de Brionne; ☎ 32 44 81 88.

HARFLEUR

St-Martin Church. – Open July and August daily from 0800 to 1200 and from 1430 to 1700; otherwise from 0800 to 1200 only.

HAUVILLE

Mill. – Guided tours (time: 20 min) Easter to 30 September from 1430 to 1830; 1 October to 11 November Sundays and public holidays only from 1400 to 1800; closed Tuesdays; 7F; ☎ 35 37 23 16.

Le HAVRE
🛈 Forum Hôtel-de-Ville, 76600. ☎ 35 21 22 88.

St-Joseph Church. – Closed Sunday afternoons in winter.

André Malraux Fine Arts Museum. – Open from 1000 to 1200 and from 1400 to 1800; closed Tuesdays and 1 January, 1 and 8 May, 14 July, 11 November and 25 December; admission free; ☎ 35 42 33 97.

Natural History Museum. – Open daily from 1400 to 1800; Wednesdays and weekends from 1000 to 1130 also; closed Tuesdays, 1 January, 1 and 8 May, 14 July, 11 November and 25 December; admission free; ☎ 35 41 37 28.

Old Havre Museum. – Open daily from 1000 to 1200 and from 1400 to 1800; closed Mondays, Tuesdays and 1 January, 1 and 8 May, 14 July, 11 November and 25 December; admission free; ☎ 35 42 27 90.

Graville Priory Museum. – Same times as for the Old Havre Museum.

Boat Trips and Harbour Visits. – Easter to 15 September, leaving from Quai de la Marine (outer harbour); contact ☎ 35 42 01 31.

La HAYE-DE-ROUTOT

Bread Oven. – Open July and August from 1430 to 1830; closed Tuesdays; open afternoons Sundays and public holidays only in April, May, June, September and October; 5F, combined visit with Sabot-Maker's: 8F; ☎ 35 37 23 16.

Sabot-Maker's Workshop. – Same opening times as for Bread Oven.

HONFLEUR
🛈 place A.-Boudin, 14600. ☎ 31 89 23 30.

Maritime Museum. – Open June to September daily from 1030 to 1230 and from 1430 to 1830; October to December and 15 February to June open weekdays afternoons only and mornings and afternoons at weekends; closed 1 January to 15 February; 10F (19F for combined ticket with Folk Art museum); ☎ 31 89 14 12.

Folk Art Museum. – Same times and charges as for the Maritime Museum.

Salt Stores (Exhibitions). – Annual exhibitions between late February and late September; contact the Tourist Office for details.

Eugène Boudin Museum. – Open 15 March to 30 September from 1000 to 1200 and from 1400 to 1800, otherwise daily from 1430 to 1700 and weekends from 1000 to 1200 and from 1430 to 1700; closed Tuesdays, 1 May, 14 July, 25 December and between 1 January and 15 February; 17F (ticket valid also for Ste-Catherine's belfry); ☎ 31 89 54 00.

Ste-Catherine's Belfry. – Same times and charges as for Eugène Boudin museum (the entrance ticket for the Eugène Boudin Museum is valid for the belfry).

Notre-Dame-de-Grâce Chapel. – Open daily from 1000 to 1200 and from 1400 to 1800; closed to visitors during services.

J

JUMIÈGES

Abbey. – Open 16 June to 15 September from 0900 to 1900; also 1 April to 15 June and 16 September to 30 October from 0900 to 1200 and from 1400 to 1700 (1800 weekends); otherwise from 1000 to 1200 and from 1400 to 1600 (1700 weekends); closed 1 January, 1 May, 1 and 11 November, 25 December; 25F; ☎ 35 37 24 02.

Parish Church. – Open for services only.

L

LAUNAY

Château. – Not open to the public; there are no restrictions on visiting the park.

LILLEBONNE

Municipal Museum. – Open May to October daily from 1000 to 1200 and from 1430 to 1830; otherwise from 1430 to 1830 daily except Tuesdays; closed 1 January and 25 December; 4F60; ☎ 35 38 53 73.

Castle. – Open all day; closed Sundays and public holidays; small entrance charge.

Notre-Dame Church. – Closed Sunday afternoons.

LISIEUX ▯ 11, rue d'Alençon, 14100. ☎ 31 62 08 41.

For information on pilgrimages, contact the Service Pèlerins-Visiteurs-Touristes, 33, rue du Carmel, BP 95, 14102 Lisieux Cedex, ☎ 31 31 49 71 Fax 31 31 71 03.

Les Buissonnets. – Open daily 1 July to 3 October from 0900 to 1200 and from 1400 to 1800 (1730 Palm Sunday to 1 July); also October to Palm Sunday from 1000 to 1200 and from 1400 to 1600 (1700 in October); closed in January; ☎ 31 62 08 70 or 31 31 49 71.

Reliquary Chamber. – Open from 0800 (0900 16 October to 31 March) to 1200 and from 1345 to 1900 (1700 16 October to 31 March); ☎ 31 31 49 71.

Display: St Teresa's Life as a Carmelite. – Open from Palm Sunday to 1 November daily from 1000 to 1200 and from 1400 to 1700; ☎ 31 31 49 71.

Diorama: St Teresa's Life. – Open 1 April to 30 September daily from 0830 to 1930 (1830 from 1 April to 13 July and in September); otherwise from 0915 to 1215 and from 1415 to 1830; closed Sundays and Mondays between 1 November and 31 March, Fridays in October, and 1 January, 1 November and 25 December; 10F; ☎ 31 62 06 55.

Old Lisieux Museum. – Open from 1400 to 1800; closed Tuesdays and 1 May; 10F; ☎ 31 62 07 70.

LISORES

Fernand Léger Museum. – Guided tours (time: 30 min) 1 April to 30 September from 1000 to 1200 and from 1400 to 1800; otherwise at weekends by appointment only; closed Wednesdays; 10F; ☎ 31 63 53 13.

LISORS

Church. – Open at weekends.

LIVAROT

Conservatory (Cheese-Making Traditions). – Open (guided tours by appointment for groups, time: 30 min) 1 April to 31 October daily from 1000 to 1200 (except Sundays) and from 1400 to 1800; November, December and March open Tuesdays to Saturdays from 1400 to 1800 only; closed January and February; 10F; ☎ 31 63 43 13.

LONGNY-AU-PERCHE

St-Martin Church. – Open July, August and September daily from 0800 to 1900; ☎ 73 33 66 09.

LOUVIERS
🛈 10, rue Maréchal-Foch, 27400. ☎ 32 40 04 41.

Museum of Theatre and Opera Scenery and Film Sets. – Open July and August daily from 1000 to 1200 and from 1400 to 1800; closed Tuesdays; otherwise open at these times at weekends and on public holidays only; 10F; ☎ 32 40 22 80.

LYONS-LA-FORÊT

St-Denis Church. – Open for services only; for information apply to the Tourist Office; ☎ 32 49 31 65.

M

MAMERS
🛈 place République, 72600. ☎ 43 97 60 63.

Notre-Dame Church. – Apply to the presbytery, 70 bis, rue du 115ᵉ-R.I., ☎ 43 97 62 14.

MANNEVILLES

Nature Reserve. – Guided tours (time: about 4 hours) by prior appointment only (May and June); groups of 20+ pay 35F per person (supplementary charge for smaller groups); maximum group size 30; for appointments and information contact CEDENA (Centre de Découverte de la Nature), 27680 Ste-Opportune-la-Mare, ☎ 32 56 94 87.

MARTAINVILLE

Château. – Open daily from 1000 to 1230 and from 1400 to 1800 (1700 between end September and end March); closed Tuesdays and also 1 January, 1 May, 1 and 11 November, 25 December; 15F (7F50 for groups of 8 or more); ☎ 35 23 44 70.

MENESQUEVILLE

Church. – Open Saturday afternoons and Sundays.

MERVILLE-FRANCEVILLE PLAGE

Museum. – Open 15 April to 10 September from 1030 to 1230 and from 1430 to 1830; closed Tuesdays; 11F; contact Mme Sutrun: ☎ 31 24 26 91.

MESNIÈRES-EN-BRAY

Château. – Open from Easter to 1 November at weekends and on public holidays from 1400 to 1800; otherwise by appointment only; 12F; ☎ 35 93 10 04.

MIROMESNIL

Château. – Guided tours (time: 45 min) May to 15 October from 1400 to 1800; closed Tuesdays; 25F; ☎ 35 04 40 30.

MONT DE LA VIGNE

Manor (Outside and Chapel). – Open 1 April to 1 October Sundays only from 1500 to 1800; otherwise Mondays only at the same time.

MONTIVILLIERS

St-Sauveur Church. – Open on weekdays only.

MORTAGNE-AU-PERCHE
🛈 place Général-de-Gaulle, 61400. ☎ 33 25 19 21.

Notre-Dame Church. – Open July to first week in September only from 1400 to 1800; closed weekends and Mondays; ☎ 33 25 12 76.

Perche Museum. – Open July to September only from 1500 to 1800; closed Sundays, Mondays and public holidays; ☎ 33 25 25 87.

Alain Museum. – Open 10 January to 20 December from 1500 to 1800; closed Sundays, Mondays and public holidays; ☎ 33 25 25 87.

MORTEMER

Abbey. – Guided tour (time: 1 hour) daily from 1400 to 1800; grounds open daily from 0900 to 1300 and from 1400 to 1800; 35F (20F for park only); ☎ 32 49 54 37.

MOULINEAUX

Church. – Contact Mme Guilbert, 1310, rue Louis-Moguen; ☎ 35 18 03 82.

N

NEUFCHÂTEL-EN-BRAY
🛈 6, place Notre-Dame, 76270. ☎ 35 93 22 96.

J B Mathon - A Durand Museum. – Guided tours (time: 1 hour) July to 10 September daily (except Mondays) from 1500 to 1800; otherwise at weekends from 1500 to 1800; 8F; groups in winter also during the week by appointment only; ☎ 35 93 06 55.

NOGENT-LE-ROTROU
🛈 44, rue Villette-Gaté, 28400. ☎ 37 52 22 16.

Perche Museum. – Open daily from 1000 to 1200 and from 1400 to 1800; closed Tuesdays and 1 November; 12F; ☎ 37 52 18 02.

St Laurent Church. – Apply to the presbytery, 8, rue du Pressoir, 28400 Nogent-le-Rotrou.

NONANCOURT

St-Martin Church. – Restoration work in progress; closed Mondays; apply to M. le Curé; ☎ 32 58 00 24.

O

ORBEC
🛈 rue Guillonnière, 14290. ☎ 31 32 87 15.

Municipal Museum. – Open during Easter school holidays and from early July to late September from 1430 to 1830; from October to March from 1400 to 1600; closed Mondays and Tuesdays; 6F; ☎ 31 32 82 02 (Town Hall).

ORCHER

Castle. – Guided tours (time: 30 min) 1 July to 15 August from 1400 to 1800; closed Thursdays; 16F; ☎ 35 45 45 91.

OUILLY-LE-VICOMTE

Church. – Contact the Town Hall: ☎ 31 61 12 64.

P

PALUEL

Nuclear Power Station. – Information Centre open daily from 0900 to 1900 (1600 during the week from 1 November to 28 February); guided tours of the plant (time: 2 hour 30 min) on Mondays and Wednesdays at 1500 and Saturdays at 1000 and 1500 by prior appointment; contact CPN de Paluel, Service Communication Externe, BP 48, 76450 Cany-Barneville; ☎ 35 57 57 89; passport or identity card is needed.

PETIT-COURONNE

Pierre Corneille Manor House. – Guided tours (time: 45 min) daily from 1000 to 1200 and from 1400 to 1800 (1700 from 1 October to Easter); closed Tuesdays, all November and 1 January, Easter, 1 May, Ascension Day, Whitsun, 14 July, 25 December; 10F; ☎ 35 68 13 89.

PIERREFITTE-EN-AUGE

Church. – Apply to the inn Auberge des Deux-Tonneaux.

PONT-AUDEMER
🛈 place Maubert, 27500. ☎ 32 41 08 21.

St-Germain Church. – Apply to the presbytery, 9, route de Corneilles; ☎ 32 41 07 06.

PONT-DE-L'ARCHE

Notre-Dame-des-Arts-Church. – Open for services only.

R

ROBERT THE DEVIL'S CASTLE

Viking Museum. – Open 15 February to 15 October daily from 0900 to 1800 (1900 at weekends); 16 October to end November from 1000 to 1800; closed Mondays; 15F, children: 8F; ☎ 35 18 02 36.

ROUEN

Notre-Dame Cathedral, crypt, ambulatory and tombs. – Guided tours (time: 40 min) from first Saturday in July to first Sunday in September Monday to Saturday at 1000, 1100, 1415, 1500, 1600 and 1700 and Sundays only at 1415, 1500, 1600 and 1700; Easter Monday to first Sunday in May Mondays to Fridays at 1500 and 1600, weekends at 1415 (1400 Sundays), 1500, 1600 and 1700; 10F; otherwise cathedral open daily from 0730 (0900 Mondays) to 1200 and from 1400 to 1900 (1800 Sundays); closed during services and 1 January, 1 May, 14 July and 11 November; ☎ 35 71 53 22.

Museum of Education. – Open from 1300 to 1800; closed Sundays, Mondays and public holidays; 5F; ☎ 35 75 49 70.

St-Ouen Church. – Open 15 March to 31 October daily (except Tuesdays) from 1000 to 1230 and from 1400 to 1800; 16 January to 14 March and 1 November to 14 December open on Wednesdays and at weekends only from 1000 to 1230 and from 1400 to 1630; closed between 15 December and 15 January.

St-Godard Church. – Open to visitors from 0830 to 1800 every day except Sundays.

Law Courts (main courtyard). – Apply to Tourist Office (syndicat d'initiative) to arrange guided tours; 26F;

Prosecutors' Room (Law Courts). – Open afternoons and also mornings during sittings; closed at weekends.

St Joan of Arc Church. – Open daily from 1000 to 1215 and from 1400 to 1800; closed Friday and Sunday mornings and during services.

Belfry. – Open Palm Sunday to 1 October from 1000 to 1200 and from 1400 to 1800; closed Tuesdays, Wednesday mornings; also closed 1 and 8 May, Ascension Day, 14 July, 15 August, 1 and 11 November and 25 December; 11F (joint ticket with Fine Arts Museum); ☎ 35 71 28 40.

Fine Arts Museum. – Open from 1000 to 1200 and from 1400 to 1800; closed Tuesdays, Wednesday mornings and on public holidays; 11F (ticket valid for Belfry also); ☎ 35 71 28 40.

Ceramics Museum. – Same times and charges as for the Fine Arts Museum; guided tours of this and Le Secq des Tournelles Museum at 1430 on Saturdays in July and August; 20F + 11F entry; ☎ 35 07 31 74.

Le Secq des Tournelles Wrought Ironwork Museum. – Same times and charges as for the Fine Arts Museum; guided tours shared with Ceramics Museum (see above).

Bourgtheroulde Mansion. – Open during business hours of the bank installed in the building; also afternoons on Sundays and public holidays.

Joan of Arc Museum. – Open 1 May to 15 September daily from 0930 to 1830; otherwise from 1000 to 1200 and from 1400 to 1830; closed Mondays from mid-September to late April; also closed 1 January and 25 December; 20F; ☎ 35 88 02 70.

Corneille Museum. – Open daily from 1000 to 1200 and from 1400 to 1800; closed Tuesdays, Wednesday mornings, 1 January, 1 and 8 May, Ascension Day, 14 July, 15 August, 1 and 11 November, 25 December; 2F; ☎ 35 71 63 92.

Flaubert Museum. – Open daily from 1000 to 1200 and from 1400 to 1800; closed Sundays, Mondays and public holidays; admission free; ☎ 35 08 80 05.

St-Patrice Church. – Closed Sunday afternoons.

Joan of Arc Tower. – Open daily from 1000 to 1200 and from 1400 to 1730; closed Tuesdays, 1 January, 1 and 8 May, Ascension Day, 14 July, 15 August, 1 and 11 November, 25 December; 6F; ☎ 35 98 55 10.

Seine-Maritime Antiques Museum. – Open daily from 1000 to 1730, Sundays and public holidays from 1000 to 1200 and from 1400 to 1800; closed Tuesdays and 1 January, 1 and 8 May, Ascension Day, 14 July, 15 August, 1 and 11 November, 25 December; 10F; ☎ 35 98 55 10.

Museum of Natural History, Ethnography and Prehistory. – Open from 0945 to 1200 and from 1345 to 1730; Sundays from 1400 to 1900; closed Mondays, Tuesdays and mornings on Sundays and public holidays; also closed 1 January, 1 and 8 May, Ascension Day, 14 July, 15 August, 1 and 11 November and 25 December; 8F; ☎ 35 71 41 50.

Botanical Gardens: Greenhouses. – Open daily all year from 0900 to 1130 and from 1400 to 1700.

RY

Museum of Animated Puppets. – Open from Easter to late October Saturdays, Sundays and public holidays from 1100 to 1200 and from 1400 to 1900 and Mondays from 1500 to 1800 only; during the week by appointment only; 20F; ☎ 35 23 61 44.

S

ST-ÉVROULT-NOTRE-DAME-DU-BOIS

Abbey Museum. – Closed for restoration work, for further information contact the Town Hall: ☎ 33 34 93 12.

ST-GERMAIN-DE-LIVET

Château. – Guided tours (time: 45 min) 1 February to 1 April and 15 October to 1 December from 1000 to 1115 and from 1400 to 1615; also 2 April to 30 September from 1000 to 1115 and from 1400 to 1815; closed December to January, first two weeks of October, Tuesdays and 1 May; 22F; ☎ 31 31 00 03.

ST-HYMER

Church. – Open May to September; apply to the presbytery.

ST-JEAN

Chapel. – Apply to the house opposite the chapel.

ST-MARTIN-DE-BOSCHERVILLE

Former Abbey Church of St Georges. – Open daily from 0830 to 1800; guided tours from 0830 to 1230 (from 0900 to 1200 at weekends) and from 1430 to 1630 (1700 at weekends); closed Wednesdays between 1 November and 31 March; 20F; ☎ 35 32 10 82.

ST-SULPICE-SUR-RISLE

Church. – Open Sundays from 0900 to 1300 and also on weekdays by appointment; apply to the presbytery; ☎ 33 24 25 12.

ST-WANDRILLE

Abbey Cloisters. – Guided tours (time: 1 hour) daily at 1500 and 1600 and also at 1130 on Sundays; 15F; ☎ 35 96 23 11.

Church. – Mass (Gregorian chants) weekdays at 0925 and 1000 on Sundays and public holidays; Vespers at 1730 on weekdays (1845 on Thursdays), 1700 on Sundays and public holidays.

STE-ADRESSE

Notre-Dame-des-Flots Chapel. – Closed Wednesdays.

ST-GAUBURGE

Museum of Popular Art and Traditions. – Open daily 1 May to 1 November from 1400 to 1900; 2 November to 30 April daily (except Saturdays) from 1400 to 1800; closed in January; 12F50; ☎ 33 73 48 06.

STE-OPPORTUNE-LA-MARE

Apple House. – Guided tours (time: 30 min) 14 July to 31 August daily (except Tuesdays) from 1430 to 1830; 1 June to 13 July and in September weekends at these times; April, May and October Sundays from 1430 to 1830 (1800 in October); otherwise, the first Sunday of the month from 1430 to 1830 (1800 in November and December); 8F; ☎ 35 37 23 16.

Forge. – Open July and August Saturdays and Sundays from 1400 to 1830; May, June, September and October Sundays only at these times; otherwise, the first Sunday of the month at these times; 5F; ☎ 35 37 23 16.

T

TOUQUES

Exhibitions in St-Pierre Church. – Open 15 June to 15 September daily from 1000 to 1230 and from 1400 to 1900; ☎ 31 88 00 07.

TOUROUVRE

Church. – Closed Mondays.

Le TRAIT

Parish Church. – Open Saturdays from 1000 to 1930; ☎ 35 37 21 45.

La TRAPPE

Abbey: Audiovisual Presentation. – Apply to the gate-house.

TROUVILLE
🄱 32, boulevard F.-Moureaux, 14360. ☎ 31 88 36 19.

Aquarium. – Open daily from 1000 to 1200 (except between 11 November and Easter) and from 1400 to 1830; closed 25 December; 30F, children: 20F; ☎ 31 88 46 04.

Montebello Museum. – Open daily (except Tuesdays) from 1400 to 1800 (1830 in July and August); closed from last weekend in September until Easter; 10F; ☎ 31 88 16 26 (Town Hall).

Exhibition Gallery. – Open July and August daily (except Tuesdays) from 1000 to 1200 and from 1400 to 1700; March to June and September to December open Wednesdays and Fridays from 1400 to 1700 and at weekends from 1000 to 1200 and from 1400 to 1700; closed in January and February; admission free; ☎ 31 88 16 26 (Town Hall).

V

VALASSE

Abbey. – Open (guided tours available) April to October on the 2nd and 4th Sundays of each month only from 1430 to 1730; 10F; ☎ 35 31 03 02 (Gruchet-le-Valasse Town Hall).

VALMONT

Abbey. – Open 1 April to 30 September daily (except Tuesdays) from 1000 to 1200 and from 1400 to 1800; also open at these times on 1 November; otherwise closed; 12F; ☎ 35 29 83 03.

Castle. – Open July and August from 1400 to 1800; 1 April to 30 June and 1 September to 31 October open at weekends and on public holidays only from 1400 to 1800; closed between 1 November and 31 March; guided visits for groups all year round by appointment; 18F; ☎ 35 29 84 36.

VARENGEVILLE-SUR-MER

Moustiers Park. – Open daily from 1000 to 1200 and from 1400 to 1800; 10F-40F (depending on season); ☎ 35 85 10 02.

House. – Guided tours (time: 30 min for house, 1 hour 30 min for house and park) by appointment only, please write to Le Bois des Moustiers, Route de l'Église, 76119 Varengeville-sur-Mer; prices vary according to size of group; ☎ 35 85 10 02.

St-Dominique Chapel. – Open daily May to September from 0830 to 1900; October to April from 0900 to 1800; ☎ 35 85 12 14.

Ango Manor House. – Open daily 16 March to 15 November from 1000 to 1900; otherwise at weekends only from 1000 to 1200 and from 1400 to 1700; 30F (house and gardens); ☎ 35 85 12 08.

VASCOEUIL

Castle. – Open Easter to 1 November daily from 1430 to 1830; mid-May to early September from 1100 to 1900; 30F; ☎ 35 23 62 35.

VERNEUIL-SUR-AVRE
🛈 129, place Madeleine, 27130. ☎ 32 32 17 17.

Tower of La Madeleine Church. – Guided tours early April to late November on the 1st Sunday of each month; apply to the Tourist Office.

Notre-Dame Church. – Open Saturdays and Sundays only.

VERNON
🛈 36, rue Carnot, 27200. ☎ 32 51 39 60.

A-G Poulain Museum. – Open daily from 1400 to 1800; closed Mondays and public holidays; 15F; ☎ 32 21 28 09.

VILLEQUIER

Victor-Hugo Museum. – Open from 1000 to 1230 and from 1400 to 1800 (1730 1 November to 28 February); closed Mondays (from October to March), Tuesdays, 1 January, 1 May and 25 December; 10F; ☎ 35 56 78 31.

White House. – Open afternoons early July to mid-August; closed Mondays, Sundays and public holidays; 5F.

VILLERS-SUR-MER
🛈 place Mermoz, 14640. ☎ 31 87 01 18.

Museum of Paleontology. – Open April to September daily from 0930 to 1230 and from 1430 to 1800 (July and August from 0900 to 1900); February, March, and October to 15 November daily (except Sundays and Mondays) at these times; admission free; ☎ 31 87 01 18.

VIMOUTIERS
🛈 10, avenue du Général-de-Gaulle, 61120. ☎ 33 39 30 29.

Camembert Museum. – Open daily from 0900 to 1200 (except Mondays) and from 1400 to 1800; 1 November to 31 December open daily from 1000 to 1200 (except Sundays and Mondays) and from 1430 to 1800 (except Saturdays and Sundays); closed January and February; 15F, children: 8F; guided visits available (except less than 30 min before closing time); ☎ 33 39 30 29.

La VOVE

Manor House. – Grounds only may be visited; if the caretaker is absent, beware of the dogs.

Index

Notes

Illustrations **EDIMEDIA** : Cabinet des Médailles BN, CdA-Hinous, *p. 15* / Collection particulière, CdA-Hinous, *p. 25* / Musée de Dieppe, CdA-J. Guillot, *p. 63* / © SPADEM National Gallery Washington, CdA-Hinous, *p. 80* - **EXPLORER** : Anderson Fournier, *p. 28* / B. Gérard, *p. 46* / F. Jalain, *p. 11*, *p. 31* / Lorne, *p. 70* / Roux, *p. 76* - **ÉDITIONS CORLET** : after photo P. Detesville, *p. 39* - **JACANA** : J.P. Ferrero, *p. 14* - **MARCO POLO** : F. Bouillot, *p. 64* - **PIX** : after photo d'Hérouville, *p. 23* / after photo D. Lérault, *p. 51* / D. Lérault, *p. 100* / after photo A. Téoulé, *p. 23* / M. Trigalou, *p. 90* - **S.D.P.** : A. Édouard, *p. 122* - **TOP** : A. Chadefaux, *p. 24* / R. Mazin, *p. 115*, *p. 116*, *p. 118* - **VIEILLES MAISONS FRANÇAISES** : B. Galeron, *p. 22* / Archives VMF, *p. 59* - **VLOO** : Kenyon, *p. 107* - With the permission of the town of Bayeux : *p. 17* - **Bibliothèque des Arts Décoratifs, Paris,** Collection Maciet, *p. 140* - **Bibliothèque Mazarine,** *p. 17*.

MANUFACTURE FRANÇAISE DES PNEUMATIQUES MICHELIN

Société en commandite par actions au capital de 875 000 000 de francs

Place des Carmes-Déchaux - 63 Clermont-Ferrand (France)

R.C.S. Clermont-Fd B 855 200 507

© Michelin et Cie, Propriétaires-Éditeurs 1988

Dépôt légal 89/3-1er trim. – ISBN 2.06.013.501-X – ISSN 0763-1383

Printed in France 01-89-20

Photocomposition : COUPÉ S.A., Sautron - Impression : I.M.E., Baume-les-Dames n° 7172

58

Brest
Quimper
St-Brieuc

1/200 000 – 1cm : 2 km

MANCHE

Pettus-Guirec • Paimpol

L. d'Ouessant

I. de Sein

OCÉ

ATLAN

MI

245

France

Provence
Côte d'Azur

1/200 000 – 1cm : 2 km

Privas ○   DRÔME   HAUTES-ALPES
ARDÈCHE   Gap
GARD   ○ Orange   ALPES-DE-   ITALIA
Nîmes AUCLUSE   ○ Digne
      ○ Avignon HAUTE-PROVENCE   ALPES-
   Arles BOUCHES-   MARITIMES
        DU-RHÔNE ○ Aix-en-Provence VAR Grasse
   Marseille   Nice
          Toulon   Cannes
                   MER
                MÉDITERRANÉE

MICHELIN